How the Web Was Won

Conquering the Digital Frontier

Authored by
Microsoft Site Builder Network members

Edited by
Cerise Vablais and Tony Leininger

Microsoft Press

PUBLISHED BY
Microsoft Press
A Division of Microsoft Corporation
One Microsoft Way
Redmond, Washington 98052-6399

Copyright © 1998 by Microsoft Corporation

All rights reserved. No part of the contents of this book may be reproduced or transmitted in any form or by any means without the written permission of the publisher.

Library of Congress Cataloging-in-Publication Data
How the Web Was Won / Microsoft Site Builder Network Members
    p.   cm.
  Includes index.
  ISBN 1-57231-917-8
    1. World Wide Web (Information retrieval system)   I. Microsoft
Site Builder Network.
TK5105.888.T73 1998
005.2'76--dc21   98-22938
                                                    CIP

Printed and bound in the United States of America.

1 2 3 4 5 6 7 8 9 MLML 3 2 1 0 9 8

Distributed in Canada by ITP Nelson, a division of Thomson Canada Limited.

A CIP catalogue record for this book is available from the British Library.

Microsoft Press books are available through booksellers and distributors worldwide. For further information about international editions, contact your local Microsoft Corporation office or contact Microsoft Press International directly at fax (425) 936-7329. Visit our Web site at mspress.microsoft.com.

Macintosh and Quicktime are registered trademarks of Apple Computer, Inc. ActiveX, Microsoft, Microsoft Press, Windows, and Windows NT are registered trademarks and CarPoint, MSN, NetMeeting, NetShow, Visual InterDev, and Visual Studio are trademarks of Microsoft Corporation.

Other product and company names mentioned herein may be the trademarks of their respective owners.

Acquisitions Editor: David Clark
Project Editor: Michael Bolinger

To William, for always loving me anyway

Contents

Acknowledgments xi
Introduction xiii

1 Wagons Ho! 2
    \<crash\>\</crash\> 4
    \<bold\>The Frontier\</bold\> 5
    \<bold\>The Pioneers\</bold\> 6
    \<bold\>"Netlers"—The Early Settlers\</bold\> 7
    \<important\>The Big Idea\</important\> 8
    The Early Publishers 9
    I Want My mtv.com (It's All in a Name) 11
    The Net Goes Hollywood—The Birth of the Live Net Broadcast 13
    Show Me the Money 13
    The Shakeout at the WWW Corral 15
    Bang, Bang, Bang Goes the Browser 17
    And So It Grows… 17
    About the Author 18

2 Braving the Elements 20
    Keep in Mind… 23
        Keeping Technology Honest 23
        Trade-Offs 24
        Where Does the Technology Fit? 25

Building a Reliable Web Site	26
What Are the Reliability Issues?	26
What Makes a Web Site Reliable?	27
How Is a Reliable System Developed?	28
Building a Scalable Web Site	29
What Are the Scalability Issues?	29
How Is a Scalable System Developed?	30
Building a Secure Web Site	32
Browser Security	32
System Security	33
What Makes a System Secure?	34
Compatibility: Designing for Almost-Standards	34
What Are the Compatibility Issues?	34
How Do You Ensure Compatibility?	35
About the Author	36
3 The Web's Oldest Profession	**38**
Why Sex On Line?	40
Anonymity	40
The Ability to Become Someone Else	41
The Promise of Variety	41
Sex Is Always Available	41
How Do They Make Money?	41
Membership Fees	42
Adult Verification Services (AVSs)	42
One-Time Payment for Services	43
Advertising Click-Thrus	43
So How Much Money Are They Making?	43
How Many Sites?	44
Adult Sites as Pioneers of Web Technology	45
How Many Visitors?	45
Regulation of Pornography on the Internet	46
Sex Does Sell	47
About the Author	47

4 Moving Pictures 48
- Building Up the Wagon Train 51
- No Troop's Complete Without a Trail Leader 52
- Poor Technology Is Never an Excuse—
  If It Doesn't Work On Line, Don't Do It On Line 55
- Know Your Audience, Set Goals, and Develop 57
- Determine Whether Various Multimedia
  Components Are Beneficial and Cost Effective 63
- Showcase the Internet's True Capabilities
  with the Intent of Pushing the Medium Forward 66
- Striking Gold on the Web with New Technologies 71
- Speculations on the New Frontier 76
- About the Author 78

5 Choosing a Partner for the Online Hoedown 80
- Pushing the Limits 82
- The Path to Finding the Right Partner 83
- Business-Related Uses for Digital Technologies 83
  - Extranets 86
  - Intranets 86
  - The Internet 87
- Four Types of Digital Solution Proficiencies 88
  - Design 89
  - Application Development 89
  - Systems Integration 89
  - Strategy 90
- Strategic Specialization 90
- The Web Shop of the Future 92
- Choosing a Digital Solution Vendor 92
  - Trade Shows 93
  - Media Coverage 93
  - Organizations 93
  - References 94
  - Qualifications 95
  - Scale 95

	Experience	95
	Staffing	96
	Conclusion	96
	About the Author	97
6	**The General Store: Generating Profits One Cowboy at a Time**	**98**
	The Store Proprietor	100
	The Wild West General Super Store	101
	Connecting Strategy with Technology	102
	The Grand Opening	104
	Marketing-Focused Web Pioneers	105
	Turning Your Web Site into a Gold Mine	108
	Designing a Site to Last into the Next Century	109
	Introducing the Silver Bullet	110
	From Cowboy to Customer	113
	Building Lasting Relationships with Your Cowboys	114
	Getting Buy-In from the Sheriff	119
	Putting Your Team Together	122
	Plan the Work, Then Work the Plan	123
	Start Using Your Gold Mine	130
	About the Author	131
7	**Pioneers Have Arrows in Their Backs**	**132**
	The Method to My Madness	135
	Where Multimedia Started for Me	136
	Some 10 Years Ago	136
	What's the Point?	138
	Cue to Enter CD-ROM	139
	Process Freaks Try to Share the Feeling	141
	The Business Model for Repurposing	144
	The Popular Perception	150
	Breaking the Three Q's (Quality, Quality, and Quality)	151
	Buyers Stay Away in Droves	153
	The Margin Call	155
	The Web Arrives Quietly	156

CONTENTS

Enhanced CD—The Last Refuge of the Truly Desperate 156
Haven't We Been Here Before? 158
The Webisodics 159
    The Good 159
    The Bad 160
    The Ugly 161
The Networks on the Web 162
What Television Is 163
    Why the Web Isn't Television 163
    MSN Builds—No One Comes 164
About the Author 166

8 How the Web Was Won: Rounding Up Online Successes 168

Chapter Overview 170
Webbed Victory 171
    Successful Goal Setting 171
    The Personal Touch 172
    Focus on Solutions 172
    Feedback 173
    Tracking 174
    Controlling Your Own Content 174
A Passel of Web Success Stories 175
    United Airlines: Translating Service to the Web 175
    Oldsmobile: Selling High-Ticket Merchandise On Line 179
    Hallmark: Building and Extending Relationships 184
Web Development Contraptions 188
    Tools of the Trade 188
    Architecture 190
    Phased Approach 190
Where We Stand 191
Web Team Organization 193
In the Web By-and-By 194
Conclusion 194
About the Author 195

**9 Conquering the Digital Frontier:
Seven Issues to Face En Route to Web Success** 196

- Topic 1: Globalization 199
  - Key Recommendations 205
- Topic 2: Convergence 205
  - Key Recommendations 213
- Topic 3: E-Commerce 213
  - Key Recommendations 219
- Topic 4: Technology 219
  - Key Recommendations 226
- Topic 5: Legal Issues 227
  - Key Recommendations 232
- Topic 6: Distribution 232
  - Key Recommendations 240
- Topic 7: Liabilities and Accountabilities 240
  - Key Recommendations 248
- There You Have It 248
- About the Author 249

Appendix Author Roundup 250

- Ron Bloom 251
- John Kim 252
- Cerise Vablais 252
- Jesse Albert 253
- Tish Hill 254
- Dan Fine 254
- Bryan McCormick 255
- Adam Heneghan 255
- Tony Leininger 256

Index 257

Acknowledgments

This book is the culmination of not only many months of hard work, but also many years of traveling down a long and winding path that brought me to my present job in the Microsoft Site Builder Network. And there are many people who I want to thank for making that journey as smooth as possible. I'd like to thank my father for always encouraging me to try new things. Without his support, I'm sure I'd be writing bad poetry on a mountain in Ireland somewhere. I would also like to thank William for showing me that I can do anything I decide to do. My thanks to Eric for giving me the best job at Microsoft and to Ralph for reminding me of the value of every minute. And most of all, I'd like to thank my girlfriends, Debbie, Cassi, Michi, and Jennifer, for always loving me and supporting me through life's ups and downs.

—*Cerise Vablais*

Writing a book is never a solo effort, and *How the Web Was Won* is no exception. I'd like to thank Site Builder Network's leadership team—Sue Bohn, Eric Ewing, Travis Howland—and my managers during the course of this project—Michi Broman and Cerise Vablais—for believing in me and for giving me the opportunity to contribute to this book. Michelle Winters was a big help in coordinating the author meetings, taping the roundtable discussion, and arranging the transcriptions. Many thanks to Carol Brown, who stepped in toward the end of the project and helped immensely to bring the text to its final form. Finally, for his support and companionship over the years, especially during the writing of this book, my heartfelt thanks to Charles "Dane" Orrell.

—*Tony Leininger*

Introduction

When I was a child, I got a toy videophone for Christmas one year. At that time, we still had the standard rotary dial phones, and videophones seemed to exist only in science fiction movies. Now, just 30 years later, videophones and much more are a reality. Being alive during a time when you can jump on your computer, find a chat room, and instantly communicate with someone halfway across the world is very exciting. The Internet has made the world a smaller place—we can get information, make travel reservations, buy things, all in an instant. Much has been written about the birth and growth of the infrastructure of the Internet, and now things are being written about how the World Wide Web is changing our society and our world.

This book represents a first among books about the Internet and the Web phenomenon. The authors represent top companies developing for the Web today. We selected the authors from the Microsoft Site Builder Network Level 3 member companies. Just like the rest of the Web community professionals, these Web developers have diverse backgrounds and came to the Web from a variety of previous occupations. But all of these authors have at least two things in common: they forged a path that has helped turn the Web into a place where corporations want to be and where online businesses have emerged, and they have helped make the Web a more exciting and enriching place.

Site Builder Network

The Site Builder Network (*http://www.microsoft.com/sitebuilder*) was created in July 1996 to evangelize Microsoft's Web technologies, including the Internet Explorer browser, with the Web developer community. The program was designed to offer different levels of membership. Anyone who registered could be a Level 0 or Guest Member, and Levels 1 and 2 were for individuals who met certain technical requirements. These first three levels attracted members from both the professional Web developer community and the Web hobbyist community. Level 3 was for Web developer organizations or consulting firms that are in business to create Web sites for other people. For each level, the Site Builder Network (SBN) offered membership benefits such as discounted software products, participation in beta trials, and free downloads. For Level 3 member companies, SBN offered co-marketing benefits, such as case study exposure on the SBN Web site and opportunities to participate in national ad campaigns. In fact, an ad featuring the Hallmark Web site, built by SBN Level 3 member Giant Step, won an award in the Thirteenth Annual Business Week Awards for Excellence in Corporate Advertising. SBN also held members-only briefings and special seminars around the country discussing Web technologies and how to use Microsoft's Internet technologies to create the most compelling and beautiful Web sites on the Net.

The Site Builder Network is the largest online resource and membership program available for Web professionals. SBN currently has more than 250 Level 3 member companies and more than 735,000 members worldwide. SBN is very proud of its success and appreciates the support and feedback from the Web community. In early 1998, SBN announced that all Level 3 companies would be eligible to migrate to the Microsoft Certified Solution Provider program, Microsoft's branded channel partner program.

In late 1997, SBN recognized the growth in the number of Web partners and decided that others should be given the opportunity to learn about these partners' successes and the challenges these top firms have faced. Eric Ewing, one of the original founders of the Site Builder Network, asked me if I'd be interested in coordinating the publication of a book written by employees of some of the Level 3 companies who had expertise in different areas. Finally seeing an opportunity to use that English/philosophy degree, I jumped at the chance! That was the birth of the book you are holding in your hands.

When I started brainstorming about the book, I kept trying to figure out a suitable analogy for the Web—when I hit upon the Wild West metaphor, it clicked. These SBN Level 3 Web professionals were truly pioneers in a digital frontier. They were trying things without really knowing what was around the next bend. They had to combat variable bandwidth, limitations of HTML, variable color palettes and screen resolutions, and on and on. Bigger questions loomed for these pioneers—what should they put on a Web site? How could they get people to visit the site? And of course, how do you make money on the Web? SBN knew that answers to these questions could be found by asking these early pioneers, and so I set out to recruit participants for this project.

It took about two months to get commitments from the various authors of this book. Then of course we had to go through the inevitable rounds of legal contracts and so forth. But we were finally ready for our first face-to-face group meeting. In honor of the book title and of our analogy, Tony Leininger and I spent some time at our local party supply store and prepared "welcome" kits for each author. Everyone received a small plastic horse, a sheriff's badge, a bandanna, and some plastic cowboys and Native Americans; and what Wild West kit could be complete without beef jerky (jalapeno flavored, of course)?

We had our first "Web Roundtable" in November 1997. One of our concerns was that the authors wouldn't be willing to share information openly since this would be a group of their competitors, but we found that they were all very open to the idea of sharing and collaborating on what we all believed was an exciting project. The authors also shared the feeling that there was enough work to go around. This definitely seemed true as we started nearing deadline time for chapters! We did get together again in January 1998, when the authors participated in another roundtable—the results of which you can read in Chapter Nine. Tony and I wanted to get the authors' thoughts on the Web of the future—what challenges lie ahead on the digital frontier. We were not disappointed, and a stimulating and thought-provoking discussion ensued. We also had the chance to visit some of Seattle's nightspots—however, those stories you will not find in this book.

Our hope is that you will learn how the Web became a viable industry and how you can use this amazing medium for your business.

Audience for the Book (Should I Be Reading This?)

Another thing that we discussed at great length was who we wanted to read our book. We had a hard time deciding whether we should target the Web professional or the business decision maker or both. We finally decided that we wanted to target both but make it easy for both reader segments to find what they were looking for. So if you are a Web developer or a Web fanatic, start with Chapter One and read the whole thing front to back. It's a great read, and you'll learn a lot and probably laugh a lot too—you might even find yourself saying, "Hey, I've been there." Our authors have shared their pains and struggles as well as their successes. If you are the busy, corporate executive type, with only a few free minutes between conference calls, meetings, flights, and rounds of golf, scan the chapter overviews and pick the chapter that addresses your crisis du jour. And I still recommend reading the whole thing front to back when you retire and are vacationing in the south of France.

Chapter Overviews

Chapter One, written by Ron Bloom of Think, Inc., introduces you to the wonderful world of the Web. You will learn about the early beginnings of the Web and why pioneers such as Ron, along with other adventurers, outcasts, dreamers, and expatriates, made the trek into cyberspace.

In Chapter Two, John Kim of Red Sky Interactive discusses the technical challenges of early and current Web development. If you've ever wondered why the colors on a specific Web page appeared different on other machines, this chapter will explain this and other such mysteries of the online world.

Chapter Three, written by yours truly, discusses adult Web sites and how they have affected the growth of the Internet. Sorry, this chapter contains no screen shots but does contain information about the number of visitors to these sites and also explores the question of how much money these sites are making.

Chapter Four, by Jesse Albert of Media Revolution, discusses how to make things move on the Web. He explains the many benefits of dynamic content and gives examples of how Media Revolution applied these techniques.

In Chapter Five, Tish Hill of SiteWerks—A Bowne Company looks at the variety of digital solutions emerging today and shows how to map a business's needs to an appropriate digital solution provider.

Chapter Six, written by Dan Fine of fine.com, looks at what companies establishing themselves on the Web need to do in order to plan, become customer-centric, and use database technologies to establish valuable relationships with their customers and prospects.

Chapter Seven, by Bryan McCormick, one of the founders of Broadway Interactive, reflects on where multimedia technologies have been, where they were supposed to go, and why they never got there.

In Chapter Eight, Adam Heneghan of Giant Step takes a detailed look at the elements of successful Web sites and focuses on how Giant Step created business solutions for three of its customers: United Airlines, Hallmark, and Oldsmobile, which, in addition to being successful, represent three common business site models: service, merchandise, and content.

In Chapter Nine, Tony Leininger records a roundtable discussion in which the authors grappled with issues currently facing Web developers. The chapter also documents their thoughts on issues that will affect Web developers in the future. These comments are a valuable starting point for anyone who is considering taking their company on line, and they touch on issues that even seasoned Web developers and corporate executives can't afford to ignore.

Saddle Up and Wagons Ho!

So there you have the background of this book. I thoroughly enjoyed getting to know each of the authors during this project, and I respect and admire their talents. Most of them have been with their companies since inception and possess the rare entrepreneurial drive that has made them successful. They truly are Web pioneers and have made the Web grow into the phenomenon it is today. When you've read our book and want to learn more, be sure to visit our site (*http://www.microsoft.com/sitebuilder*). And if you're ready to start building your own site, you can also read the book, *Survival Guide to Web Development,* written by Mary Haggard. It's a hands-on approach to building a Web site. But enough of my talking—now it's time for you to grab a tall, cool glass of lemonade and sit a spell and read their stories. Enjoy!

Cerise Vablais, April 1998

"There I was, sitting, with nothing but my rusted 386 and a smoking modem!"

Ron Bloom

CHAPTER 1

Wagons Ho!

It was a cold winter in 1994… at least it was cold somewhere. I, however, was comfortably ensconced in the office of my Los Angeles entertainment production company, supposedly working on the musical score for an upcoming and most likely soon-to-be-forgotten feature film. It was a romantic comedy. You know the plot: boy-has-good-girlfriend-gets-tempted-by-bad-girl-gets-caught-fooling-around-kicked-out-comes-back-makes-up-happy-ending-smooch-end-titles-over-happy-song. (Forgive me; sometimes I rant.) At least it was better than last night's recording session, featuring a used-to-be-famous pop star making a comeback, doing a bad remake of an old ballad that no one needs to hear again. Yeah…*this* was the life.

I was well into my morning ritual, having just finished a healthy breakfast of last night's cold pizza and this morning's coffee, and I was, uh, surfing the Net via my now-defunct regional Internet Service Provider (ISP), on my now-defunct Web browser. I noticed a single cloud in the sky and thought, "Ah...Christmas is coming." Caught up in the sentimentality of the moment, I blasted off a few e-mail messages to my East Coast friends, reminding them that the holidays are nicer when you're wearin' a Hawaiian shirt, smokin' a fat ceegar, and sportin' a pair of cheap sunglasses. (To create real envy, I attached a pic of yours truly in said getup.) In short, I was doing what I do best—contemplating life.

Over the last several months, even with all of the super-tech toys at my disposal in my state-of-the-art audio facility, I had been spending more and more time at my crusty 386, living on a steady diet of MS-DOS and the Internet, drawn by some mysterious energy. Looking back, it wasn't the technology; it was the connection. I was hooked on the Web, and I didn't even know it.

<crash></crash>

The symptoms—getting up in the middle of the night to check my e-mail; that unfocused, I-wanna-go-home-and-log-on-so-I-can-see-what-has-changed-in-the-last-twenty-minutes mind; and the gaze of almost addicted longing when passing the Comp USA store on La Cienega—were mystifying to my big-shot Hollywood friends. (Somehow I always gave directions that took us by the place.) Soon I was uncontrollable, adding a new hard drive (a whopping 100 MB!) for extra storage, getting the latest 14.4 modem (mind-boggling speed), adding a second phone line, even learning a bit of HTML. Eventually I was eschewing my bigtime Hollywood buddies for my new friends, Eddie the programmer and his sidekick, Rick—who didn't bathe much but could fix anything by the time he finished a six-pack.

But the Net became more than a mere compulsion as I began to imagine a different type of world, a *wired* world where the lines of communication would become beautifully intertwined in a holistic network, changing the way people met, related, thought, and acted. Most important, I could sense it would change the way businesses did business. It felt good, and it felt right.

Then one day the system crashed. There I was, sitting, with nothing but my rusted 386 and a smoking modem. I had lost my connection, and I went immediately into withdrawal. Panic calls to Rick and Eddie, an all-night vigil (it took a case of beer that time), two trips to Comp USA, and I was *back!* Connected. I was one with the world, at peace. Able to breathe again, I sat there, in my worn-out terrycloth robe and worn-in MS-DOS T-shirt, and contemplated. In a world where society was putting up bigger walls, I saw how important it was to be able to connect. I saw this as a simple, fundamental truth of human existence, one that had been slipping away as society "holed up." Then it came to me. The Net wasn't only a medium; it was a movement, and I was caught up in the soul of it.

From that moment on, I had a mission. This must have been how the original pioneers felt. There was a new wild, wild West; only this time it was the wild, wild Web, and I had to be a part of it. There was a voice (it always sounded a bit John Waynish) in my head saying, "Go Web, young man." So along with other adventurers, outcasts, dreamers, and expatriates, I journeyed out into cyberspace.

<bold>The Frontier</bold>

The history of the Internet traces its roots to our beloved United States government creating the Advanced Research Projects Agency Network (ARPANET) in an enlightened effort to ensure communication between computers in the event that the Soviets (or others) dropped the big one on a major metro area. By developing a simple language that all computers could speak and then creating a network or web of *pipes* (connections that pass data) to which any type of computer could connect, the makers of the ARPANET provided a simple and effective means for the spooks from the East Coast to ensure communication with the geeks from the West Coast. So even if, let's say, Denver became nuclear toast, computers could literally bypass the hole in the Web and still find one another. Looking back, I believe that in many ways the explosion created by the Net has been greater than any it was designed to mitigate.

The early Internet was text only, a world of simple type on simple screens: no images; no audio or video. The key was the connection. The initial connection was a large pipe between the East Coast and the West Coast called the backbone. This backbone let anyone exchange digital text efficiently with any one else who could connect to that pipe. Since universities were often the seats of research, more and more schools connected their pipes to the backbone, utilizing it to exchange all types of information, even personal greetings and news. By the late eighties, pipes had multiplied, and the Net had been extended over a large part of the world.

<bold>The Pioneers</bold>

The early Net-pioneers were an eclectic group of people from businesses, government agencies, and colleges across the globe. They were a ragtag bunch of researchers, students, hackers, and hobbyists forming virtual villages, exchanging information, and learning the Net craft through various rites of passage handed down by those who had gone before. Their language was rich and full of the jargon of the times. They spoke multiple dialects of UNIX, the then-dominant computer language utilized by networks, taking pride in understanding its sometimes enigmatic command-line protocol. They communicated via BBSs, chat, finger, and telnet, forcing new developments by their intensifying will to communicate in a more effective and interesting fashion. In those days, the Net grew by word-of-mouth; as each apprentice became more masterful, he or she would reach out to other newbies across the Net and spread the gospel.

What was the original attraction of this new frontier? In its early stages, the Net was cantankerous, inefficient, and limited in its scope. The magnetism that attracted early settlers to the wild Web was strikingly similar to that which attracted the West's original pioneers: no one *owned* it! Although the government subsidized the Internet, inherent in its very nature was anarchy. They did not control it. And there was the anonymity. One of the original sayings coined by the pioneers was "On the Net, nobody knows you are a dog!"

The Net culture grew in the soft underbelly of the communication generation. As Madison Avenue and the telecommunications and entertainment industries attempted to channel users, the Net became the communication alternative. Early pioneers valued the privacy of communication on the Net. As with the code of the West, the code of the Net was rigorously adhered to, and justice was meted out with an iron keyboard. It was perhaps this very anarchy and lack of sophistication that kept the Net invisible to big business. The Net was not considered a commercial enterprise, and its potential went virtually unnoticed by large telecommunications companies and software giants (an oversight that Microsoft eventually corrected, in an effort that has become a case study in managing business dynamics).

Wagons Ho!

So why did the Net continue to grow? Disillusionment with the media, the trend toward cocooning, and other factors were creating a culture starved for new ways to communicate. Attempting to explain the explosion of the Net, historians will likely fall into two camps: one touting the Net as the cause and the other as the result. What is important to remember is that while the Net started as a medium, it evolved into a movement. This movement has become a sophisticated culture of communication that has changed the world forever.

\<bold\>"Netlers"— The Early Settlers\</bold\>

As the Net grew, the pioneers were followed by settlers—hardy souls who staked claims to virtual real estate and began to plant and build. Virtual villages became virtual communities, populated by an increasingly interesting lot. Early netizens were libertarian, fierce protectors of freedom of communication. Many who were social outcasts in traditional society were finding themselves virtual gurus in this new culture. In many ways, Net culture enabled type B personalities to emerge as type A personalities (creating an interesting cultural mix in the process). Everyone on the Net had both a voice and anonymity. On the Net, you could speak your mind to thousands of netizens without having to identify yourself. To a great extent, everyone was equal, although some were more equal than others.

Eager to take advantage of these emerging communities, young entrepreneurs, both the visionaries and the carpetbaggers, descended upon the Net, looking for ways to profit in the new world. Some sought to create alternative, private communities for profit, and others sought simply to control access. The impact of these early Netlers is being felt today, as many commercial enterprises stake their fortune on the ability to generate an online community around their products or services. Eventually, structured communities, in the shape of enterprises such as America Online (AOL), Prodigy, and Quantum Online, or GeoCities and The Microsoft Network, emerged to help new netizens get a taste of frontier life. By many routes and for many reasons, the Net continued to grow. But in the early days, something was missing.

<important>The Big Idea</important>

The Net was based on two simple elements: availability of plenty of pipe and the ability of all computers to communicate through it in a common language. In the beginning, the Net carried text only or, more exactly, digital bits and bytes that represented text. This was fine for researchers exchanging files of facts and figures, but the communication culture wanted more. As the desire to communicate strained the ability of the Net to enable it, new technologies were required. At a university in Urbana-Champaign, Illinois, a young netizen named Marc Andreesen was one of the dissatisfied. But this netizen decided that he could do something about it. His thought was that if bits and bytes of text could be communicated, anything that could be converted to bits and bytes could be sent across this network. With that in mind, Andreesen went to work, further developing his idea.

In early 1993, Andreesen debuted a software bundle that enabled not only text but also images and other elements to be published on the Net. He made use of a concept called hyperlinking, which had been developed by another pioneer, Tim Berners-Lee. With simple commands and a rudimentary knowledge of how to use them, anyone could publish content on the Net. This content was assembled on a page, much like a mosaic, with text, images, and other elements linked together and transmitted through the Net along with the commands necessary to have a computer place them on the screen. And the viewing device for these pages was a simple but elegant piece of software called a browser. Andreesen was a true netizen and, as such, wanted the world to use his invention. So he did something that was anathema to any budding capitalist—he gave it away! This turned out to be a major event for the Net, and eventually not bad for Mr. Andreesen. Word spread across the Net like wildfire, and people rushed to download this free browser software, aptly named Mosaic.

The browser became the spark that ignited the hearts and minds of the information generation. In an information explosion, the World Wide Web was born. Mosaic changed the Net from a network of text-only channels to an image-rich world in which artists joined technologists in creating locations, or sites, each site with its unique address, style, look, and feel. Visitors began to pour into this world with increasing interest, surfing this Net and exploring the creations of burgeoning digerati. As had been the case with the anarchic Net, Andreesen's idea quickly evolved into something no one individual might have imagined. Creators and creations came from around the world. Almost every day, someone added an element, a design, or a line of code that improved upon the beast. It was only a matter of time before the World Wide Web began to catch the attention of buyers, sellers, and others, ranging from the civic-minded to the commerce-minded. Many saw gold in the Web, and the rush was on.

The early Web gold rush was not for the faint of heart. Entrepreneurs leaped onto the Web with the fierce intensity of prospectors throughout history, staking claims to real estate across the Net. Each was as sure as the next that his claim would yield the strike and that the riches would come pouring in. All you needed to join the rush was a computer, an address, and a connection to the Web. No one knew where the gold was, but the hunt was worth the risk. As wagonloads of prospectors headed on to the wild, wild Web, word began to spread and the press began to take notice.

By the fall of 1995, the World Wide Web, was touted on the cover of books, magazines, and newspapers across the globe, and the gold rush was running at full force. Mr. Andreesen had seen the light and had struck his own mother lode, founding Netscape with Dr. Jim Clark and James Barksdale and launching the company with a successful Initial Public Offering (IPO). Others soon followed (eventually including my own company, THINK New Ideas). Fortune 500 companies began to take notice, and a few of the brave ones decided to open outposts on the Web. But in order to get there, they needed help. And help was to be found in the shape of a small group of Web site builders, early artisans in tiny shops that had sprung up to build Web sites for the early homesteaders of the gold rush. Like the wagon masters of yore, these Webmasters offered their services to the city slickers who yearned for a taste of the wild, wild Web. Early shops typically were forged from either the design or the technology world and sported such names as Organic, Avalanche, and On Ramp.

The Early Publishers

As the Net continued to evolve, it began to establish itself as a publishing platform. The beauty of this platform was that it enabled all users to have the same voice (although that is beginning to change). Anyone who had a computer could be a publisher, and anyone who had content or opinions could share them with the world. More important, open discussions could be held among and between people from across the globe, enabling not only information but also individuals' opinions to find new audiences. One of the early publishers found his Net niche in an exodus that began in the entertainment industry. Adam Curry was already a guru of a different sort, a popular veejay of the then-exploding MTV Network. During the day, Adam pulled down long dough introducing the likes of Poison and Beavis and Butt-head, but by night, Adam led a secret life. Every afternoon upon leaving the taping of the show, Adam would scurry home, secrete himself in the attic (yes, his haven was the attic), and log on to the Net. The secret eventually came out. One of the most popular veejays in the history of MTV, the man with the golden hair, was, yikes, a closet nerd!

Curry had caught the bug as early as 1987, subscribing to The Source and Quantum Online (later becoming Prodigy and AOL respectively). Adam was one of a small group that had already starting publishing on the Net. He parlayed his MTV profile into creating an online musical information exchange via finger and Fidonet, using that system in a manner that eventually morphed into the concept of newsgroups. Fidonet and the noncommercial spam-free USENET newsgroups were the primary resources for finding communities of like-minded folks to share ideas and information with. Where else could you find as lively a discussion as that in rec.sewing.thimbles? Unlike today, the creation of a new newsgroup required merely a Request For comments and a minimum number of positive votes for inclusion in the Net-wide bulletin. Early pioneers even took their conversations into their own "private" space such as the text-based BBS system the Whole Earth 'Lectronic Link (WELL), consisting of pre–Silicon Valley pioneers.

Not satisfied, Curry looked to broaden his publishing efforts, obtaining a "dial-up shell account" from New York–based Panix, a pioneering ISP. He knew that fans from around the world wanted to know more about the goings-on behind the scenes of the music biz than they could learn from any television network, even MTV. He used his connections to create a network of information feeds about the entertainment industry. From this account, he began what has become one of the Web's most entertaining and beloved virtual newsletters, *Cybersleaze* (*http://metaverse.com/vibe/sleaze/index.html*). Traffic was so strong that Panix threatened to close Curry's account. *Cybersleaze* has evolved to include television and radio segments and is still popular, drawing thousands of readers and subscribers.

Meanwhile, the metaverse had sprung up on the Net. This realm of chat rooms established the Net as a place where people of like minds could go and share interests, meeting in virtual anonymity and having the ability to converse in groups or one-to-one. Since their inception, metaverse chat rooms have been responsible for many meetings in person and even several weddings and divorces. Other broad communities revolved around music and entertainment (the Internet Underground Music Archive) or local events and social issues (the WELL). Still more communities focused on narrow interests (such as bass fishing and wines), creating the first inklings of what has emerged as a new commercial environment, the affinity group.

At the time of their introduction, these affinity groups were unique in that, for the first time, people from around the world with a common interest could meet in an unmanaged environment and share thoughts, resources, ideas, and feelings. This seemingly insignificant development came at a time when traditional lines of communication were being questioned, and it resulted in an explosion of alternative communities across the Web. Due largely to these initial community environments, today marketers are reengineering the way they approach target audiences, defining not by region but by cybergraphic interests and tendencies.

I Want My mtv.com (It's All in a Name)

Today, as the commercial aspects of the Web become more prevalent, one of the biggest issues is the ownership of ideas in virtual space. Beyond the ownership of ideas is the right to use pictures, sounds, text, and even trade names. Although many saw the Net as exploding onto the scene, big business and their big brands chose to ignore this young upstart medium. As has often been the case, legislation was even further behind, not even beginning to address the potential complications caused by being able to "broadcast" ideas, images, sounds, and other elements in cyberspace. One of the key areas where legislation eventually had the greatest impact was in the formalized registration of Web site addresses.

When an individual wanted to create a Web site, he or she merely needed to register a Domain Name System (DNS). Early Web aficionados set about registering names in an anarchic frenzy. Some of the world's best-known brands saw their trademarked brand names being registered by individuals with completely different interests in mind. One of my first clients, Budweiser, saw budweiser.com taken by a Bud drinker in Phoenix. In this case the name was returned based on a deal that brought the satisfied Bud fan a case of beer and a Bud autographed by August Busch III.

Other transactions were not so simple, as Web entrepreneurs sought a fast buck by registering all types of corporate names. To this day, no clear-cut laws have been established governing trade names in the online world, and case law is equally far behind. In the meantime, DNS registration, once controlled by the government, has been privatized and promises to create a completely new set of issues: companies may be able to register not only dot coms and dot orgs but also suffixes such as dot lawyer and dot bank.

One of the first cases regarding naming conventions on the Web involved Adam Curry. Convinced that the Net was going to change the world, in mid-1994 Adam went to MTV and asked them to back his venture to create an online MTV network. (I am relating *my* impression of this story, as Adam remains in a vow of silence, subject to the terms of a settlement with MTV.) The executives at MTV didn't see things his way, seeing the Web as a going-nowhere fad, and did not back his plan, but Adam went ahead and created mtv.com anyway. Adam's online reputation soon grew, as did his dream of using the Net as a new communications network. During this time, Adam's Internet efforts had come to the attention of Marc Andreesen. He was taken with Adam's efforts and felt that Adam might be able to use his new software. So Andreesen sent Adam an e-mail, suggesting he might find use for his new browser, named Mosaic. Meanwhile, MTV online had become a success, and with that success, MTV's interest grew. Suddenly, they wanted their mtv.com! The subsequent publicity (and legal case) focused attention for the first time on the issue of name registration rights on the Net. Eventually, MTV got its mtv.com, but from that link, a company was born. Adam changed his MTV site to MeTaVerse, named his new company On Ramp, and went to work, assisted by a couple of hackers in an 8-by-8-foot office in New York and supported by a brother team in San Francisco with a server in their bedroom.

The Net Goes Hollywood—
The Birth of the Live Net Broadcast

Meanwhile, back at the ranch in Los Angeles, I was developing my Web expertise. I was part of a growing group of Web users who felt that the Web was a new medium becoming a new culture, but I saw no real examples of what I thought the Web could become. I believed the Web would enable us to combine information and entertainment, creating what is called *infotainment*. If the infotainment were compelling enough, people would flock to see it. If people flocked, we might be able to sell sponsorships or advertisements to the event. At least that was the thought. It had never been done. So I went searching for a project that would demonstrate this concept. In late 1994, I approached the National Academy of Recording Arts and Sciences (NARAS) with a plan to broadcast the Grammys on the Web. The Rolling Stones had done an Mbone concert, attempting to broadcast live via the Internet backbone to those precious few with high-bandwidth connections. I had developed a different concept that would combine the Net with television and radio, creating a simulcast in cyberspace. I called Mike Greene and described the concept. Searching for a word to describe it, I blurted out, "It's…a…cybercast!" His initial response was less than enthusiastic since he had heard of the Web's reputation for wildness. But he did agree to meet.

The problem was that I had a concept but did not have the team to produce it. Panicked calls to friends led me to go to New York, where, I had heard, an ex-veejay (Adam Curry) was building a smart Web company named On Ramp. Adam and I met and decided to team up to produce this cybercast. But first we had to get the rights.

Show Me the Money

Full of confidence and a business plan, we flew to Los Angeles to meet the Grammy Execs at their posh offices. After pleasantries were exchanged, we sat down to discuss the project with NARAS executive Rob Senn. After listening to our preamble, the first words out of his mouth were, "The Internet is a solution looking for a problem, and the Grammys aren't interested!" NARAS had turned the Grammys into a multimillion dollar brand and didn't want to have it tarnished. Undaunted, we proceeded to present our plan and extol the virtues of this new medium. As the conversation continued, Rob gradually began to see the benefits of the concept and actually began to contribute some strong ideas. An hour later, he sat down at his word processor and typed a one-page license. Brandishing the document, he turned to us and said, "How much are you going to pay me for this license? Our typical fee for something of this nature is over one million dollars."

At that moment the world froze, and all you could hear was the sound of two men gulping. Without beating an eyelash, I said, "Rob, we were thinking of paying you nothing!" Before he could react, we went on to explain how it would help the Grammys become the first global entertainment brand on the Web. We were creating the first cybercast—a historical event. We offered to produce the event at our cost, hoping to make money from the sponsorships we thought we could sell. Of course, we didn't have the money to pay for the costs. We were convinced we could sell the sponsorships simply by approaching current TV, print, and radio sponsors with the cybercast as an add-on. Sometime during our conversation, I think that Rob just decided to take a chance with us. In any event, he simply put the license on his desk and signed it. We thought we had it made. We shook hands and headed for the door. Rob called out, "One condition: you must not approach any of our current sponsors!"

Adam and I left in a combination of euphoria and panic. The Grammys were eight weeks away, and we had a cybercast to create. In those early days of sites and browsers, no one had really worked on a promotional Web event before, although advertisers had begun to take a chance by purchasing space on more popular Web sites and placing small advertising elements—what came to be called banners—on key site pages. From our New York and Los Angeles offices, with the help of the sales staff of Media America (Adam's On Ramp investment partners), we went out and started trying to find sponsors for our cybercast. Initial forays produced few results, and time was running out. Meanwhile, I had spoken with CBS television, owners of the Grammy TV rights, about the cybercast. Although they were not overly thrilled with the idea, they did give us rights to certain key areas that they were not going to be able to cover during their live telecast. These included backstage areas and other behind-the-scenes events that we felt would be exciting and interesting to our cybercast viewers. We also decided to begin our cybercast three days before the television broadcast, following the setup and the rehearsals at the Shrine Auditorium, creating a live "making-of-the-Grammys" online event.

Showtime was nearing; we had assembled a location team of 12 as well as a support group in New York. We were dropping a T1 line into the Shrine and flying in servers, computers, and even some emerging technologies. What we needed were sponsors. At the last possible second, the first sponsors came through, and the 37th Annual Grammy Awards were the debut of the world's first cybercast. The show featured the first use of RealAudio in this environment; the first use of a live digital camera as an update device (donated by Casio); trend-setting uses of update cams, behind-the-scenes reporting, and promotions; and other elements that are now standards on the Web. Sponsors included Casio, IBM, VISA, and Zima. Even more important, the Grammys went on to become the first million-dollar online brand, generating new and more valuable sponsorship for NARAS; they're still popular today.

Adam and I were reluctant to break up the Grammy team, so at his invitation, I joined On Ramp. We went on to create events for the NFL, Major League Baseball, a live concert from the Arctic Circle, the Mike Tyson comeback fight, and a host of others, firmly establishing the cybercast (now sometimes called NetCast) as a meaningful and profitable Internet event. On Ramp prospered as well, becoming both one of *Fortune Magazine*'s Top 25 new technology companies and *Advertising Age*'s interactive agency of the year in 1995.

The Shakeout at the WWW Corral

As the hot summer of 1995 eventually gave way to the cold winter of 1996, not all early Web pioneers were left standing. But you couldn't read any periodical or watch any news show without hearing about the Internet. Big business began to take serious notice. Those who had predicted the demise of this cantankerous upstart medium began to join the converted. Netscape, the lone dominant player on the Web frontier, saw a new and formidable opponent appear. One of the most important business contributions that came from the explosion of the Web was that it opened the door for a host of new entrepreneurs, giving them the opportunity to change the face of communication in both a business and a personal sense. Armed with big ideas and often venture capital, young businessmen and businesswomen were forming companies that would define and change Net space. The activities of these companies ranged from developing programs for finding things on the Web (Yahoo, WebCrawler, Lycos, and so forth) to creating communities (Geocities, Parent Soup) to building cutting-edge software that enabled more information to fly over the phone lines into your computer (RealAudio).

Other companies initially thought that the Web's culture could be re-created in private environments that could charge a premium membership. An early advocate of this business model was the successful AOL. Taking its cue from the AOL success story, a new player, a sleeping giant, began awakening and would soon be looking at the Internet with newfound respect. Microsoft had basically ignored the Net, instead focusing on dominating the desktop operating environment. (Windows 95 had just been successfully introduced.) When the Web initially caught Big M's eye, the response was to attempt to create a Web-like environment in which private members could meet and find specific content. The Microsoft Network (MSN) debuted amid much hoopla but quickly found itself mired in the difficulties relating to its attempt to be an alternative network. It soon learned that the Net as a culture could not be contained in any one environment. As a matter of fact, users would tolerate significant rubbish and unfocused content to maintain the freedom and holistic nature of their information network. This was a powerful lesson for Microsoft and one that it is still attempting to implement. However, within about six months of its debut, The Microsoft Network joined the Internet at large. It has become a meaningful destination for hundreds of thousands of Web users. Interestingly, AOL chose to join the Net in a hybrid environment, offering private and public content—successfully so far. In the process, AOL determined that its future lay in providing a content environment for its users, and it shed its cable and technology elements. The future of MSN and AOL will be interesting indeed.

Bang, Bang, Bang Goes the Browser

Simultaneously Microsoft faced new issues with MSN, and the technology architecture that supported the Web caused a rethinking of business networking. Gradually, it was becoming apparent that the network was the ultimate computing environment. Microsoft had focused successfully on the individual desktop. It was rapidly becoming evident that a computer that was not connected to the Net might soon be a thing of the past. This was a problem for Microsoft. Networked computers could use a different environment to manage their desktops, an environment dominated by the browser! And who was the king of the browser world? Netscape.

This was a showdown that Microsoft understood. It owned the desktop and would fight to the death to keep it. Gates and team saw this and reacted, making a legendary shift in the company's destiny. Microsoft determined it would own the browser market. So it strapped on its six-guns and stepped out into the morning sun. At the other end of the street stood Netscape, the new kid in town. There just wasn't room enough in Net town for the two of them. When the gunfight ended and the smoke cleared, Microsoft had taken a simple browser product originally licensed from Spry and engineered a completely new desktop environment. With its Internet Explorer, Microsoft became the formidable force in browsers and networked or common desktop environments. At the other end of the street lay Netscape, wounded but not yet mortally. But as the browser gradually becomes indistinguishable from the network and the desktop, this historian sees the writing on the wall for Netscape. The company is already seeking suitors for a sale.

And So It Grows...

As you are reading this book, new information and technologies are dating these comments about the Net. But as the Net emerges into a profitable and productive environment, it will owe its success to the early pioneers. These early Net pioneers have given us a rich heritage. They took chances, risking bankruptcy, forgoing perks that ranged from salary to bathing, living through countless 20-hour days, while breathing life into a network of wires and chips. Many of them didn't last. But they all contributed. Across the Internet, early settlers laid the foundation that has given us e-mail, commerce, promotions, database-driven sites, banner advertising, content publishing, and more.

I was one of the lucky ones. On Ramp has grown to become THINK New Ideas, Incorporated, emerging as a global award-winning technology and communications company. As president of THINK, I helped take the company public (still another book) in 1995. With about 300 employees and five offices, we have created a formidable consultancy and interactive solutions provider, helping Fortune 500 companies prosper in the information age.

Perhaps the most important point made in this chapter is that the Web has won. The Net has influenced society deeply and widely. It has created or been created by an overwhelming desire to connect. If has fed on the idea that networking information provides more powerful resources for everyone. Because of the Net, much information, once the currency of elite power brokers, has now become a powerful tool in the hands of the everyday person. Just as the automobile and the telephone enabled people to connect in a way that changed society, so has the Web by providing the foundation for people to share ideas and have access to an almost unbelievable depth of knowledge in a common environment.

About the Author

Ron Bloom, president and chief operating officer of THINK New Ideas, is a contributor, speaker, and author in the interactive community who has helped to shape the concepts of marketing and communications on the Internet. On occasion he has been quoted as saying, "Just when we think we have built the perfect idiot-proof system, someone invents a better idiot."

"The security of any computer system can be breached, and the methods for cracking the security are well known to hackers."

John Kim

CHAPTER 2

Braving the Elements

I started playing with computers as a kid—and to this day I still consider what I do with computers as play—soon after I moved to America. I was born in South Korea, but when I was ten, my father's work in the logging business required a move to Singapore and then to Kent, Washington.

I was a very social kid in Korea, where I had a lot of interests and friends. Then I came to the States, a completely different culture, where I couldn't understand or communicate in the English language. Not speaking English, I found it really hard to make friends.

But even without English skills, I found that my classes were easy enough, so I did all my homework at school. With few friends and my evenings free, I turned to computers. Playing on computers—sometimes through the night—became a way for me to master a universe, whereas in the real world I felt I was losing control. I started out playing games on a Magnavox Odyssey game console, and then I convinced my parents to buy one of the first new computers—an Apple II Plus. For fun, I began to write my own games in 6502 assembly language on the Apple and then quickly graduated to Pascal and Forth.

As my English improved, I actually came to have a social life, and my interests broadened to music and theater. I had played the clarinet since I was eleven, but in high school, I learned to play the sax, sang in a choir, toured with my high school jazz band, and jammed with my own bands. In theater, I played nearly every role possible—actor, director, stage manager, and lighting and sound designer—particularly as part of the Asian-American Acting Coop, which I cofounded at Wesleyan College.

A few years out of college, in 1993, I first heard about this new thing called multimedia. I got a glimpse of a career that would combine my two real interests—computers and art, particularly theater—in an atmosphere of play. I bought a computer and some software, and for three months I listened to anyone who would talk about multimedia, all the while teaching myself to program. Then I hired myself out as a freelance developer, creating everything from "edutainment" games and demos showcasing the Apple Macintosh to networking software accessible for interactive television.

This work made it clear how very creative programming is. Sure, it's technical, but it requires creativity because you're solving problems, and there's always more than one way to solve a problem. You have to figure out what the parameters are and, given the objective, try to come up with the best way to find the answers. That's what I really love about what I do.

It was an easy transition to the highly inventive environment of Red Sky Interactive, which had been around for just a year when I joined as their first full-time engineer. Now, two years later, as Director of Engineering, I work in an environment that requires constant innovation as we try to synthesize aesthetic expression with technological performance.

Braving the Elements

Keep in Mind...

Before we get into the technical challenges of designing a Web site, remember that the Internet at its inception was not designed to do what we're trying to push it to do today. It was never intended to accommodate a large volume of traffic, nor was it designed to transmit huge files with music, animation, and other multimedia content. It was designed for a relatively small group of people to exchange information openly, primarily in the form of text. Furthermore, it was developed specifically to be decentralized. Independent networks and organizations are connected together, governed not by a central authority but by the voluntary acceptance of collectively developed standards. This technological legacy is the source of many of the problems that arise as site builders try to create Web sites that inform and entertain their visitors.

Keeping Technology Honest

Keep in mind that the Web is simply another medium for your business. Approach it as you do all new business ventures, and make sure that the technology serves your business objectives and not the other way around.

Technology can be very seductive, and Web developers have a tendency to get caught up in it. This is understandable—it's exciting and fun, and those who work in this field obviously want to exercise this technology, so they stay on the cutting edge. But technology is not a magic bullet—you can't just shoot it at a business problem and expect a solution. It's crucial, therefore, that your Web know what a tool can and cannot do. At Red Sky Interactive, we constantly interview technology vendors who pitch the latest version of their product. "Great new features," I tell them. "Now fill me in on the drawbacks of using this new tool." I know we can't fully comprehend technology until we're comfortable with its limitations; only then are we able to work around any potential issues that may come up.

We begin our work with the client by getting a very clear grasp of the core competencies of the business, its customers and competitors, and the market conditions. Before even *thinking* about the technology, we carefully explore the core business problem that the Web site is intended to solve. Only when we have a solid sense of the business and its objectives are we ready to consider the tools and methodology appropriate to achieving the business goals.

For example, one of our clients wanted a searchable database for their Web site. Before we even thought about the implementation, we examined the customer profile, the type and potential use of information in the database, and how we'd access and maintain the database. These deliberations led us to realize that creating tools that would help our client easily update the database information was as critical as the actual Web database the customer would use.

And in fact, we have at times recommended an approach that was not the most technically advanced because it didn't need to be. We were developing a Web site for resellers of Toshiba laptops and desktops. *Push* technology, examples of which are BackWeb and Pointcast, was very hot at the time, and Toshiba wanted to use it to disseminate new product information. (Push technology allows users to subscribe free to a Web site and to customize the information they receive; the information is then delivered to them regularly on a schedule they determine.)

In evaluating the feasibility of using push technology, we discovered that the computers of most of the resellers weren't powerful enough to receive push information, the modems were too slow, and the phone lines didn't have a ready connection to the Internet. In addition, Toshiba didn't have the resources to maintain or support such a system. So we recommended an e-mail system that all the resellers were equipped for. We delivered the content in two formats: text-only for those with very old computers and modems; and for those with more up-to-date systems, content that incorporated graphics, tables, and so on.

Trade-Offs

As an engineer, I can make anything if you give me enough time and money. Technical decisions are influenced by the scope of the project, development time, cost, and the desired quality of the final product. You must weigh all these factors to arrive at a technical solution that works for your business objectives. So there will always be trade-offs.

For example, let's say you want a corporate Web site to coincide with a product launch in six weeks. It could be an extremely expensive proposition to hire and manage the team necessary to develop an extensive, deep site in such a short time frame. (For example, we had about a month to make our first Nike site, which required several teams working virtually around the clock to produce it on schedule.) To bring the project within the budget, you might cut scope—for example, implement the most critical part of the Web site to meet the deadline and phase in implementation of the rest later. Or you could cut development time by being discriminating about how much "flash" you wanted on your site and where it could be placed for maximum effect. Your Web developer will discuss these tradeoffs with you to develop the parameters that will lay the foundation for the design of your Web site.

Where Does the Technology Fit?

Building a successful Web site combines all the techniques of successful software development, the production processes that form a magazine, and the creative insights that go into a work of art. It requires a team that contributes a diverse set of skills.

At Red Sky, every Web project starts with the strategic services department, which does account planning and management. The creative department conceives the design with engineering, which deals with the technical aspects of building and testing a Web site. The production team builds and maintains the site. All these people with specialized skills from different departments have to cooperate. Any successful team must have a common purpose and a clear understanding of everyone's role. While it may not seem obvious, such clarity and collaboration are major factors in determining the success of a project.

For example, we pair a technical lead and a creative director to ensure that the creative team develops ideas that can be implemented. Often a technical person is able to offer ways of implementing something that the creative person might not otherwise come up with. Once there is an agreement on the creative elements of the Web site, the technical lead generates the technical specifications and works with the production group to implement the technical portion as well as provide support.

The kinds of Web sites that this chapter addresses are those that are pushing technology to the limit. These are not the point-and-click, text-only sites of yore (a couple of years ago!) but those that provide some kind of transaction—checking a telephone bill, buying everything from a pound of coffee to a car, researching a vacation, and so on. These Web sites hold essential data and are important, even crucial, to a company's core business.

These sites are important to users as well, whether it's in the moment (getting the running score in a live sportscast or the latest stock price) or over the long term (banking on line). These are also high-volume sites, with hundreds of thousands, if not millions, of hits.

You must consider four major aspects of Web architecture in the development of a Web site: reliability, scalability, security, and compatibility.

Reliability   refers to the sturdiness and stability of a Web site—a reliable Web site is always accessible.

Scalability   refers to a Web site's potential for accommodating additional, sometimes exponential, demands and growth—for example, a stock trading site that could withstand a market crash, or architecture that would work whether an online store sold 200 or 2000 items.

Security   is an issue for users: how secure is the data, such as a credit card number, that they put out on the Internet? Companies with Web sites, on the other hand, are concerned about the vulnerability on the Web of proprietary information, such as customer data and trade secrets.

Compatibility   concerns the visitor's ability to view a Web site as it was designed to be viewed. The most prevalent compatibility issue is the existence of different browsers, such as Internet Explorer and Netscape Communicator, and all the different versions.

Building a Reliable Web Site

A reliable Web site is like a tugboat that can still do its job amid high winds and giant waves. In the stormy environment of the Web, a reliable site has enough redundancy so that it doesn't crash—it is sturdy and stable.

What Are the Reliability Issues?

Reliability is a concern of Web developers because virtually nothing on the Web is stable. It's your concern too because when a Web site fails to provide a requested page, customers will usually see a blank page or an error message. They don't understand *why;* they simply assume it's *your* fault, and this can result in the loss of business and credibility. There are many reasons for this instability.

The Internet is still in the process of being invented. Coordinating organizations such as the Internet Activities Board (IAB) and the World Wide Web Consortium (W3C) are improving the underlying protocols in the form of new standards. But it takes time for them to propagate through the user community. In the collaborative spirit in which the Internet was born and raised, complying with any standard is voluntary. Even after companies agree to the standards, it takes time for Web servers, browsers, and so on to conform. And it takes longer for individual and business users to upgrade their software (and even hardware) to take advantage of the new standards.

In addition, the Internet is growing at a furious rate. For example, the number of Web sites multiplied more than 10 times, from 100,000 sites in January 1996 to 1.3 million in August 1997, only 20 months later. New programs are constantly being launched. For example, personalization software, such as Firefly, was less than a year old before it was widely used to give individuals personalized service or content—news or book recommendations, for example. And existing programs, such as RealAudio (which lets you hear sound on the Web), NetMeeting (which enables virtual meetings over the Web), and the various browsers are improving frequently!

Several problems result from this rapid pace. Because the development pace is so accelerated and the cycle of testing and bug fixing is so compressed, there's little time to test the software adequately or work out all the compatibility issues. The results can sometimes be buggy and unstable until a newer version comes out. But even then, with software being released every three to six months, there's no guarantee that a Web site developed for today's technology will work with the latest version of that software tomorrow.

The problem of creating reliable Web sites is exacerbated by the fact that people use different browsers and different versions of each browser, forcing the developer to support many versions. And as if this weren't enough volatility, I can guarantee that at some point your hard disk will fail. Servers will crash. Internet connections will go down. It's not a matter of *if*, but *when*.

What Makes a Web Site Reliable?

In this capricious environment, nevertheless, it's vital to keep the connection to the Internet. Each minute lost is a potential customer who cannot access your site, representing a loss of business at some level. Redundancy is the key to reliability. The more important your data is, the more important it is to build backups to the server system so it can accommodate the inevitable breakdown. (A server is simply a very fast computer with a very large hard drive.)

Companies typically purchase Internet access from an Internet Service Provider (ISP). The Web servers that make the connection to the Internet can be located either at the company or at the ISP. (Very large companies can use their own servers.) The latter arrangement allows the company to own (or rent) the servers but allows access to the ISP's data center infrastructure. Typically, the ISP would offer such services as multiple high-speed connections to the Internet, emergency backup power generators in case of power failures, and 24-hour monitoring. It should also offer some kind of uptime guarantee (a promise that the site will function a certain percentage of the time—98 percent, for example); it could also include a money-back guarantee for each hour the system is down. If the servers are kept in-house, make sure that there is at least one additional backup connection to the Internet, preferably from another ISP. (Some companies, such as Amazon.com, with millions of hits a day, back up their systems through as many as nine separate ISPs.)

How Is a Reliable System Developed?

How does a Web builder plan for and design a Web site that will work, and work well, in what can be an extremely unstable environment? At Red Sky, we manage the risk using several techniques.

Rapid prototyping is a method for testing sample features in many browsers. It's best used up front to find out what features are possible without spending a lot of time and money. There are two kinds of prototyping: wide and deep. Which one the Web shop uses depends on the functionality being tested. If, for example, you wanted to provide personalized Web news, the Web developer could build and test all the different kinds of news that someone might request—world, financial, sports, weather, and so on. Or the developer could focus on one type of news and implement every aspect of that feature—how the news feeds would be handled, how all the links would work, and so forth.

Collaboration with vendors can be a great solution. Often new technology is crucial to the success of a project, but for the reasons mentioned earlier in this chapter, its use may not be a good risk. In exchange for the use of their software on a client's Web site, vendors may agree to give special support—top priority to answering technical questions, fixing bugs upon request, and even customizing features to work more efficiently with the site.

Chapter 2: Braving the Elements

Solid scheduling is essential for completing projects on time. When creating a schedule, your Web developer should build in a number of milestones, each with definite deliverables. At each checkpoint, you should re-evaluate the approach—is it going to work? Should you continue, or change direction, or go with the fallback? Mostly because of the mercurial nature of the Web, projects always take longer than expected no matter how carefully they are planned or how experienced the developer is. Your site builder should pad the schedule to solve the unpredictable, but inevitable, problems.

Building a Scalable Web Site

Scalability refers to the ability of a Web site to accommodate the demands on the site—even exponential demands—and to grow gracefully as a result or as business objectives change.

A trading site provides a perfect example. A crash on the stock market could result in a huge spike in the number of people trying to access their accounts at the site and sell stocks. The servers and the rest of the Web site infrastructure must be built to manage that additional load—perhaps even a 100 percent increase in the normal volume. Furthermore, the site must be designed so that it's easy to expand and change—adding options trading or Frequently Asked Questions (FAQ)—as the company gets a better feel for its targeted audience.

What Are the Scalability Issues?

Obviously, such design does not come free, and you must weigh the possibility of success against the cost of developing for it. How much disruption and delay can you afford?

For example, there would be no question of going to extra lengths to ensure scalability for a site that handles stock transactions or a one-time cybercast of a live event, such as the Academy Awards. These obviously have a high priority in accommodating increased usage. Some sites, however, might require fewer resources to make the site scalable. For example, a Web site that mainly gives such information as a list of stores or a company history might tolerate delays or server problems that take it off line for an hour or two. But in this age of instant information and the resultant expectations, such sites are increasingly rare.

If the site builder doesn't design a site to be scalable, it can be costly and disruptive later to accommodate changes. It's like building a bridge for which you initially estimate that no more than 1000 cars will travel over every hour. What happens if 2000 cars an hour drive over it? Or 10,000? That kind of traffic may require closing the bridge for a short period to reinforce the stress points or closing it for a very long time to rebuild it from the ground up.

In addition, if the Web developers haven't planned your site to be scalable, they most likely won't have anticipated the organizational requirements of a larger site. Typically, a small team that's building a modest Web site won't make notes about their process because it's easy to communicate changes. They hold site information in their heads—directory paths, file names, and all the little idiosyncrasies of the site.

But if the site is wildly successful and the client wants to showcase not 200, but 2000 products, a handful of people are not going to be able to handle it with that low-key approach. In fact, sometimes the hardware and software are perfectly capable of handling the volume, but no process is in place to accommodate the increase in work. (There is software on the market developed specifically for managing large sites, but like most Internet tools, it's immature.)

How Is a Scalable System Developed?

With the issues firmly in mind, an experienced site builder will use some of the following up-front strategies to ensure a scalable Web site. Of course, they're easier stated than done. The headlong growth of the Internet makes it difficult to predict user demand accurately and even throws available market data into question. It's also difficult to estimate potential hits on new online businesses that have no counterpart in the "real" world, such as businesses offering subscriptions for renting software (word processor, contact manager, and so on) and hard disk space through WebTV.

Quantify your target. This means setting up a baseline of service using such criteria as the number of visitors you anticipate and the maximum acceptable delay. For example, the speed of the average target modem would govern the maximum file size of a Web page—as the page gets bigger, the display of the site slows.

The Web developer must also consider the importance of the transaction. Is it OK for a user to wait or to have to try again? For example, if electronic postcards (multimedia "cards" that are sent from a Web site) are a feature of your Web site, the Web builders would establish the maximum number of users that you would anticipate sending postcards to simultaneously. Or they might limit the size of a video clip or animation so that most visitors would wait no more than five minutes for it to download.

Anticipate services. Anticipate additional services wherever possible because a future addition may affect the design of those already installed. Is it likely you'll want to add technical support, a link to human resources, or an e-mail suggestion box? Returning to the bridge example, it's much easier to add an exit later if the original builders considered the possibility and reinforced the bridge footings near the potential exit.

Plan for the unexpected. This is somewhat akin to earthquake-proofing a bridge. The Web developer will install enough servers and server connections to handle the unexpected—an extreme spike in usage, a power brown-out, and so on. The capacity of a Web site depends in part on the speed of its connection to the Internet; the flow of data is analogous to the flow of water through a pipe or a hose, with a T1 connection represented by a kitchen pipe and a T3 connection represented by a fire hose.

If you're calculating a baseline of 5000 visitors per hour to your site and your system is at 95 percent capacity handling this, that's probably not enough leeway. You could expand by adding more Web servers, but that's only half the solution—a kitchen pipe can deliver only a certain amount of water, even if the water (data) is flowing from a fire hydrant. You will probably also need to increase the server connection to the Internet (like adding more pipes)—for example, by adding an extra T1 connection.

An important component of such planning is testing the Web site using software that simulates what could happen; it's a lot like the kind of crash testing that is conducted on cars using life-size dummies.

Document the process. Even if your Web site starts small and you think it will stay that way, it helps to have a process in place that documents how the site was built and the processes used to maintain it. Documentation is even more important when you put mission-critical information on the Web.

The documentation should include the initial objectives, a site map, and site specifications—design guidelines, technical specifications, how the site was produced, and how it's maintained. Site specifications should also include a record of the "postmortem" conference that occurs soon after the site goes live. All the team members and the client convene to discuss what went well, where the problems were, and how they'll improve the process and the site on the next round. (This is an iterative process, so there's always a next round!)

As a client, make sure that you have copies of the documentation and that it's kept up-to-date. I've seen situations in which Web developers created documentation when the site was started but never updated it, so when changes needed to be made a year and a half later, it was as if there were no documentation at all.

Building a Secure Web Site

There are two aspects of security on the Web. Of primary concern to users is the security of their data—their address, credit card number, secret love note—as it traverses the Internet. The foremost concern of companies with Web sites, on the other hand, is the security of proprietary information, such as customer information and trade secrets. Remember that the Internet was originally designed as an open environment for the free sharing of information, and the legacy of that architecture is weak security.

Browser Security

People are concerned that someone could steal their credit card number or read their private e-mail on the Web. The media have fueled this concern with a lot of attention to browser security. But browser security is actually quite good. (In fact, I'm not aware of any documented case of credit card interception over the Internet.) Most browsers can encrypt information, such as the credit card number during a purchase, before sending it to the server. (Note that encrypting information requires more processing time, so encrypted transactions are as much as 50 percent slower than those without encryption.)

Given enough machines with enough power and enough time, it's technically possible for someone to decode encrypted information. Decryption has proven to be unlikely, however, because it's time-consuming, excruciatingly meticulous work that requires profound mathematical knowledge to do. It's far easier to dig up old credit card slips in the garbage behind a retail store or sift through office trash than it is for a hacker to try to crack the browser encryption. However, a number of standards are being developed to address this concern. The major one, called Secure Electronic Transaction (SET), is being developed jointly by VISA and MasterCard. Unlike an ordinary credit card transaction, in which you hand over your credit card to the merchant or phone in the number, with SET the Web retailer will never see the number. Rather, a bank verifies the number and the line of credit and then informs the merchant of approval. SET is still in its pilot phase, and a number of implementation issues remain to be resolved.

Some of the fear concerning browser security can be attributed to the newness of making purchases without any human contact at all. There's evidence, however, that these fears have abated somewhat, as measured by the growth in online sales.

System Security

But browser security is not really where significant problems lie. Data and server security are much bigger risks. Data can be read, stolen, or even changed without any control by the company that "owns" the Web site. The security of any computer system can be breached, and the methods for cracking the security are well known to hackers. (IBM has a team of ethical hackers. These experts, who test the security of corporate systems, gain entry 85 percent of the time.)

Operating systems such as UNIX and, to a lesser extent, Microsoft Windows NT have well-documented vulnerabilities; there are also widely publicized security holes in browsers. Hackers can use Web servers to break into a system (for example, by having an external packet of information masquerade as an internal packet) or to cripple a Web site (for example, by flooding it with thousands of requests per minute using a method known as SYNFLOOD). There is even freeware that automates the process of testing passwords. Furthermore, the relative immaturity and swift innovation of software mean that security holes might not be detected before the Web site goes live.

The scope of the problem could be wider too because many security intrusions are never reported. The Federal Bureau of Investigation estimates that fewer than one in eight hacker attacks are reported. That's understandable—no bank, for example, wants it to be known that an unauthorized person has gained access to the information in a customer's account.

What Makes a System Secure?

The more important the data and the transaction, the more important security is. Start with the expectation that attempts will be made to compromise the site if it is highly public or holds important information. Even if a site is small, is not highly publicized, and does not contain any critical data, you should still maintain some minimal security.

Of course, the best security is no access at all, but that would defeat the purpose of a Web site. The goal is to manage your risk by controlling and monitoring access. A company can use a variety of strategies to do this. One is to limit access by using passwords. Another is to create an internal firewall—a computer that protects a corporate network from the Internet and keeps intruders from breaking into it. But the most effective thing you can do is to charge someone with the responsibility of developing and maintaining a security system. Whether a company employee or an outside security firm, they should:

- Review potential security issues, and obtain fixes or coordinate with the ISP responsible for hosting the servers.
- Conduct security reviews at regular intervals and when a change is made to the site that affects security.
- Keep current with available security software and with security industry information.

Compatibility: Designing for Almost-Standards

Compatibility concerns the browser's ability to view a Web site as it was designed. Compatibility is an issue because different browsers are competing for market share on the Internet. Internet Explorer and Netscape Communicator are the prominent ones as of this writing, and each of these is available in several versions as well.

What Are the Compatibility Issues?

While browsers are based on industry standards, these standards are so loosely defined that two different browsers could implement them differently enough to cause a problem. Even worse, it might be such a small difference, an odd difference, that you don't really discover the problem until you start testing. For example, fonts are used differently enough in browsers to throw off a line length in a meticulously designed online brochure or to relegate a caption intended to lie under an image to the marginal hinterlands.

Not only do browsers implement the standards differently, they each have their own sets of features, and supporting a feature specific to one browser can cause problems with another. For example, some versions of Netscape can detect whether a user has certain plug-ins such as RealAudio or Shockwave and can take the user automatically to the appropriate Web page. Internet Explorer 4 does not have this capability, so we have to ask the user if he or she has it in order to know what page to serve.

Occasionally, you might be lucky enough to develop a Web site for just one browser, such as for an organizational intranet or extranet. (An intranet is an internal Web not connected to the Internet. An extranet is a Web site with access limited to certain people. For example, Red Sky puts its calendar on an extranet so that its public relations firm can read it and add events to it, but there's no access for anyone else.) In this case, the organization has probably standardized on a certain browser, so you can take full advantage of its features without spending time and money making them available in other browsers.

The bottom line? Research your target market. Find out what browsers your prospective clients will most likely use, and decide which browsers to target.

How Do You Ensure Compatibility?

Once the target browsers have been identified, the Web site developer will make sure that your site works at a certain basic level for all of them. The developer will constantly weigh the costs of creating and maintaining the site with the return in consumer impact. One way to keep the cost down is to design a system that requires writing each page only once rather than design a customized version for each browser. There is readily available code that detects what browser and version the visitor is using.

For example, we developed a Web site that used different images for each section of the site as context markers to help visitors navigate the site. We designed the page using tables. Version 2 of Netscape, however, can't have a background image in a table. Because it was one of our targeted browsers and because the images were critical to navigation, we dumped the idea of tables and made the entire section of those pages (including the text) an image map.

Once the Web developers make sure that the Web site works for all the targeted browsers, they have the option of customizing a page (or even an entire Web site) for a certain browser or browser feature. This adds time and cost to development because it still must be tested on the other browsers to ensure that it doesn't cause any conflicts. For example, one of our clients wanted animated rollovers with sound. (Rollovers are the little tips that pop up when you pause the mouse cursor over something on screen.) Users with browsers that couldn't combine rollovers with sound saw the rollovers alone. And for browsers that couldn't display rollovers, we duplicated the effect using animated images.

Once the site is built, the site builder must test the performance of your Web site with each browser. Currently we test for five different browsers based on their market share: Internet Explorer versions 3 and 4 and Netscape Communicator versions 2, 3, and 4. Our statistics show that a sizable number of people still use each of these browsers, so we can't ignore them. And while people will be constantly upgrading to newer browsers, Web developers will continue to have to provide multiple browser support in the foreseeable future.

About the Author

With his career in classical ballet cut tragically short by a knee injury, John Kim currently spends his days as Director of Engineering at Red Sky Interactive in San Francisco, working with such clients as Lands' End, Nike, and Absolut Vodka.

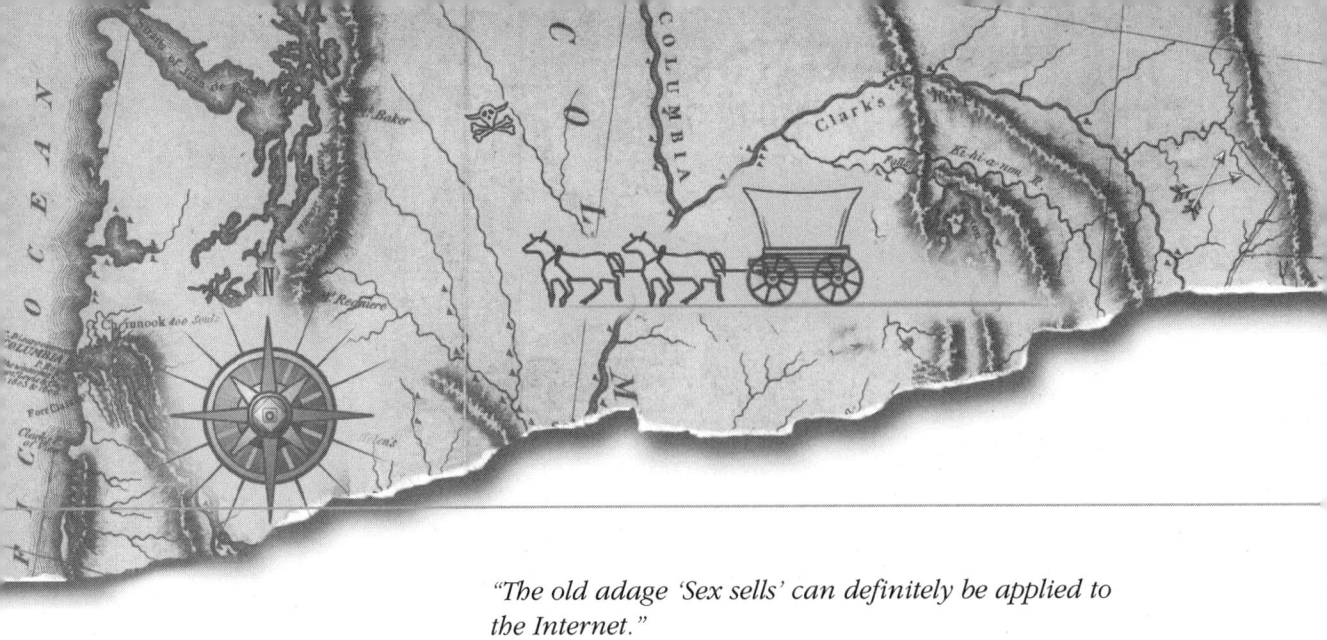

"The old adage 'Sex sells' can definitely be applied to the Internet."

Cerise Vablais

The Web's Oldest Profession

It was a dark and stormy Seattle night. At about 1:00 A.M., I logged on to my laptop and jumped on the Internet. I went to Yahoo and typed in the word "sex." I picked one of the first sites I saw that offered video and connected to the site. After clicking through the various age disclaimers and filling out the registration form, I took a deep breath and started to watch my first online adult video. My first reaction was really just, "Why? Why would anyone watch video that is of such low quality?" I figured that someone must watch adult video since there are so many sites that offer it. I went back to Yahoo and visited a few more sites, including some foreign sites that promised "more action" or "live sex." After viewing several of these sites as well, I truly couldn't tell the difference in content from site to site. Then it hit me. Before I began writing this chapter, I knew that adult sites had contributed to the growth of the Internet. I also knew that many times adult sites were the first to adopt new technologies and ways of doing business. But after cruising the sites for several hours at a time over the course of a few days, I figured out why. They were selling the same thing over and over again: sex. And the only way to differentiate their content was to put it in a new package. So the adult sites used the latest and greatest technology to keep their users coming back for more.

Now for a little background on me. I don't make it a habit to cruise these sites. In fact, Microsoft has several policies and technologies in place to make sure that employees don't spend their days surfing the porn sites. At the same time, I felt that this book wouldn't be complete without addressing the issue of online porn. Just like the growth of the VCR and cable-TV industries, pornography helped the Internet grow into the social, cultural, and business phenomenon it is today.

Why Sex On Line?

Sex still seems to be a topic that our society has trouble discussing. During my research, I did come across articles in which psychologists claim that this Victorian attitude toward sex has added to the huge interest in online adult content. And of course, a significant amount of Web traffic involves international visitors, especially in countries in which traditional forms of adult content may be illegal. But there also seem to be some unique qualities of the medium that make it more appealing to a larger audience.

Anonymity

A lot of people have asked, "Why sex on line?" The quality of online video is much lower than the quality of video tapes. It seems that the beauty of the Internet is its anonymity. The users of the sex sites are known only to their credit card companies and to the Webmasters of the adult sites, who, much like adult mail-order catalogs, bill their customers very discreetly. For the first time, purveyors of porn don't need to face the clerk at the local video store to view or buy pornographic material. They simply need to go to their computer, log on to the Internet, and visit their favorite Web site. Some adult site proprietors believe that eventually the Internet will replace adult cinema. People will simply choose what they want to watch in the privacy of their own homes.

The Web's Oldest Profession

The Ability to Become Someone Else

Adult chat rooms also give their users the sense of being able to become whoever they want to be. In online chat rooms, men can be women, teenagers can be adults, and no one knows what you look like. There seems to be some anecdotal evidence that people are more able to express themselves in the total anonymity of the online environment. If you have ever visited a chat room, you have probably felt that people are more candid there than they would be in other situations. After a while, this type of honesty and rant just becomes rather boring and innocuous. But if you find yourself offended by fellow chatters, just remind yourself how frustrated they must be with struggling to type their pickup lines at the mercy of a 4800-baud connection.

The Promise of Variety

Unlike the video you've rented or the evening's programming on an adult cable TV channel, the Internet offers literally millions of bytes of adult content. If you become bored with one site, it's a simple click of your mouse to find a new site that is more interesting to you.

Sex Is Always Available

The Internet is available 24 hours a day, seven days a week. And there's no need to wait for a certain show to come on. As with a rented video, the user is in control of the experience. Granted, it might seem a little strange to be sitting in front of your PC at 3:00 in the morning, but it's always an option. And unlike using traditional forms of media, you can even disguise your viewing as work!

How Do They Make Money?

These sites are making money—lots and lots of money. "But how do they do it?" you ask. Well, primarily, adult Web sites make money in four ways, as you'll see in the following sections.

Membership Fees

Most adult sites charge users weekly, monthly, or more extended membership fees. Most of these services are set up to be automatically renewed (much like AOL or MSN), so when, for example, one month is up, your monthly membership is renewed and billed to your credit card. Many of the sites boast hundreds of thousands of members. Membership fees generally range from $6.95 a month to around $29.95 a month. But this doesn't mean you have access to all the services of the site after you pay your monthly fee. Most sites offer basic chat rooms, bulletin boards, a few pictures, and other teasers as part of your basic membership fee. But most sites charge additional amounts to view live video, download pictures, or join chat rooms with "entertainers."

Adult Verification Services (AVSs)

As part of the federal Communications Decency Act (CDA) passed in February 1996, all Internet users must prove that they are over 18 years of age in order to view adult material. In addition, the Telecommunications Act of 1996 requires adult sites to screen users by requiring that they have a valid credit card and other age verification. Although the Supreme Court put a temporary injunction on the CDA, because of the growing controversy over children having access to pornography on the Internet, many Web sites now require that their users have a password from one of the AVSs. And guess what, both the AVS and the participating sites are making money. Most of the services charge between $16.95 and $25.95 for a one-year membership. Part of this revenue is then paid to the Web site the new member linked from to join the AVS. One of the AVS sites, AdultWatch, claims to pay the highest commission. It pays participating Webmasters $8.50 for each unique user that signs up for a $16.95 six-month membership. Some sites require that a user subscribe to a particular AVS in order to view their content. So one day you might go to your favorite porn site and find that you now have to subscribe to an AVS. What if you already have a subscription to a different AVS? Too bad, you'll need to purchase a subscription to the second service as well.

The Web's Oldest Profession

One-Time Payment for Services

A few sites still allow you to buy services for a one-time fee. Many of these services require you to become a member of their program but don't charge you for membership. Instead, they charge you a flat access fee and then a per-minute fee for video content. And of course, much like 900 number providers, these services usually require the purchase of a minimum number of minutes.

Advertising Click-Thrus

Many adult sites also make money from click-thrus to other sites. *Click-thrus* refer to those banner ads you see on sites, adult and nonadult alike. For every user who "clicks-thru" to the advertising adult site, the original site is paid a small amount (usually between $.02 and $.07, although some sites pay up to $.11). The goal is obviously to drive traffic to the other adult sites, but it is also interesting to note that many of these sites are owned by the same company. Some of them even broadcast the same live content.

So How Much Money Are They Making?

While it is often hard to measure the true revenue generated by any sector of the adult entertainment industry, most estimates are that the online porn business will generate $1 billion a year by the year 2000. Opinions differ regarding how much these sites are making right now. Forrester Research in Massachusetts estimates that adult content sites account for close to 10 percent of all revenue generated by Web sites in the United States. If this is true, that would result in revenue of over $100 million for 1997. However, some estimates go much much higher, with some industry analysts putting the current amount of worldwide revenue from online adult sites in the $2 to 3 billion range. Within this huge range of estimates, only one thing is certain, and that is that the online adult sites *are* making money, unlike nearly all of the nonadult content–oriented sites on the Web. Consumers won't pay to get their news or movie listings on line, but they will pay for sex. Sexual content is always in demand, and its suppliers can charge whatever they want and still make money.

How Many Sites?

The number of adult sites on the Internet is hard to peg. In an August 1997 *Newsday* article, *USA Today* was quoted as reporting that there were between 4000 and 6000 adult sites on the web. And a June 1997 *Wall Street Journal* article estimated that there were some 10,000 adult-oriented sites on the web. When I went to Yahoo (December 1997) and typed in the word "sex," there were 166 category matches and 1917 sites in those categories. Just three months later, there were 170 categories and 2080 sites! For comparison, I typed the word "computer," and Yahoo returned 25,902 site matches spanning 966 categories. The word "food" returned 245 category matches with a total of 6501 sites. Three months later, there were 269 food categories and 6561 sites—a much smaller increase than with the sex sites. So while there are a lot of adult sites on the Internet, they are not as prolific as everyone might think, although they do seem to be multiplying faster than other types of sites.

There are even new search engines that list only adult content. One of these, Naughty Linx, is run by JMR Creations in Boston. Jonathan Lieberman, the CEO, provided me with a lot of information about the real size of the online market. Naughty Linx looks like and acts like a traditional search engine but has one important additional feature. If you search on a keyword and get a list of sites back, Naughty Linx will tell you whether each site is up or down. How and why do they do this? The how is easy; they regularly "sniff" the sites that are listed in their directory to see whether each site is still operational. JMR Creations added this feature to the Naughty Linx search engine to help alleviate the frustration a user might experience when trying to connect to a site only to find it nonoperational and sometimes permanently gone but still listed in a search engine.

Lieberman estimates that there are approximately 28,000 adult sites on the Web, with about 50 percent of these created by commercial ventures and the other 50 percent created by individuals just for fun. He also estimated total revenues of the online adult industry at $1.25 billion for 1997. He told me that the bulk of the revenue comes from subscriptions and video-conferencing fees, with a much smaller but growing revenue stream from the sale of adult videotapes, CD-ROMs, and adult sex toys. He said that he definitely felt that product sales would increase because of the privacy afforded by buying on line.

CHAPTER 3
The Web's Oldest Profession

Adult Sites as Pioneers of Web Technology

While speaking with Jonathan Lieberman, I asked him what he thought about the influence of the online adult sites on the growth of the Internet and particularly on the technologies used in these sites. He cited several "firsts" among the online adult industry—these Web proprietors were the first to aggressively bill their visitors. They were also some of the first sites to try online video, long before the video was even of seemingly reasonable quality. I believe that the success of offering video content made other industries, such as the news industry, incorporate streamed content into their Web sites.

Adult sites were also the first to build shopping carts. So I guess you could say that the adult Web site proprietors were the early pioneers of these technologies, and it makes sense because they could take the risk. They were nearly guaranteed that they would get their money back—sex sells in any form.

How Many Visitors?

The March 1998 Media Metrix World Wide Web Audience Ratings report stated that 28.9 percent of all home Internet users were accessing adult sites. The most popular adult site was cybererotica.com, with a total of 1,898,000 hits in the month of March. During the same time period, Yahoo received 16,945,000 hits and of the top 50 domains, four were adult sites. What I found more interesting is that users are spending more time on adult sites compared with time spent on other sites, with an average of 12.0 minutes of use per day for the month of March. Next highest was the news/info/entertainment category, with an average of 9.3 minutes a day. Visitors to adult sites are also more likely to visit more pages within the site and return to the site on a more frequent basis than visitors to other types of sites. I think that part of the reason for this loyalty is the fact that they are paying for the content and often have a subscription to a service. This makes them come back to the same site more often. I also think that they are more motivated to wait for the content to download and therefore spend more time on the sites.

Regulation of Pornography on the Internet

As with most other adult industries, the government began to worry about the *availability* of online pornography. The debate over regulating online content heated up after the publication of the now infamous Carnegie Mellon University study of pornography on the Web in 1995. This study found that a high percentage of images downloaded from bulletin boards and newsgroups were pornographic. More interesting, the study found that a large number of the downloaded images contained content that the federal government has defined as obscene and even illegal, including images of child pornography and bestiality. The study was later discredited, but the research proved to add impetus to the fight for the passing of government regulation for online content. The proposed Communications Decency Act of 1996 was the first bill to attempt to regulate the online adult entertainment industry. This bill sparked off a huge fight over First Amendment rights, and many Web sites went as far as to make their home pages black in protest of the proposed legislation. Nearly all proprietors of adult sites felt that the bill, initiated by Democratic Senator James Exxon of Nebraska, was unnecessary. They felt that they were already doing enough to ensure that minors were not accessing the content on their sites.

To control access to their images and video content, most adult site proprietors require users to confirm that they are over 18, and most require the entering of a credit card number. The government concluded that entering a credit card number would provide ample proof that a site visitor was over 18 years of age. This actually helped the online adult industry make money because visitors were required to enter a valid credit card number, making it much faster and easier to purchase content.

In the midst of the controversy surrounding the Communications Decency Act, several options for limiting Internet accesibility for minors emerged. Net censoring software, such as NetNanny, became available, allowing parents to restrict access to certain Internet sites. Some sites voluntarily rate themselves using ratings from organizations such as the Recreational

Software Advisory Council on the Internet (the RSACi ratings) and SafeSurf. Parents can use Internet Explorer and other browsers to recgonize these self-imposed ratings and block out the sites with ratings higher than what they want a child to access. The obvious problem with self-rated sites is that the Webmaster can rate the site however he or she chooses. Nothing's perfect, but parents can be reassured that there are at least minimal protections in place.

Sex Does Sell

The old adage "Sex sells" can definitely be applied to the Internet. As with other media technology, such as VCRs and cable TV, it didn't take long for the adult entertainment companies to realize that the World Wide Web was a new delivery mechanism for their content. And as was the case with home video in the late 1970s and cable TV in the 1980s, the demand for pornography has helped the Internet grow to become a major cultural and business phenomenon of the 20th century. And because sex sells, the number of adult sites that will give you their content for free is decreasing, which is not the case with most other types of sites. And unlike a news site or a corporation's Web site that provides additional information, these adult sites exist for only one reason: to make money. And so there you have it—the adult entertainment industry was one of the first to use the Internet as a true commercial venture, and in that venture it has been quite successful.

About the Author

Cerise Vablais has been on the Site Builder Network team since early 1997. She is still trying to figure out how, with an English/philosophy degree, she ended up at Microsoft. In her spare time, she likes to run marathons and look at the stars.

"Now that's one hell of a captivated audience!"

Jesse Albert

CHAPTER 4

Moving Pictures

Once again it was 7:30 A.M., and I was a little impressed with myself for arriving at work at such an early hour when I didn't leave the night before until well after midnight. I may have been impressed with myself, but Angela, my fiancée, was getting more and more frustrated. "I'm glad you proposed before these crazy hours started. I don't know what kind of answer you'd get now," she said.

As you can tell, my work life has been a bit overwhelming, but when you work in a medium such as the Internet, it has to be expected. We at Media Revolution have a lot of work ahead of us as we add our contribution to the development of this burgeoning industry. The Web is still in its infancy and everyone involved is a pioneer, so charting this new territory takes a lot of time. Angela understands this, knowing very well what we plan to do. She just wishes it didn't take so many damn hours to do it.

On this particular morning, I pulled into the Media Revolution parking lot and headed upstairs to the main entrance. After fumbling for my keys, I realized the door was already unlocked. I walked in and, finding no one in sight, went to the back of the offices to investigate. Perhaps someone was in the server room; why at this ungodly hour I didn't know, but perhaps. Upon entering the server room I found proof that we are in fact conquering a new frontier. Like a cowboy whose campfire has deteriorated to ash, huddled in the fetal position on the floor was our senior programmer. Surrounded by the glow of four halogen desk lamps that were resting on the floor encircling his sleeping body, Yush Yuen, the ultimate pioneer, was sound asleep. Having worked well into the wee hours of the night, Yush had decided to not waste the time driving home to sleep but rather had stayed in the office and held down the fort till the morn. With no couch and no heat, he had sought shelter and warmth from the slight heat radiating from the four halogen bulbs arching over his prone body.

This, in a story, is what Media Revolution is all about. The members of this team are on a dedicated mission to transform the multimedia and entertainment potential of the Web into a reality. If, in fact, the Web is the latest unconquered frontier, the individuals that Media Revolution comprises are not only some of the pioneers of this new medium but also part of the wagon train.

"Open from 9:00 A.M. to very late at night" is what you hear when you reach the message center at Media Revolution's office, and it's a clear indication of how we work. During the past year and a half, we have helped transform the Web by developing some of the highest-profile and most creative Web sites for the Hollywood community. Our recent projects have included campaigns for blockbuster movies such as *Independence Day* (Twentieth Century Fox Home Entertainment), *Alien Resurrection* (Twentieth Century Fox), *Air Force One* (Sony Movies), and *Amistad* (DreamWorks). We have also developed projects for Sega GameWorks, Reba McEntire, and a host of other site seekers.

"The whole is greater than the sum of its parts" may be applicable to Media Revolution, but each part is incredibly strong on its own, and it's the variety of experiences that makes our digital communications company tick. Each core member of our team comes from a different media background and focus, and therefore each one of us is able to bring something fresh to the table. The two things we have in common are a desire to take risks and an entrepreneurial nature. In such a new industry these qualities are imperative to achieving successful careers. Together we have been able to build a remarkable company dedicated to creating compelling entertainment on line and committed to finding new methods of effective communication for this high-tech marketing world.

Building Up the Wagon Train

We're not quite sure whether Jason Yim, our creative director, hired someone to steal his car so that he could use the insurance money to start a business, or whether he just has a natural ability to turn terrible situations into extremely successful ones. Either way, that one unfortunate experience steamrolled into quite a successful career.

While in college, Jason took his advertising background and the advice of a professor and decided to give this "Web thing" a shot. Already an accomplished designer (having worked summers with the design staff of McCann-Erickson's Auckland, New Zealand, office and the Nestle, Inc., account for Medicus PDA in Sydney, Australia), Jason returned to the States and dedicated his senior year of college (1994–1995) to Web design and development.

Jason learned one very important thing while in college, and it has carried over into his work today. He was taught that there are two basic types of Web adventurers on the Internet. One type of person sees the Web as an information resource and wants content delivered quickly. The other is more exploratory and often in search of some form of entertainment. To keep both schools of thought happy, he learned early to keep file size down and to make sure each piece of art has a purpose, yet to use the medium to its fullest potential by getting his point across through more than just words. Our mantra has expanded: to keep Web design effective, you must keep it small, pertinent, and accessible.

Jason and several classmates (including Sharon Yang and Yush Yuen, current members of the Media Revolution staff) decided to use the 1995 Digital World convention in Los Angeles as a litmus test to see if their vision of content on the Web would fly with consumers. Receiving a green light from many convention goers, Jason and company set up shop in the spare room of their apartment. The rags-to-riches story continued as they soon paired with Twentieth Century Fox to utilize the then new Director technology from Macromedia to produce some of the most creative and animated Shockwave games and screen savers for movie Web sites such as *Down Periscope* and *Chain Reaction*.

Early on, Jason's group had designed graphics for Media Ventures Entertainment Group, the company owned by Academy Award–winning composer Hans Zimmer and Grammy Award–winning producer Jay Rifkin. Media Ventures quickly saw the potential not only of the Internet and multimedia on the Web but also of this team and knew it was time to venture into new territories.

Media Ventures was impressed with Jason and company's commitment to pushing the boundaries of this new medium. They knew, though, that as beneficial as it was to have fresh minds working on this fresh medium, it was still a service industry and needed an experienced marketing approach to be successful. Media Ventures—along with Jason, Sharon, and Yush—was at a great starting point, and I was fortunate enough to be breaking the same trails at the same time. So we all hitched our horses to the same wagon and off we went.

No Troop's Complete Without a Trail Leader

I came to the Media Revolution team with a wide variety of marketing experience. I had spent several years touring with an array of bands, including a stint with Aerosmith. But I had been a news junkie since the age of seven, when I began selling *The Sun* newspaper outside one of London's tube (subway) stops. I abandoned music to turn my love for communications into a career. In time, I obtained a position at the international public relations agency Manning, Selvage, and Lee. From the beginning, I used e-mail to communicate with editors long before most individuals in the communication industry knew what it was. At that time the Internet really was a new and undiscovered frontier, and I was incredibly lucky to witness its infancy. It was love at first site, if you will, as I saw early on that this medium offered us the chance to create new communication paradigms.

I followed MS&L with a brief stint at an advertising agency, and then I opened my own consulting firm, Advanced Media Marketing, Inc., where one of my first projects was to create and subsequently implement an Internet marketing strategy for Epson America. It was around the time of first generation corporate Web sites. Often these sites featured what we called *brochureware*—your basic text-based site with a reiteration of a company's traditional brochure put on line verbatim. With a limited number of people on line at the time, I saw pretty quickly that the marketing advantages weren't quite there yet. We were still using the 9600-baud modems, there was a complete lack of true commerce capability, and the Internet's limited abilities to track users and establish valid benchmarks made the investment suspect at best. However, the potential for customer service applications and the need for alternative and cost-effective solutions to help desks and phone support centers were enormous. So we presented a successful strategy that emphasized customer support. However, I wish we knew then what we know now, and I certainly wish we had the tool sets and capabilities then that we have now.

Today, with significantly increased modem speeds, better animation tools, and streaming technologies, we are able to do so much more. Imagine if Epson had been able to animate the setup process of a printer step by step or proactively push new printer drivers to customers in 1994. Well, you know what they say: hindsight is always 20/20.

After developing the Epson site and working with several other clients, including Candle Corporation (a technology company), Xatrix Entertainment (makers of the hit PC game Cyberia), and GameFan Online (from *GameFan Magazine*), I was introduced to Jason and the others. I immediately saw in them the talent and drive to create something successful, and more important, the desire to push the medium dramatically.

We formed Media Revolution in mid-1996 and began to work immediately. We grew very quickly in the first nine months.

As a staff grows—and ours quadrupled in the first year—the ability to track and forecast new technologies becomes crucial. It is always important that we carefully select enabling technologies, which are palatable to our clients and their audiences. It is also important that we're right as often as possible, since constantly training a staff is expensive and time consuming, and our reputation and those of our clients are at stake.

You see, the entertainment market space can often be intense, with each project trying to be heard above the fray. This gives us not just the incentive but often a charter to push the limits, whether with a technology or by creating some form of immersive user interactivity. So it's working with projects as edgy as Alien-Resurrection.com and as solemn as Amistad-thefilm.com that makes the challenge so appealing. We sought to push the current limits of multimedia with the *Alien Resurrection* Web site by integrating multiple audio, visual, and animation technologies to create a completely immersive experience. And we tastefully animated the *Amistad* Web site to match the emotional feel of the movie, which on a Web site is sometimes a difficult thing to do. The common mentality of much Web design today is to provide in-your-face splashy graphics to an audience with an incredibly short attention span. It's MTV all over again. With *Amistad,* we sparked emotions by means of streaming mood music and Flash animations depicting slavery images. It was much different from most things found on the Web today.

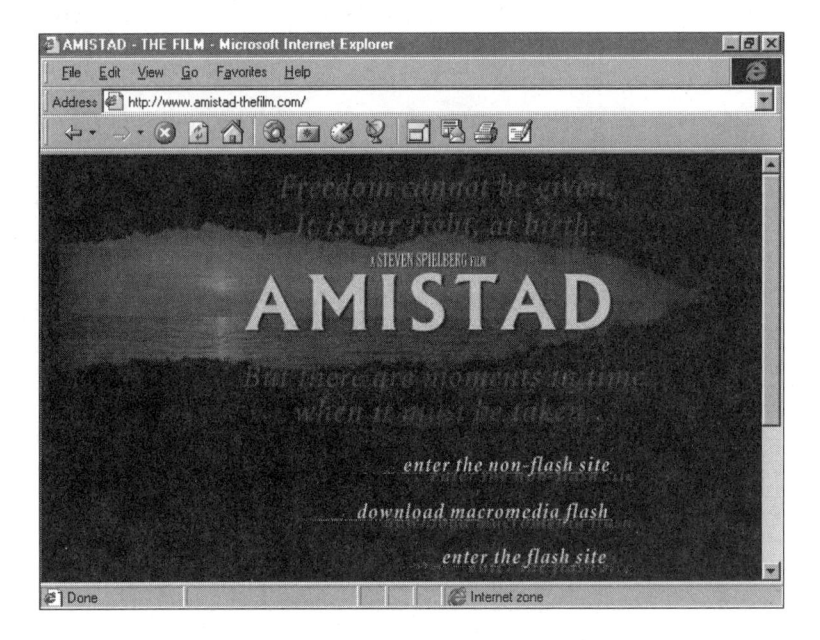

We have also learned how vital it is to provide value to a Web site beyond development of a cool presentation. On numerous occasions we've seen companies make a conscious decision to scale back money for the Web because they are not seeing a financial return on their investment beyond that cool impression it makes on people. I think Media Revolution has been successful at respecting those boundaries and has been able to concentrate on making sites utilitarian—meaning making sure a site offers something that is a true value-add to the user. Multimedia can often pro-

Moving Pictures

vide that value-add in an inexpensive package. For example, you can add streaming media to present a more compelling message; you can integrate Shockwave games to generate more traffic or create more branding opportunities; or you can use interactivity to create a more targeted and personalized site and enhance the ability to develop relationships with the audience.

Today when Media Revolution brainstorms with clients on Web projects, our concern is that what we create must be functional, of value, and yet different from anything our client has seen on the Web in the past. By thinking out of the box and utilizing multimedia in unusual and captivating ways, we are often able to create that uniqueness that will keep users on the site and enhance the brand and/or sell the product. Remember that consumers still like to see what they are buying. They may not be able to actually touch the product on line, but by using a variety of technologies end users can at least see what they are shopping for and perhaps even visualize the product in use.

Poor Technology Is Never an Excuse—If It Doesn't Work On Line, Don't Do It On Line

A commitment to make the Web a viable medium on its own should continually force developers to never let the limitations of the Internet be an excuse for poor work. If the early pioneers of the West could brave weather, lack of food and roads, and disgruntled native peoples to make their way, we can take the extra effort to make multimedia a little more palatable on line. We should always be hunting to create the most rewarding experience for the smallest file size. If we can't have one without the other, we need to return to the drawing board until we hit that magic combination.

Our creative director, Jason Yim, is quite outspoken about this. He gets really angry when he hears Web content developers use the excuse, "It's the Web, it's Shockwave (insert your favorite multimedia application), and therefore it can only do so much." Settling for subpar interactivity or graphics only subverts the overall quality of the Web. We want people to surf, play, and enjoy the Web without any excuses.

Regardless of how cool or fun the site is, its purpose is still typically to generate revenue either through actual sales, through enhanced brand awareness, or by driving potential sales to more traditional distribution channels. In the movie marketing scenario, this is elegantly termed "butts in seats." Games for games' sake or multimedia for multimedia's sake is not enough. Granted, games can be an excellent draw. However, it's our feeling that multimedia is an opportunity to integrate a message or a brand with a creative environment that makes the traditional marketing approach more palatable and even fun to interact with.

Extending your message and your brand is integral to any campaign. Why create the equivalent of a billboard and speak to your audience for 3.2 seconds, when you can develop a multimedia experience that enraptures your audience for one to five minutes (or possibly more)? In the nonentertainment world, the LifeSavers Web site (*http://www.candystand.com*), designed by Skyworks Technologies (Maywood, NJ), effectively integrated games and added Macromedia's Flash technology to its site. While we can't vouch for the company individually, it's a sure bet that there was a considerable increase in traffic and, more important, lengthier visits when the new technologies were introduced.

Often the most popular downloads from our movie sites are movie trailers. These files can range from 11 to 13 MB or more each, and in the days of 14.4 and 28.8 modem speeds, downloading one could require leaving the Internet connection on all night. This is evidence that the Internet audience is starved for compelling multimedia content on the Web. They certainly seem willing to go to extensive lengths. We look at our job as making that content as accessible and entertaining as possible, and multimedia in its many and various forms is typically the solution.

Whether we are working with a movie, a game, a consumer product, or a corporate identity, enhancing brand awareness and giving the user a compelling "why to buy" experience is the ultimate goal and holds true for each. While the audience for entertainment may differ slightly from that for the consumer product, we can still implement the same technologies to achieve the results we desire. What follows are several case studies culled from our recent experiences developing for entertainment clients. These studies detail the integration of multimedia, why and how it was implemented, and what degree of success was achieved.

Moving Pictures

Know Your Audience, Set Goals, and Develop

Whenever a company begins construction of a Web site, whether it is a corporate site or, in this case, a site promoting the launch of one of the most high-profile video campaigns ever, there has to be a strategy that guides the design of the site regardless of the multimedia used. For example, Twentieth Century Fox Home Entertainment needed to sell *Independence Day* home videos, and lots of them, within a tight window for the 1996 Christmas season. It was counting on the Internet to drive traffic to the retail outlets and build anticipation for the video release of the blockbuster movie.

Because the movie had been released so recently, our primary development goal was to differentiate the video from the movie. We needed to offer the audience a compelling reason to come back to the Web site and participate in the Independence Day 4 (ID4) campaign one more time (having just gone through it over the summer). We needed to re-create the hype. Once the viewers were on the site, we felt that we could effectively convince them that the opportunity to relive the ID4 experience in the sanctity of their homes was a compelling reason to purchase the video.

Our first job, as should be everyone's first job when planning a Web site, was to identify our audience and its technical capabilities. According to Kathy Barton, our client at Fox Home Entertainment, this media campaign was very unusual because the target audience included everyone: all ages, both sexes, and all demographic categories. Fox had found from surveys and registered users that its online audience skewed toward young males 18–35, but it also found that young girls and female adults were altering the bias. We also determined that our audience had most likely already seen the movie, and because they enjoyed the shoot 'em up excitement of this film, we assumed they often played or were interested in video games on the side. We knew that the movie's success also afforded us the opportunity to build something that would in all likelihood attract an audience. The question was, could we hold them?

A complication with this site's development was that we had a limited time to generate interest in the marketplace. We had a 12-week window from launch of the site to the video hitting the retail shelves. So knowing these constraints, we set out to create a site that was just as over the top as the rest of the marketing campaign proved to be.

We decided the best way to remind former audience members of the film's excitement was to create a completely immersive and involving experience that would highlight many of those climactic moments in the movie that audiences worldwide had loved. Similar to the way in which the movie theater creates an immersive experience with the pitch-black room and digital sound, we believed we could create an experience that exploited many of those same elements of visual and audio stimulation but that used the Web to its fullest capacity, with its capability for interactivity and personalization. Our solution was to create a site where the users hopefully become so engaged in what they are doing that they completely forget that the site's purpose is to market the video to them. "So," you ask, "how does one do this?"

In conjunction with Fox, we developed three principles to carry us through the creation of the site. Because of the over-the-top nature of the movie, we believed this site should feature the best multimedia available at the time. To that end, we acknowledged that there might be a constituency on the Internet that would not avail itself of the newest plug-ins or technology. To those users we would offer a limited version of the Web site with access to a wealth of static content, limited interactivity, and no immersive experience.

The issue of appealing to the widest audience possible and designing for that "lowest common denominator" is a difficult one, and one we struggle with every day. There is no real agency policy other than to address such issues on a case-by-case basis. In this instance, we were fortunate to be given the charter by Barton to create a site that was immersive and over the top. She wanted the coolest site on the Internet. Also, Fox believed that the studio's audience on the Internet came expecting to be entertained and had an expectation of quality that had been instilled through the more traditional media of film and television. Its philosophy was that for Fox to live up to such standards, it might require some additional time and effort on the part of the audience to download content or plug-ins. Fox believed audiences would be more willing to work for this entertainment and therefore deemed using plug-ins and downloadable content acceptable.

We also felt that the site needed to be episodic in nature to enhance the reliving of the movie experience. The concept of episodes on the Web was new at the time, and offering them gave us a means to attract our audience. By implementing continuous and extensive changes to the structure of the site and the content, we guaranteed that we would get an audience that would keep coming back, a philosophy that holds true to this day. Repeat visits obviously meant that we were generating more enthusiasm and additional opportunities to promote the film and its marketing partners.

Finally we determined that the site needed to be personalized so that we could create an individualized experience. This would allow us to communicate with our audience and, in doing so, enable us to generate a database of names and demographic information to continue the process proactively for future studio endeavors as well. Once these guidelines were established, we went to work.

It's worth mentioning that much of what we attempted to do here just a year and a half ago is now either commonplace or much more easily done at this level without extensive and expensive databases. Microsoft's SQL server product allowing for Active Server Pages (ASP) is readily available, inexpensive enough to purchase and implement, and much more robust than the thousands of CGI scripts and several databases we were forced to create at the time.

Because we wanted to attract traffic from other Fox-owned sites, we created a rolling countdown clock to build anticipation for the new site's launch. To this, we added the ability to sign up and be notified when the site launched via what remains today as the true "killer app," e-mail. This gave us time to work...and the clock was ticking.

Initially we felt compelled to develop a gateway page because of the use of multiple applications and plug-in technologies, as well as the need for some form of registration to allow the user to participate in the full, personalized experience. This page would initially greet each user and attempt to detail, in a compelling manner, what kind of experience was in store, encouraging the visitor to register. From that point on, it was up to visitors to decide to what degree they wanted to participate in the site (Shocked or non-Shocked, for instance). It should be pointed out that at that time, plug-in detection was not as sophisticated as it is now, and it is still not as sophisticated as it needs to be. However, browser technologies were also not as unique as they currently are. From the gateway page we were able to make our argument for participating in the full multimedia experience and, where necessary, downloading the applicable plug-ins. (Again, at that time this was not an automated process, as it is now with many of the browsers.)

We asked those who chose to register to pick a city in the United States they wished to defend in the fight against the attacking aliens. If, for example, they registered in Los Angeles, they would see a Los Angeles cityscape the next time they logged on. For New York they received a New York cityscape, and for America Online, we created a special AOL cityscape. As the site's episodes progressed, there would be changes to the cityscapes and updates as to how the city was faring against the aliens, as well as in comparison with the other cities. Once we had the users registered, we were able to communicate with them as well. Not only did we personalize their experience, but we also sent them "in-character" e-mails letting them know when the next episode of the site was up and running, with various calls to action encouraging them to join the fight to save the world and so forth.

This enabled us to form a direct relationship with consumers and to create another level of excitement. While we find this concept to be extremely effective with the entertainment and immersive sites, it also works just as well with the more traditional sites, which may be looking to enhance customer service by providing regularly updated information. The key here is to solicit only those who request to participate and to be reasonable about your interaction. You may eat and sleep widgets, and to you they are the most important things in the world. But to the customer they're still just widgets. Anyway, back to the ID4 site.

We decided that we would tackle the site in four stages. When a registered user came to the site in the first three weeks, the home page appeared as any theatrical home page would, with lots of ID4 content, a personalized welcome, and the cityscape. The page offered the traditional navigation bar, graphics, and other elements one might find on a site. At this point, no "aliens" had been "detected." It was simply a cool Web site for a great movie. The user could view 3-D wire frames of the movie's various planes, missiles, weaponry, and so forth and, using Shockwave technology, could move the elements and view them from any angle. We also created monitors showing pseudo newscasts from around the world, on which visitors could watch "current" broadcasts.

Moving Pictures

In addition to the above content, Media Revolution also created an interactive and personalized comic book as part of the Web site. In doing so, we offered a compelling reason for user participation and a product that users could download and print off line when it was completed. This was a first on the Internet, and it helped create just the type of publicity we needed for the site to differentiate itself in such a short period of time. To engage users further, we gave them their own story to follow. We took the concept of a series of cells that make up a comic book, and we animated and personalized them. For example, users began the comic book, in the first weeks on the site, as mere trainees being sent to flight school. They clicked through a series of cells that charted their progression in flight school. The comic book referred to the users by their call signs and showed them getting their hair cut, putting their uniforms on, and preparing for training in the flight simulator. Then the users came across a final screen. They clicked on the screen and were launched into a Shockwave flight simulator, which we also created. How the players performed in the game determined the next episode of the comic book. In reviewing the site logs and tracking registrants, we found that many of the participants were intrigued enough by the comic book and the resulting game ending each episode to return to the site repeatedly to participate.

Other areas of the ID4 site offered opportunities to retrieve the more traditional information on the cast and the crew, including written biographies of the stars and downloadable pictures and trailers from the movie. (Despite their large size, these were still some of the most popular files for downloading.) Also, because of the large marketing efforts for the film, there were numerous marketing partners who each wanted a presence on the site and a link to their site. We worked with the studio to create a new experience for each partner and the consumers by taking the products, modeling them, and then putting the 3-D version on line with accompanying copy and link. Overall, this offered a much better and more cohesive presentation of the partners' products, and it provided them with a value-add for participating on the site. At the same time, doing this enabled us to retain more control of the overall user experience.

In the following stages of the ID4 site, we began to truly exploit the multimedia capabilities of the Web at that time. In stage two, we flashed emergency broadcast messages across the top of the users' screens to warn them that something unidentified was out there and was approaching earth. We took news clips from the actual movie, created animated GIFs from them, and inserted them into the original world news monitors. Overall, there was a distinct atmosphere that something was happening, although no one quite knew what.

Stage three re-created the actual alien attack from the movie. On the home page, there was visible battle damage to the Web site. Graphics and links were broken and users could see behind the site, as if they were peering into the core of their monitor. The cityscape that welcomed each visitor was visibly damaged, with buildings toppled and burning. Alien craft were visible in the background. We also featured audio and visual alarms, sirens, and broadcast commands ordering people to "Report to Base" and "Prepare for Attack." It was a full multimedia affair, complete with confusion and overstimulation.

Determine Whether Various Multimedia Components Are Beneficial and Cost Effective

Believe it or not, we were actually cautious with our use of multimedia, as its impact is effective only if the memory and bandwidth complications don't take away from the overall effect we are trying to create. Barton from Fox will be the first to tell you, and I'd agree, that multimedia today still overdelivers because of the extremely cumbersome bandwidth limitations, which prevent end users from truly experiencing everything the medium is capable of delivering. In the end, acceptable levels are going to be a judgment call when weighed against the experience or message being delivered and the degree to which multimedia contributes to that message. We always evaluate every project to determine whether various multimedia components are really beneficial and cost effective. Every studio we've ever worked with does this as well, and it's an important principle to keep in mind. After all, the misuse of multimedia or of any application for that matter can drive audiences away from content. Sometimes you need to acknowledge that the development dollar goes further without participating in some of the latest technology trends. It's truly a judgment call based on a careful needs analysis.

With the grand finale in sight, we created the climactic fourth stage of this episodic site. (This version of the site remains on line as of this writing.) Barton believed that some of the most effective components of this ID4 site were the Shockwave games that we built because they were challenging and fun, and they contributed to the immersive experience we were striving for. While a client testimonial is always appreciated, the truth is in the numbers, and this site produced some "shocking" numbers.

The final episode re-created the part of the movie in which the world fought back, and on the site, that's just what they did. We created a contest around a Shockwave game with an online leader (score) board where our visitors could fight aliens, save the world, and at the same time compete with other site visitors. The leader board enhanced competition among players and created a multiuser experience to some degree. With the top 50 players posted at all times, each player was constantly aware of others playing simultaneously. Playing Shockwave games on the Web was no longer an isolated experience. The contest featured dozens of prizes and pitted city against city as well as person against person in a battle to see who could kill the most aliens. The enthusiasm raised on this portion of the site went beyond our wildest dreams, as we tracked users' behavior on the site and compiled astounding results. We had individual users who spent over 70 hours on the game over the course of the contest and shot down more than 200,000 aliens. Now that's one hell of a captivated audience!

While it's impossible to substantiate how many of those contestants bought videos, it's safe to say that we were able to generate more excitement and word of mouth through the millions who visited the site then than any billboard or print ad could possibly have hoped to achieve.

When we at Media Revolution reflect on this site, we still believe it stands the test of time and remains conceptually over the top. As I alluded to earlier, with the advent and growing acceptance of certain technologies in the last year, such as Macromedia's Flash (which we love), Microsoft's SQL server, and RealNetworks' improved audio and video applications, we would have been able to create faster and more efficient applications and certainly better streaming audio and video capabilities. However, those technologies only give us hope for where the Web is going. Not only have the issues of memory and bandwidth become less prohibitive in the last year, but also back-end database issues are receiving more attention in the Internet marketplace. Flash has far fewer memory or bandwidth issues than the cumbersome technology we used a year ago. Likewise, today a SQL server allows you to track and personalize data on the back end without having to spend the money to purchase or develop on the larger and more complex Oracle or Informix servers. When we created ID4, we had to create our own database with CGI scripts and store information on the server. Today a SQL server has those capabilities and the price point to warrant the purchase. Investment in Internet technology is difficult because the often fleeting nature of Web sites discourages many businesses from investing in the more expensive infrastructures required to create a site of this caliber. But with technology advancing as quickly as it is, I would expect to see sites with capabilities such as those developed for the ID4 site more and more. These profile sites showcase many of the true capabilities of the Internet. But when only a few take full advantage of all the Web's potential, the Internet's capabilities become hype and the less robust and less creative mainstream becomes the reality. In the end, everyone is left disappointed.

Showcase the Internet's True Capabilities with the Intent of Pushing the Medium Forward

A perfect example of the advancement of new technologies is our more recent work for the DreamWorks film *Amistad*. During the 1997 Christmas season, we created a full-fledged multimedia affair that transformed the poignant nature of the epic Steven Spielberg film into a dramatic Web site. By implementing Macromedia's Flash technology, we designed an intensely informational site that discussed the history of slavery in a powerful, animated fashion yet still had all the components that compose a traditional Web site.

The main challenge of this site was putting forth an educational resource that featured background information on the film yet still served as a publicity vehicle to promote the film and in the end sell movie tickets. As poignant as this subject matter is, we couldn't forget that we had the job of putting butts in seats.

What makes this site unique is that it's based on a historical incident, so we can provide a lot more information. When you are working with a fictional movie, there are certain limitations, such as the requirement that you not divulge the movie's magic or give away the end. With *Amistad*, everybody already knows the conclusion of the story. Our goal was to spur interest in the story—find out what background information was going to click with the end users so they would be compelled to go see the film.

To begin with, we received two years' worth of research from Dream-Works on the Amistad incident, and we needed to find a compelling way to present this vast amount of information to spur interest in the subject. Utilizing Macromedia's Flash capabilities, we were able to create an interactive historical timeline, which features over 60 dates ranging from 1475 to 1977. The dates run across the screen, but when a user wants to view a specific event, he or she can access the controls that pause, play, and jump to any point seamlessly for a more detailed explanation of the event. With file size always being a concern, the creation of elegantly designed content was an issue. The beauty of creating this timeline in Macromedia's Flash is that Flash operates in an extremely small file, which in this case is filled with an immense amount of information. If you haven't guessed yet, we are true proponents of Flash, and we believe Flash has the capabilities to substantially broaden what we can do on the Web in the near term. For example, if this timeline had been created in Shockwave it would probably have been around 10 times the current file size or larger, but when created in Flash the file is only 210 KB and the download process is more seamless.

Flash applications are vector-based drawings that define the points of a figure and then draw the lines together to fill in the picture. The benefit of vector-based programs is that an image can be blown up to a very large size without increasing the file size or shrunk with ease without degradation of the image.

In addition to the Flash timeline, we provided detailed essays discussing the institution of slavery before the Amistad incident and after. According to Michael Vollman, member of the marketing department at DreamWorks, what was of great interest to DreamWorks was the Internet's ability to function in essence as a large library. It would be impossible to send people a 15-page essay on what slavery was like in the 1840s; but on the Web we can present it in a compelling fashion, and not only will people learn, we will be able to generate more interest in the film.

Another requirement of DreamWorks was that the Web site mirror the look and feel of more traditional marketing methods yet still stand on its own as a separate entity. We knew we had the capabilities to engage people in an experience as we had done in our previous work, but now the challenge was to evoke emotion and thought to the point that people were compelled to see the film. We drew the users into the site with a dramatic home page animation combining tasteful uses of Flash with select samples of music mirroring the tenor of the movie. It's a truly moving experience.

As Jason so aptly pointed out in the brainstorm process to develop the site (and I hope we're not spoiling the movie for anyone at this point), the words are the most powerful part of this movie. The characters didn't physically fight their way out of slavery; their court case was based on understanding and intelligence. We needed to get that across in the introduction, which I think we did by successfully but subtly matching words with sound and motion.

On the splash page, the word "Amistad" appeared in stark white on a black background. Animating, the letters of the word then separated and moved to transform into a quote about freedom. A variety of quotes were served up depending upon when the user logged on, to create a new experience every time. The quote then faded into the background, leaving only certain letters highlighted. Those letters then re-formed in the word "Amistad." While this splash page animation unfolded the movie's title, African tribal music played hauntingly in the background.

The beauty of *Amistad* is that the subject matter itself is so compelling that we could rely on that to sell our message. With this site we were confident that if we gave users the background story, they would naturally want to see the movie. It was a much more subtle sell than the ID4 site.

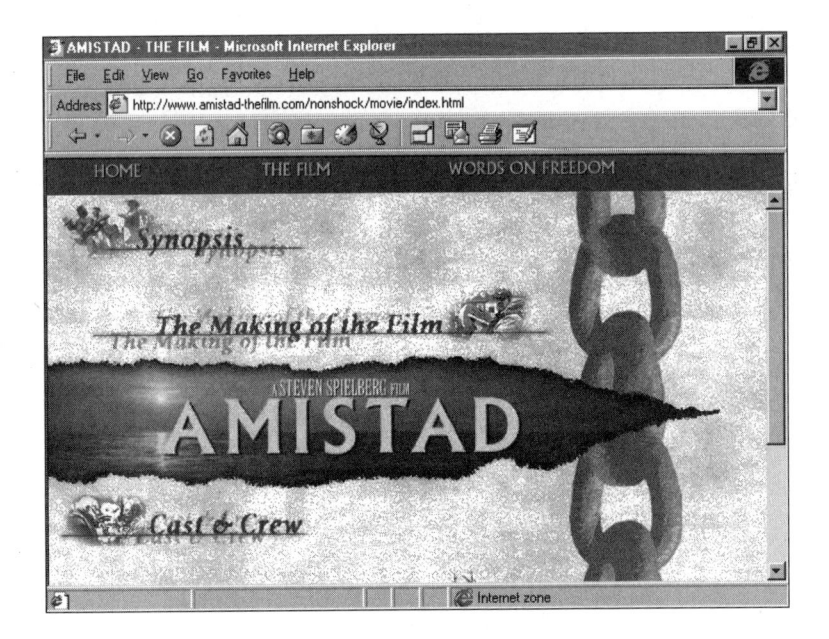

When we decided to use Flash, it was a new technology in the marketplace, but it was provided by Macromedia, a very reputable vendor that sells many useful development tools such as Shockwave and Director. We looked at some sites that were already using it and were unable to find any that really keyed into an emotional experience. We were determined that in every Flash sequence we used, we would give a little piece of the story, whether it be look, feel, sound, or actual narration.

To subtly enhance the mood further, as this is what we were relying on to promote the film, we designed a home page with a background resembling a ship's sails with the word "Amistad" subtly scrawled repeatedly across it. The entire image rocked back and forth as if it were sailing over ocean waves. A main theme of this film is the nature of freedom, and we wanted to use images that would illustrate the struggle the slaves were experiencing. Our art director, Sharon Wang, designed this page to capture the slaves' journey and give the viewer the sense of moving from freedom to servitude, from light to darkness. The shift in color and movement made you feel as if you were on a journey, and we hoped people would realize just how painful a journey it was.

Technology advances such as Flash have enabled us to create much bolder marketing messages, ones that we never would have been able to make two years ago. Just looking back on what we did with the *Amistad* site is quite interesting. It's obvious that the visual medium is always going to be the most appealing, and by adding the audio component to this site we were able to successfully establish a mood and tone for the Web site. It's much more dynamic than how sites were previously presented to the users.

When we discuss the potential of the Web and whether it is a viable medium for marketing and content delivery, it's always compared to much more substantial media such as television. However, we'd guess that the Web has more developers and marketers than television ever had, and that's a powerful force pushing forward. Simply observing the behaviors of marketers on the Web in the last few years gives us faith that people really see the Internet as a viable marketing medium. Traditional marketers have become more aggressive and competitive on the retail front, striving to use every advantage they can to develop the most intriguing and interactive point-of-purchase displays as they fight for consumers' eyeballs and shelf space. So too have marketers on the Internet been fighting for consumers' eyeballs, with that same level of competitiveness and sophistication. The only way companies, brands, and products on the Internet can stand out is to use multimedia. It's a natural extension of the Web's progression. With the written word you could only do so much, but now you have the opportunity for visually and aurally appealing messages through animation, visuals, and sound.

In the past, marketers have also tended to present their messages to the lowest common denominator; and even to this day, they often shy away from programming advanced technologies on their sites. Because of the growing popularity of the Web (various estimates call for approximately 50 million users on line in 1998), there is more reason than ever for marketers to accommodate every user based on that user's technological capabilities. So the same message is often created in multiple formats. For example, on our Flash-intensive *Amistad* site, we offer users a Flash site; a non-Flash site; or, for those without the Flash plug-in, the opportunity to go to the Macromedia site and download Flash so that the full capabilities of the site can be appreciated. With more marketers seeking to take full advantage of what multimedia offers, I think we are going to see an increase of this accommodation in the upcoming year as more Internet technologies (style sheets, DHTML, various plug-ins and browsers) fragment and until some semblance of standardization actually occurs. The lowest bar for entry into a site will still remain low, but at the same time the bar for capturing the mindshare of all the users is going to continually increase and become much more competitive, aggressive, and sophisticated.

Beyond simply getting the marketing message across, multimedia can be used for many companies in the service and support role as well. Take a company such as IKEA (not a client), for instance. Nearly every piece of furniture bought from the company requires some form of assembly. A natural extension of its business would be to create animated Flash applications to demonstrate the actual assembly process, step by step, of its most complicated products. Imagine if electronics companies produced animated demonstrations on how to program their VCRs. It would be convenient for the customer, and it's an absolutely cost effective method, driving traffic away from the 800 phone lines, which any CFO can tell you are incredibly expensive. For a long time what we saw on the Web was the "brochureware" concept, whereby written "why to buys" or assembly instructions were simply pasted on line. The Internet in general, and multimedia in particular, provide the marketer with the opportunity to offer a much more detailed and inexpensive exhibition or showcase of a product to the customer. The beauty of multimedia is that this application can be a video of a person, an audio message, or a Flash animation or movie.

Moving Pictures

There's a very interesting yet simple way of looking at the marriage between entertainment and the corporate arena on the Web. For every business, especially those on the Internet, there are two types of information: what a customer needs and what the business wants the customer to know. Information that a customer requires does not need to be sold to that customer; it just needs to be quickly and easily accessible. But information that a business wants a customer to know is dependent on some enhancement or value-add if the business hopes to successfully market it. Multimedia allows you to do just that. It allows a business to get across its marketing message but still allows the customer to enjoy the process. Sometimes content is best delivered in this manner. Always keep in mind that good multimedia should never be superfluous.

We know that many businesses can benefit from a strong Web presence, but what are the best technologies out there to do the job? In the following section, I discuss the pros and cons of some of the more prevalent technologies on the Web today. An obvious start would be with one of Media Revolution's favorite vendors, Macromedia. We've been using Macromedia products from the beginning, and although they have their shortcomings, they truly are the best and some of the most important technologies on the Internet to date. Macromedia can take much of the credit for bringing the Web out of its static state.

Striking Gold on the Web with New Technologies

Like many developers for the Internet, we had always used Macromedia's Director product when we were designing CD-ROM projects, so it was natural for us to embrace Shockwave for Director when it was first released. Shockwave is very powerful. We've created numerous screen savers and successful online games with the technology. However, the file size issue with Shockwave still makes it prohibitive to use for integral parts of a site such as navigation or primary content. There's a difference between asking a user to wait for an 80-KB game to download and to wait for an 80-KB navigation bar. Because Flash works with vector files instead of pixel-type files, we are now able to create fluid and colorful animations with minimal increases in file size. Another consideration for Macromedia products is that Macromedia has done a fantastic job with achieving acceptance in the Internet community for its necessary plug-ins, making them some of the most widely accepted on the Internet. According to Michelle Welsh, Macromedia Director of Flash product marketing, by December 1997 there were 121,000 downloads of the Flash player per day. Macromedia has determined that it has achieved an 80 to 90 percent saturation rate with its products. It's these types of numbers that give you reassurance in using the products to develop sites. We are confident that when the average user enters a site with Flash or Shockwave on it, most likely that user will already have downloaded the plug-in, and we won't have to worry as much about compatibility issues.

The newest version of Flash (3.0) will be released in May 1998, and many of the new features will give developers even more flexibility when they are creating. One of the most interesting additions deals with the constant problem developers face, user bandwidth limitations. In Flash 2.0 we had the ability to export a little text file that let us see how large each element in our file was so we could make changes to reduce file size. Now, in Flash 3.0, there is a bandwidth timeline that has been added to the top of the screen that allows designers to adjust the modem speed to what the majority of their audience is connecting through. This way, developers can see in advance what portions of their animation go beyond the acceptable speed and where exactly the delays are. This will help designers keep file sizes manageable and know exactly how well their files are designed.

However, even within our agency there's dissent. Some of us believe that certain portions of the Web are already at the point of oversaturation with the Macromedia technologies. As much as we like and depend on Director and Flash, what we've found is that the technologies don't work perfectly from browser to browser and from platform to platform. There's also the issue raised earlier in this chapter of using technology for technology's sake. Sometimes people just want to get the information they need and not wait for the plug-in to download or the animation to complete. Often those people will go to the non-Flash or non-Shockwave versions of our sites. It's appropriate to use these technologies when they add to the experience and you can't get the same experience without it, as on the *Amistad* site. However, on information-based sites, it can be inappropriate. If the need is to get information quickly and Flash or Shockwave interferes with this, the technologies should not be implemented.

Moving Pictures

Macromedia is aware of the inconsistencies and lack of standardization issues that we developers are constantly facing. It has recently outlined its Universal Media Initiative, which is intended to assure playback of all its multimedia products whether the user has the necessary plug-ins or not. The initiative will allow Macromedia Shockwave, Macromedia Director, and Macromedia Flash to automatically generate the HTML and the JavaScript that will allow the browsers to intelligently detect what is loaded on the individual's system. The developer can then program, with a single script, the application to determine which browser is currently queuing the pages and default to that browser to optimize playback. This is definitely not the end-all, but it could save developers a lot of time, and we will be better able to serve our varied users.

Another technology that has the potential to be extremely powerful but is currently plagued by bandwidth limitations comprises the streaming technologies, both audio and video. Considerable progress has been made in this area, especially from the work of RealNetworks and to a lesser degree Microsoft NetShow, but the technology is still sporadic. We've seen all streaming technologies behave erratically at times, where they will either stop and start or skip so many frames that it's not even worth watching or listening. A simple solution when working with streaming technologies is to rely on the serverless technologies until the others are more robust, because currently they're more consistent. Those serverless technologies include the popular QuickTime streaming video and Macromedia's Shockwave streaming audio. From a production standpoint, Macromedia's streaming audio for Flash works well, but synchronizing the audio to the video is an extremely time-intensive process.

Recently, though, new developments between Real Networks and Macromedia have taken place that seem to justify the amount of time it takes to synchronize the audio with Flash. Today we are able to add streaming audio from RealNetworks to enhance the Flash experience. RealNetworks and Macromedia have formed a partnership, announced in early October 1997, for a new product named RealFlash. Now Flash-based content can play back in RealSystem 5.0, synchronized with RealAudio. End users can now see and hear long-format animations in real time over low-bandwidth connections. This advance should improve the overall Flash experience, and fortunately it is not much more intensive to create than the current Flash audio.

Also, Microsoft's latest release of NetShow is trying to resolve the majority of our complaints about the streaming technologies. With NetShow 3.0, due for release in the first half of 1998, Microsoft intends to bolster the end user's experience through a number of improvements.

One of the touted changes that we really hope comes though as advertised is the ability to encode at two different rates within one stream. What this means is that when a client's bandwidth connection to the Internet drops down, NetShow will be able to seamlessly move to a version of the file that is built for lower bandwidth. So rather than getting jerky-quality video that we're all too used to, the user will receive a file that is optimized for the lower bandwidth rate. This could be a godsend and could widen the use of streaming video and audio applications.

Another Microsoft development that should increase the use of streaming audio and video in intranet business applications is enabling NetShow to integrate with other Microsoft applications. Microsoft is now delivering commerce integration and personalized ad insertion capabilities into NetShow via Microsoft Site Server. If the streaming video capabilities are as dynamic as we've been told, corporations will be able to find many cost-saving uses for the applications. From broadcasting corporate messages over the network to using streaming video for training sessions and customer service, the opportunities are really endless. But that all depends on the actual quality of the product.

RealNetworks, Microsoft, Intel, Adobe, and other multimedia vendors are working to establish a single format that's optimized for streaming multimedia. If a format goes through, it will eliminate content developers' worries about format type and what tools to use because they will all be standardized. Competition will remain in the server arena, but this could mean big strides for the overall quality of streaming media.

Let us remember the bottom line, however. Just as Shockwave games are only as good as the gameplay, so is streaming audio and video dependent on the content. The concept of synchronizing sound with your visual is very compelling and if done correctly can create a complete experience for the user. With music, streaming audio can be used to augment the entire atmosphere of the Web site. Again, on *Amistad* we created an entire package, one where the animation, information, and music all went hand in hand. The music was able to provide the emotional context for what the visitor was watching.

Moving Pictures

Another important technology is Dynamic HTML, which allows the animated HTML content to be delivered to users' desktops on the fly. It is similar to Flash in this concept, but it doesn't require a plug-in. Rather, the animation, sound, and other objects are embedded into the HTML itself. The problem with this technology is that it is often much better understood by the programmers than by the designers. What this means is that designers are often begrudgingly forced to rely on and to turn over more of the implementation of the creative process to the programmers. Because of this, there are two factors to consider in the future of Dynamic HTML vs. plug-ins: the amount of acceptance and the ease of use. To end users it doesn't matter what technology is used, as they will not be able to tell the difference, especially if the plug-in comes integrated with the browser. Therefore, the most important factor to consider is authoring. Given a choice between two applications to provide the same content, creators will naturally choose the easier and more familiar one. That is where Flash wins today.

However, Macromedia has released another product, DreamWeaver, which eases some of the programming burden of Dynamic HTML. This visual Dynamic HTML editor creates dynamic content without requiring the designer to use code. Whenever a designer needs to implement a JavaScript into a file, he or she attempts to translate the message to the programming staff; and, similar to the game of telephone, something inevitably gets lost in the translation. This is an area of designing that DreamWeaver aims to facilitate. Although our art director, Perry Wang, doesn't believe this visual editing tool will be able to replace most designers' favorite tool, BB Edit, he does think it's superior in its Dynamic HTML and JavaScript capabilities.

Other integral components of DreamWeaver include its ability to create frames easily without any coding. We don't often use JavaScript in our programming because of the translation issue mentioned earlier in this chapter and because it works differently on every browser version and on every platform. We never know how it will work until we test it, and it often is too time intensive to leave to chance. DreamWeaver eliminates this risk taking by allowing us to check what target browser we are aiming for in advance. If our client wants to hit only Internet Explorer 3.0 users on a PC, DreamWeaver presents us only with choices that will work on Internet Explorer 3.0 for the PC. It also lets us make our content available on all the different browsers through the same process. It will let you know immediately if something isn't going to work.

Push technology is another area that is filled with debate on how and where it should be used. Many individuals are distrustful of having information pushed to their machines. Often they have a valid reason to be wary, as some push technologies will push many megabytes onto users' desktops without their knowledge. It's rather complicated for the average user, who usually winds up with too much information and not enough memory. For the time being, we at Media Revolution believe the best place for push technology is on the intranet level, where the inner network can control what is being delivered. On the intranet, push—and BackWeb in particular—is an extremely powerful technology, especially where there is a need to seamlessly deliver robust content to a highly targeted, receptive audience. It is unfortunate that push technology has received such a bad reputation on the Internet, but in essence it is quite similar to e-mail spamming. It is not the technology that is necessarily corrupt but rather the irresponsible people who are using it. People haven't shunned e-mail because individuals are sending unsolicited advertising to their in-boxes, and they shouldn't write off push as an irrelevant technology. We need to put things in better perspective and understand that technology is merely the means to an end. Technology is just technology, so don't shoot the messenger. Push simply needs to be placed in more responsible hands.

Speculations on the New Frontier

With the state of the Web constantly evolving into more and more of a full-fledged entertainment and informational medium, we like to pontificate on its future. We all see big changes ahead for 1998–1999, and most of them rely on some transformation of the bandwidth dilemma. If we can get a large percentage of the people who are on the Web off desktop modems and onto cable modems or any other alternative high-speed connection, we will see a lot of explosion. But how does this explosion affect the online marketplace and impact the current concept of the Web presence? Obviously, more bandwidth will result in the ability to transmit more robust multimedia, a boon to any marketer looking for better or more enhanced means of communicating a message or delivering a product. As it stands, this more enhanced content that content developers are creating, with its larger byte sizes, inevitably impacts the Internet's ability as a whole to transmit the additional content peer to peer without massive congestion and subsequent potential Internet brownouts (an issue that the telephone companies are left to deal with currently).

However, even with bandwidth improvements, the Internet is not equipped to compete with television, so this enhanced content needs to take a form more suited to the type of interaction and interface found on the Internet rather than mirror that of television. Television is a passive experience, while the real power of the Internet is in its ability to offer an interactive experience. This interaction will allow the content provider to offer more robust multimedia content, in a more targeted and palatable form, and to deliver messages in a manner tailored to and most acceptable to the end user.

Let us not forget the issues brought on by the merger of the two. The Internet and television are on a collision course. Currently there are two courses for this merger. WebTV takes the Internet and places it on the television monitor. Other technologies, not too far in the future, take the content of both and marry them on the larger screen. This idea can already be seen today. If you took a look at the commercials for the 1998 Super Bowl, you saw that Intel aired a commercial that told viewers to go to their computers, log on to Intel's site, vote for a promotional campaign, and determine the outcome of the commercial. The results of the online survey were aired in the second commercial, the conclusion. The advanced technologies aren't available yet to prevent the user from having to move to his or her computer, but the ideas for how to marry the television with the Internet are already brewing. Many of us see enormous potential in interactive television technologies, in which the best of the Web and the best of television can be combined.

There's obvious marketing potential in developing co-content with television—instant access to more detailed information or the instant gratification of making the purchase on line. Consumers could be watching a commercial on television and immediately purchase the product to have it delivered to their doorsteps the next morning. The opportunities are endless. However, such a concept implies that the Internet will merely become an adjunct of television and that the power will remain with the networks and owners of broadband distribution.

The potential of interactive television is great and looming, but the Internet is here to stay. Continue to invest in your Internet presence, and continue to watch the entertainment sites. The entertainment sites offer the best potential for furthering the acceptance of and aiding in the distribution of new technologies to the general Internet populace. These new technologies are the ones that make the best bet when it comes to investing in your next-generation Web site. Also, never be afraid to test new ideas. Remember, this is a new frontier; there's no limit to the amount of pioneers it can hold.

About the Author

Despite the protestations of his first grade class, Jesse Albert is not related to Jesse James. He did, however, spend a number of years on the road touring with various rock and roll bands prior to coming to marketing and new media.

"Knowing what combination of options will best suit your business goals puts you on the right path to choosing an appropriate vendor to work with."

Tish Hill

CHAPTER 5

Choosing a Partner for the Online Hoedown

One of the first databases I helped put on microsoft.com exploded the servers. It was the event database, which allowed Microsoft clients to sign up for events around the country and the world. People could search for events and register on line. It was a hit, except that there was just too much traffic. That was something I never expected to happen, and it brought all the servers down.

Blowing servers might come across as a negative, but in this case, it was a win. Luckily, my client, Microsoft, was willing to experiment and to push the limits of what the Internet could do and what a Web site could do. As partners, we were ideally suited to one another. Because we were willing to push the limits together, we ended up with a quantum leap forward in understanding. In that particular case, we both learned about the tremendous interest in using this new technology and saw what it would take to sustain the amount of hits this kind of functionality could and would draw.

I also worked with Microsoft to put the first big Microsoft database on line, but it never actually went live. It was a database to give potential clients the ability to search for information about Microsoft Certified Solution Providers (MCSP). Information was loaded into it so folks could search for the right MCSP based on vertical industry or other criteria. Let's just say that when we tested it we didn't always get what we were looking for. We had to scrap the project. But again, together we learned an important lesson, probably one of the more significant lessons that we picked up in the early days: how much effort it would take to scrub data and make sure user interfaces were working properly. It was a valuable experience, and it grew out of a balanced and mutually acceptable partnership in which both sides were willing to push the limits.

Pushing the Limits

Sometimes a potential client will ask, "Didn't you build that thing that totally bombed?" Well, yes. And the fact is we can and do take chances when we work with a client who shares our sense of adventure. We go into certain projects knowing that an experiment might not work perfectly. In those cases, our partners understand that what looks like a failure can often be a tremendous success for reasons that we could never have anticipated.

We're constantly trying new processes and new technologies, and at times there are some exciting results. Sometimes we see results in the technology—not always in such dramatic terms as crashing servers but frequently on the same scale in terms of the move forward in technical knowledge. Business results can be very exciting as well, such as sudden and substantial cost reductions or the enormous gains that can come from expanding a local business to a global scale.

We never really know exactly what's going to happen when we experiment in such a quickly changing field, but we work in close contact with clients to design what we think is going to happen. Obviously, positive results are what we're aiming for, but we don't always get them right away. We constantly encounter surprises.

The Path to Finding the Right Partner

Surprises will continue to happen because Web site builders and their clients are pushing technological limits. Without these adventurous collaborations, technological and business boundaries won't expand.

Not all businesses, however, are willing or able to push boundaries in this way, and for some, a more cautious digital solution partner may make for a better and more satisfying relationship. This chapter looks at the variety of digital solutions emerging today and shows you how to map your business's needs to an appropriate solution provider.

As the Internet has evolved and new ways of networking such as intranets and extranets have appeared, site builders have begun to focus their efforts on strengthening certain core abilities and rounding out their overall competencies. To put those competencies to work for your company, you will first of all need to understand your own business's needs and how these new digital technologies can help you meet them. Then you'll have to match those needs to providers that can deliver the specific technical solutions that will help your business succeed. Most important, to partner your business successfully with a digital solution provider you will need to match your company's level of adventurousness—its personality and culture—to a site builder that has a similar style.

In the following pages, we'll look at the business needs that are being fulfilled by the Internet, intranets, and extranets. Then we'll look at the core competencies that digital development companies are beginning to hone. Finally I'll discuss ways to choose an appropriate partner to maximize your business's chances for success.

Business-Related Uses for Digital Technologies

Some companies are early adopters of new technologies. They push hard to get results by using new digital tools. Other companies go a little slower and do not adopt so quickly. That doesn't mean those companies aren't adventurous—they may not need all the options right away. Still other companies are reckless: they go after the new technologies for technology's sake, with little or no thought about how these new tools are related to their business's mission. What's true across these types, however, is that the business community as a whole is embracing the Internet.

The results of adopting Internet technology used to be most visible in terms of marketing. Now results are really showing up in return on investment and other mission-critical issues, things that touch the essence of the way companies are doing business.

At Sitewerks, we work with a large financial group that wanted to more quickly establish rates for lending. They have a central office and many subsidiaries that work with clients to negotiate rates depending on different criteria. That process used to take months because of the paperwork going back and forth and the time involved in evaluating the risk to the lender. Sitewerks put that process onto an intranet, which allowed the parent company and the subsidiary to speak in real time and negotiate a rate on the spot for a borrower. Now that transaction can happen within a few minutes instead of months. That's a quantum leap forward for a mission-critical aspect of their business.

Can you imagine changing a process that once could have taken up to three months to one that takes about three minutes? That's how digital technologies are changing businesses now, and that's going to happen in more and more ways as this technology evolves.

Still, that solution didn't come about because someone walked into a Web shop and said, "Build me a Web site." It was the result of a successful partnership, and it points to an important lesson: when business leaders and technology pioneers work together to understand both the business's needs and the potential of these newly emerging technologies, amazing things can happen.

That leads to a crucial question: what factors do most companies have in common? Let's look at for-profit companies, although some of the issues are the same for nonprofit companies. Most companies have input from partners, suppliers, and so forth. They also need to communicate effectively within their organization. In addition, they need to communicate with both established and potential clients. Information needs to flow through nearly all companies in these ways. The new digital technologies are having tremendous impact by streamlining this communications continuum.

Choosing a Partner for the Online Hoedown

Today's technologies are able to enhance all these forms of communication. In the simplest terms, when I talk about the Internet I'm talking about information that flows from a business to its customers. Intranets, on the other hand, allow a business to communicate within the business itself. Extranets enable business-to-business networking. The evolution has gone from Internet to intranet and finally to extranet. Looking at it from a business perspective, it probably should have gone the other way. But that's just the way it happened.

In the illustration here, the largest box represents a typical company. On the left, double-ended arrows entering the box represent extranets—communication between the business and its partners, suppliers, and so forth. Within the company, an intranet makes possible more effective communication between employees, project teams, departments, and so on. On the right side of the diagram, an arrow coming out of the box indicates communication via the Internet. The tip of the arrow leading away from the box is large, representing the greater focus on communication from the company to its market audience. A smaller tip on the end leading back into the box represents a company's ability to receive comments and questions from the visitors of its Web site.

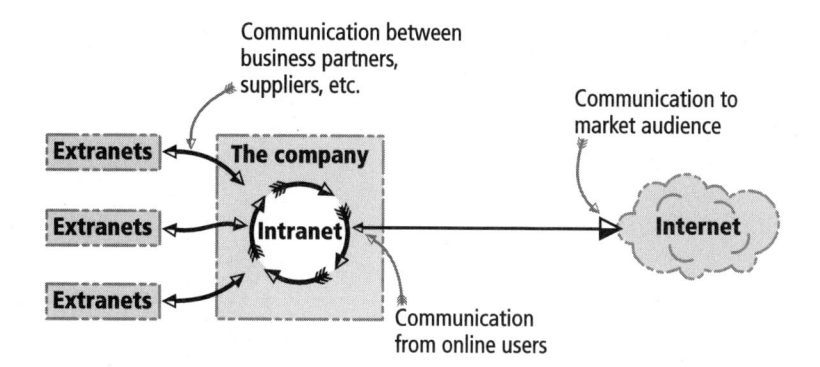

Early on, the Internet focused only on the right side of the picture, on output, which is looking more at sales and marketing content such as brochureware. Now people are looking at the way processes, communication, and information flow within the company, and that is where intranets fit into the picture. An even newer concept covers input into the company, the extranet component, which enhances the company's relationship to suppliers, partners, and so forth.

The following is an example of how extranets, intranets, and the Internet can work together. Let's look at a hypothetical company, such as a car manufacturer, and see how information flows from extranets to intranets and ultimately to the Internet.

Extranets

Extranets—private networks that enhance communication between organizations—are becoming popular. Extranets give businesses the ability to negotiate with suppliers and to do things such as put requests for bids on line so subsidiaries can compete with one another and communicate with the parent company. This is a popular area because the return on investment is very high.

In the case of our car manufacturer, an extranet could allow a particular dealership to know how many cars are coming off the line. That's important to them because it notifies them when they need to prebuy because there's going to be a shortage. Extranets can also allow companies that ship the cars around the nation or around the world to communicate their availability or rates.

These types of communication, of course, already happen without new technology. However, digital technologies are allowing them to happen much more quickly and in a much more cost-effective fashion. That ultimately lowers the cost to the consumer or increases the company's profit margins. That's why the Internet is selling itself—because the results are so good.

Intranets

On our communication continuum, information moves from extranets to a company's intranet. A car manufacturer needs to communicate within its organization, from management through to the folks that are building the cars. Intranets are accessible only to users within the company, and because of that they can hold many kinds of private information. There may be financial information for employee shareholders. There may be product information, testing results, and so forth that would be important to workers within the organization, such as data that helps the company's salespeople understand what the latest products and services are.

Intranets help spread the word about human relations issues—information about benefits and health care, training, and so forth. These issues are common to all companies, and the information needs to flow through any group of employees.

Intranets are invaluable for collecting comments from field sales people, consultants, and company reps, whose experiences need to get back to the company so that the company can change its service offering.

You're not likely to find an "off-the-shelf" intranet solution. Usually, a developer goes in, has a look, and tries to figure out how to use digital technologies to automate something that's currently done manually: faxing, filling out forms, making phone calls. Parts of an organization might already have automated systems in place. In those cases, a digital solution provider would work on systems integration—ways of pulling data from one area, synthesizing it, and then delivering it to another part of the organization.

The Internet

The Internet is the most familiar component here. It is a very quick and inexpensive way to facilitate communication. For a car manufacturer, the Internet can facilitate communicating with people who are interested in finding out about the latest models. Potential clients may also want to see which local dealers offer the cars. With e-commerce, there's even the potential to purchase on line. Microsoft CarPoint, for example, allows Web site users to look inside a car and make an evaluation. Site visitors may also be potential investors. The Internet can make it easier to share information such as you might find in an annual report.

Before, the information on a Web site was always generic. Personalization issues are now coming into play. With the recent innovations in personalization, you can shape the experience to the individual. You can use technology to provide a personal look at your product or service.

Four Types of Digital Solution Proficiencies

Just as a variety of business functions make up a successful enterprise, successful digital development requires a combination of wide-ranging skills and expertise. A good site builder will combine the capabilities necessary to meet clients' development needs across the business communication continuum—extranet, intranet, and Internet.

We at Sitewerks recognize four areas of expertise that are integral to providing a complete solution. The solution provider you choose should demonstrate significant skills in each of these areas:

- **Design.** This involves developing concepts for marketing, advertising, and merchandising and includes creating the graphics, narrative, and branding of a site.
- **Application Development.** This comprises building and integrating online applications, such as e-commerce engines, online banking, and custom applications.
- **Systems Integration.** Businesses may need Internet commerce applications to be integrated with existing inventory, order processing, and accounting systems. At a minimum, database integration is a common requirement.
- **Strategy.** This glue holds the other components of the business solution together to bring significant value to clients.

You won't find a combination of these capabilities in related service businesses, such as advertising, strategy consulting, or systems integration firms. In fact, part of the reason that the Internet development business has sprung up independently of these service providers is that these businesses lack the skills to meet clients' digital development needs. Even among leading Internet development businesses, it is uncommon to see strong capabilities in all of these areas. Most tend to emphasize only one area, usually systems integration or design.

Design

Many competent Internet companies are doing a good job with design. Many digital developers have honed a strong sensitivity to branding issues and the user's experience. They are adept at personalization and have the ability to support localization from a front-end perspective.

As a client, you have many folks to choose from who are skilled in this area. When you get into the other areas, expertise becomes a little bit scarcer.

Application Development

The skills required to provide good application development closely resemble those required for traditional software development, but they also require familiarity with new programming languages and Internet technologies. Relatively few companies are highly technical and can develop applications that run on the Internet.

This area is where Microsoft, Netscape, and IBM—big players that are going to dominate—are focusing a lot of their attention. However, more companies are starting to specialize in this area and are having some great results.

Systems Integration

Many digital solutions are an extension of existing business processes—things such as existing databases and Human Relations systems, or databases full of customer information. Many companies have a variety of systems and processes in place—some of them manual, some of them automated—and they're trying to make sense of all this data.

When information is stored in mainframe systems, companies have to run reports. That generally means having to work through someone in the Internet Technology group, a time-consuming and therefore costly process in many cases. Systems integration allows a company to pull out some of that data into a smaller database that has a Web front end, making it usable by many people at a low cost.

Strategy

We often find that our clients do not yet fully understand the potential of the Internet or how it will affect their businesses. They need assistance to identify the opportunities and develop an Internet strategy.

There has always been strategy in developing Web pages. What is emerging, though, is Internet business strategy. What should this Web site do from a business perspective? What are the business-related reasons behind an extranet, intranet, or Internet site? What does the business hope to achieve? This has normally been the area of the management-consulting firms, but they won't touch anything under a million dollars.

Many digital developers are making a commitment to understand more fully the businesses they choose to work with. Increasingly, digital developers are honing their skills in looking at the business strategy of a particular industry. This way they can find better ways of implementing, fixing, or assisting a business in doing what it is trying do.

Strategic Specialization

What would happen if digital solution providers really analyzed where the inefficiencies were within a specific industry and proactively designed a solution? That would be different from how things have been. Until now, Web shops have been constrained by a lack of funding, which has meant they could focus only on the jobs they have been asked to do. Now they're starting to take on investments and design solutions on their own initiative.

In a sense, this industry has been putting out fires. Businesses have been going to Web shops with specific needs in mind, and Web shops have built solutions for those problems. Now more Web shops are able to approach businesses and say, "There's a fire here, and you may not know it, but there will be a fire there. Here's what we can do to help."

There are tons of Internet companies, and most of them—when they specialize—are specializing only in design, applications, or systems integration. We are not seeing much specialization in strategy. More often the big management consulting companies are reaching into this area.

Choosing a Partner for the Online Hoedown

Digital solution providers of the future will need to deliver all of these services. However, they won't be able to do that across vertical industries. We can't offer a full service solution for both a financial company and an apple grower. Web shops will soon begin to refine their offerings and combine them into solutions that relate to a specific vertical industry.

Internet companies that don't do that won't be able to offer the right services to your company.

Let's take banking, for example. Suppose an Internet company focuses on financial vertical solutions. They have developed a way of doing business that can give banks a proven return on investment. Because they've invested the time to develop something that really works, they have a digital solution that all banks need. Moreover, because they didn't develop the solution for a specific bank but created something for the banking industry, they can work with all the banks in town.

The useful specialization we will be seeing will not be in design or systems integration but will focus on the strategic needs within a certain industry. Of course, not all companies work exactly alike, and successful digital solutions do not come shrink-wrapped. They're the result of systems integration, application development, graphic and user interface design, and strategy. So these solutions won't necessarily be plug and play. Nevertheless, you're going to see a lot more industry specialization.

I took what I learned from the surprises I had with my early experiences into my company, Sitewerks. Those lessons taught me how important issues such as usability, databases, and system integration really were. Consequently, we made the decision to hire more frequently from within the software engineering area, which was revolutionary in 1995. Most Internet companies at that time were more focused on design, advertising, and marketing and had employees who knew HTML. We were hiring database designers and information architects, a practice that was ahead of its time but that paid off in spades as the Internet quickly grew up. We had the right resources with the right skills to support the needs that were emerging.

The Internet has grown up very quickly. Most business leaders recognize that the Internet offers serious potential for success. It used to be that the Web comprised only marketing and brochureware. Then intranets and extranets arose, demanding different skills, different technologies.

The Internet, in combination with intranets and extranets, will provide support that is more mission-critical for businesses as time goes by. For Sitewerks, this has meant hiring more management consultants, more MBAs, and more business process reengineers. That way we can stay ahead of our clients and help support them in issues that provide real returns on investments. You're going to see a lot more of that.

The Web Shop of the Future

So what will a digital developer look like next year? Well, it's going to have software engineers, HTML programmers, designers, and writers. However, it's also going to have business analysts and management consultants.

No digital solution provider can do all things for all businesses. Within each industry, businesses are going to be looking for a different mix of these proficiencies, and every digital solution provider is going to have a different mix of strengths.

Some businesses have limited scope and do not require services based on all of the components of this business model. However, to adequately service a client over time and across multiple extranet, intranet, and Internet sites, this combination of skills and focus on a specific industry will become essential.

Web developers are going to start to narrow their focus so they are not all things to all people. The best shops will begin to look at return on investment issues and pinpoint their efforts on building digital solutions that work across a vertical industry.

Choosing a Digital Solution Vendor

We've seen three basic ways digital technologies can help your business to operate better, and we've looked at four areas of expertise in which digital solution providers tend to focus their energies. Now it's time to face the big question this chapter set out to answer: how will you find the right digital solution provider for your company?

The most important step in the process is to make sure you understand what you need to make your company successful. Then look for a vendor that can deliver that.

Where should you look? The usual approach has been to keep your ear to the ground and pay attention to hearsay and word of mouth. Let me suggest some other approaches: trade shows, media coverage, and organizations.

Trade Shows

Because of the specialization that is beginning to happen, Web developers will be making more of a commitment to specific industry niches. This means you're going to find them not so much at the Internet trade shows but at the legal trade shows, the manufacturing trade shows, and the financial trade shows. In other words, they will be entering your world a lot more.

If you go to the Internet trade shows, you'll probably find generalists, which is fine if all you're looking for is a general solution. However, if you're looking for mission-critical help, you should start to find digital solution vendors within your own industry.

Media Coverage

Again, because of specialization, industry trade journals will become increasingly helpful in the search for a digital solution vendor. Soon you're going to see articles in business magazines on using Internet technologies to solve problems.

Generally, you'll find coverage of this kind in the technology area of a trade journal. Still, it's going to be about both the technology and the business behind the solution.

For example, a health care journal may run stories about digital solutions that are helping to bring about business-related successes. Look for case studies about ways businesses are using these technologies to solve industry-specific issues. References to the companies that are providing these solutions will be an integral part of those articles.

Organizations

Several organizations independent of the technology producers are trying to come up with lists of vendors so business leaders can look there. So far, however, these efforts have not produced any reliable results.

If you are interested in using specific technologies, check with the manufacturer to see whether they can refer you to preferred vendors. For example, the Site Builder Network (*http://www.microsoft.com/sitebuilder*) is a good place to look if you are planning to use Microsoft's Internet technologies. Other companies are also making an effort to recommend approved vendors that might be able to support you technologically.

Once you have made a list of candidates, you'll have to start cutting away at that list based on a variety of criteria. A good place to start determining what these criteria comprise are vendors' Web pages.

A list of questions to ask yourself when looking at these vendor Web pages follows:

- Has the vendor worked with companies similar to yours in size?
- Have they worked with other companies within your industry?
- Have the sites they've built been successful in ways that you would like your site to succeed?
- What is their record in terms of return on investment?
- Do you like the vendor?

The Internet is so new and fast-paced that sometimes people are carried away by the sexiness of the technology, or the skateboard and dreadlocks attitude, or whatever. It's important to evaluate a potential site builder as you would any other partner. You will need to narrow down your list by checking references, investigating qualifications, and evaluating things such as the scale of projects the company has tackled or other criteria related to the company's staff and experience.

References

Ask potential candidates for references. They should be able to point you to successful sites they've built for other clients within your industry. Get specific names of clients and contacts so that you can call and ask them what the work was like and how they felt about their collaboration with the candidate.

Have references walk you through the process they faced so that you understand what happened and why. Ask to see the creative brief, and find out about their business goals. Find out about any systems integration issues as well. Call the reference's IT department and ask about the experience.

Ask a lot of questions. Here are a few to get you started:

- What was the methodology behind the vendor's design?
- If an application was built, what technologies did the candidate use and why?
- Is the client continuing to receive support, or did the vendor just build the solution and run?

Qualifications

Narrowing down your list of candidates is not just about who has a great client list. It's related to the work that was done. Don't settle with just the marketing stuff. Find out about technical certifications and industry awards.

Make sure that a potential partner has received professional training in using the technologies you need. Verify that they have certified staff and that those people will be working on your project. It isn't just that the director of the technology group has X, Y, and Z certification: is there proof that the people who are working on your site have that knowledge?

Is the vendor a preferred supplier to either a colleague company or a competitor? Being a certified supplier could mean that they've provided superior service for a period.

Scale

Look for a vendor that has experience delivering solutions on the scale that you need. If you're a large enterprise, look for vendors that have worked with large enterprise companies. If you're a small company, look for vendors that have worked with small companies. That's very important, particularly for big companies, because small vendors may take on more than they can deliver.

Make sure that your ideal candidate is a good match for the scope of the project you have in mind. In addition, remember that once you get started, these projects can become a lot bigger than you originally thought.

Experience

Experience is not always necessary. A startup that has a great management team and design team and is well funded might be just right for the job you have in mind. Generally speaking, however, companies that started early and are still in the business are obviously doing the right thing and would probably be a better place to start if you have a major project to complete.

If the expectation is for a mission-critical type of Web site and the candidate has not done any of those before—beware. Always look for specific experience on the particular type of job you need to have done. Don't just settle on a company that has a bunch of big names on their client list. And don't fall for the marketing stuff.

Staffing

The staff's credentials are also important. Vendors need to have the right people to do the various types of work and enough people to solve problems as they come up.

Are the employees shareholders in the vendor's firm? Are there financial incentives for the staff to do a good job? Is there some tie between the quality of the service they provide and the financial rewards they receive?

Conclusion

The business partners you choose to work with can obviously have enormous impact on your success. This chapter has looked at issues concerning collaboration with digital solution providers, including three types of digital solutions available to businesses today, four basic core competencies of digital development firms, and various ways to find and evaluate potential vendor partners.

To choose the right partner, the essential first step is to look at the goals of your business and map those goals to the types of digital technology solutions that are available. These solutions are generated by the use of extranets, intranets, and the Internet.

Knowing which combination of options will best suit your business goals puts you on the right path to choosing an appropriate vendor to work with.

As the technologies and their uses have grown and evolved, the garage Web shops of the mid-nineties, which once were able to tackle projects across industry boundaries, are maturing. They are beginning to specialize to serve clients within specific industry niches more effectively and provide ever-greater returns. At the same time, the scope of the types of projects that are being sought by today's increasingly tech-savvy businesses has demanded that to stay competitive, vendors must deliver complete solutions within their chosen market. The successful Web shops of the future will seek to balance their staffs to offer design, systems integration, applications development, and business strategy in complete and balanced ways to serve their clients best. However, since no digital solution provider can be all things to all clients, understanding the core strengths of potential vendors will help you choose the best digital solution provider for your needs.

As vendor specialization becomes more widespread, you can expect to begin seeing digital solution providers who have chosen to focus on your field at your industry's trade shows and in business journals that focus on your field. When you evaluate potential vendor candidates, look for all the benchmarks you would expect to find in any other professional partner candidate. The digital networking industry has grown up quickly, and unless you are looking for a general solution, it is unlikely that a startup company will be able to deliver the specific types of services you need.

Before you choose a partner, check the vendor's references, ask hard questions, and expect to get solid answers that prove the candidate's reliability. Most important, be sure you choose a vendor that is a good match in terms of your business's personality and culture. If you see your company as a maverick, you'll want to work with a company that is eager and able to push the technological envelope in all directions. If you aren't willing to take certain kinds of risks, you may need to find a partner that is more cautious in its approach.

About the Author

Luticia (Tish) Hill is one of the twenty-something co-founders of Sitewerks—A Bowne Company, which is a Seattle-based Internet development company. Tish took the company from a two person start-up to its recent acquisition by Bowne Internet Solutions, an international professional Internet services firm. With a focus on keeping company culture, Tish is responsible for the start of now-regular events such as "Beer Friday" and can often be found stoking up the rooftop barbecue on a sunny afternoon.

"After all, if you don't make dust, you'll eat dust."

Dan Fine

CHAPTER 6

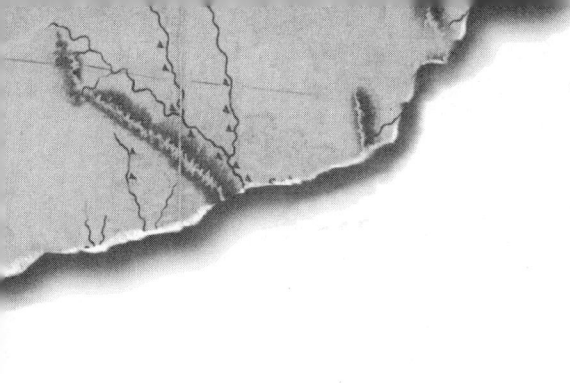

The General Store

Generating Profits One Cowboy at a Time

The Internet has opened up opportunities for many trailblazers. The question is whether they'll pick the right trail. Like many of the entrepreneurs who opened up shops in the Wild West 100 years ago, the majority will fade away without ever making a dent in the landscape. Since starting our Internet development company, my partners and I have met hundreds of entrepreneurs who want to become trailblazers but ignore the fundamentals of building a successful business.

A business that studies and learns from the past could become the next Sears, Roebuck and Co. This means that companies trying to establish themselves on the Web need to plan, become customer-centric, and use database technologies to secure valuable relationships with their customers and prospects.

This chapter will help you lay out the strategies needed to establish a powerful Web site that will enhance and extend your brand image, increase the lifetime value of your customers, and lower the cost of acquiring them.

The Store Proprietor

As the bright morning sun bends itself around the drapes and invades the bedroom, my squinting eyes peel open. That foreign light, called sunshine, is quite unusual during a Seattle winter. I roll over, dragging the comforter half off my wife. This starts an immediate tug of war; however, my mind is already drifting to another place. I'm thinking of last night's dream. I've been having elaborate, incredible dreams since I was a young tot with oversized ears and a buzz haircut. I don't know what has caused this intense dreaming. It's entirely possible that I was dropped on my head when I was an infant, and the sudden jar shifted something.

James Cameron, the Hollywood director, would be proud of some of my dreams. I usually create them with the production budget of *Titanic*. My fantasies are so real they look like they've been filmed in 70 millimeter with THX sound. Even though I'm pushing 40 years old, my dreams haven't slowed down. I'm sure you can imagine how the content of my dreams has changed since I was a kid. I'd mention some of the recent themes, but I'm afraid Special Prosecutor Kenneth Starr would indict me.

As a kid, my fantasies would focus on other eras. In my fourth-grade classroom, I'd be sitting at my tiny wooden desk with pale blue metal legs, usually staring blankly out the window. My very stern fourth-grade teacher, Mrs. Kemly, would launch into an exceptionally exciting topic, like the daily routine of the pilgrims during harvest time. My gaze was fixed on the playground. My mind drifted to a different era. Then daydreams would kick into high gear, and soon I was living another life during a very different time, in a strange and distant place.

In one particular dream, I was transported back to King Arthur's time. As a knight, I mounted the back of a beautiful, chestnut-colored horse. Although I was a child in the present, somehow I was a full-size adult in my dream. I was face to face with the enemy. He resembled Richard, the kid sitting next to me. Like Richard, he was low-life pond scum. Somehow

CHAPTER 6
The General Store: Generating Profits One Cowboy at a Time

I introduced modern weaponry into my arsenal. My favorite was the laser-guided photon pistols. The scoundrel I faced was equipped with medieval, primitive arms, such as a sword. No match for my photon pistols.

There is no doubt that my path to becoming a successful Web entrepreneur started in the fourth grade. My role as chief executive officer of a fast-growing Internet company has its roots in these recurring dreams. Along with my fellow classmates, I would head into fantasies of the late 1800s, the time of the wild, wild West. We each would jump immediately into the role of the cowboy. We'd ride high on our trusty horses, six-guns ready to draw for almost any reason at all. We slept outside every night around the campfire. In the morning, our mothers never told us to make our beds.

Sometime during high school, my daydreaming shifted. Instead of dreaming about being brawny, I would dream of being the brainy type. I'd sit somewhere in the middle of the swarm of my fellow students, and my teacher would gush on about the poetry of Blake. I'd stare out the classroom window, my eyes drifting up and down the bricks of the gymnasium, and I'd dream about various profit-making scenarios.

The Wild West General Super Store

I've always been a little different from the other kids. At least, that's what I've been told. In high school, my recurring dream about the wild, wild West usually deviated from the standard fourth-grader fantasy. The cowboy thing—riding a horse most of the day and sleeping on the dusty trail—never really appealed to me. My calling in life is talking with and meeting folks and leveraging my work into bigger things. I had this fantasy that I was the proprietor of the general store. Local folks would visit me all the time, and I had a never-ending supply of goods for them. I'd entertain the kids, my next generation of customers, and give them candy when their moms had their noses in new bolts of fabric. All the action in our small Western town seemed to swirl around the general store.

With my unlimited production budget, I could make time stand still and inject magical powers into my dreams. So I was able to create a shopping experience at the general store unlike one they'd ever seen before. I had tactics that kept customers for life and kept them happy. Across the entire West, no other store compared to mine.

The store was merchandised to perfection. I commissioned a customer traffic flow study to maximize impulse buying and cross-selling. Products, displays, and aisles were set up to capture the attention of customers and get them to spend additional time and dollars in the store. Extra dollars were allocated to great store fixtures that put products in their best light. In the dimly lit back room, I hired the only market analyst west of the Mississippi to build a customer database out of index cards. I used the information from this database to identify, segment, and act on upselling and customer retention opportunities.

The local newspaperman hated my guts. I was the only merchant in town who was able to measure the advertising effectiveness of his publication. Of course, I spread my knowledge around town, which really irritated him. I was able to negotiate a better advertising rate with him because I insisted on paying only for results.

To see if I could improve customer satisfaction and increase profits, I commissioned a survey of my customers. I found out they wanted the convenience of having the store open every day. To see if this was profitable, I committed to opening the store seven days a week and extended the evening hours. Some of the customers said it was a pain to ride all the way into town only to find out the store was closed. To improve service, I created a training program for the staff. To pay for it, I had it funded by the manufacturers. Finally, to create additional loyalty and to clear unwanted inventory, I created a shopping club. Those belonging to the club who spent certain amounts at my general store received additional privileges such as free delivery.

Store owners around the West flocked to monitor my progress and mimic my strategies. In the late 1800s, there was no other store like it. Actually, here we are in the late 1900s, and there still aren't many stores like my dream store.

Connecting Strategy with Technology

In New York City during the early 1980s, I spent several years working in some great advertising agencies. Some evenings, a few of the other young ad execs and I would go to the bar at Smith & Wollensky's and debate ideas about the perfect ad agency. In my perfect agency, everything would be run from start to finish with computers. Prospecting for new clients would be done with a database, conference reports would be prepared with a word

The General Store: Generating Profits One Cowboy at a Time

processor, and ads would be transmitted over an electronic network to a hundred newspapers simultaneously. The only thing done the old-fashioned way was entertaining the client, of course.

In the early 1980s, finding computers in advertising agencies was like trying to find an episode of Star Trek in which Captain Kirk didn't kiss a sexy alien. I saw this as an opportunity to build a new type of agency.

I wanted this agency to be in a perfect town, so I moved to Seattle. I started an agency that focused on using technology to the maximum. Great dream, but since I didn't have any money, I had to be creative. I needed to get some business, pronto. To pay the bills, I delivered pizzas at night and prayed that none of my clients had ordered one. Talk about embarrassing.

My new agency was fairly successful. The strategy was paying off. It was one of the first to use this integrated technology approach, and it provided a clearly visible competitive advantage. We proved to clients that we could get things done quicker, cheaper, and better than our competitors that were stuck in the Dark Ages.

In the fall of 1993, I started my research on small and medium-sized advertising agencies. What I learned troubled me. I delivered a speech to the International Association of Advertising Agencies (IAAA) entitled, "Are Small Agencies Becoming Dinosaurs?" My speech focused on the decline of small and medium-sized advertising agencies. Clients had MBAs to head their marketing departments, media buying services had started taking over the buying function for a fraction of the cost, and computer programs had made it easy for clients to produce their own collateral. A big vacuum existed in how clients connected technology with their marketing strategy. I introduced the audience to database marketing, multimedia, interactive voice response systems, fax-on-demand, and marketing through online services such as CompuServe.

Two things went wrong with that speech. First of all, I delivered it to the leaders of small advertising agencies. Most of them had been in business for decades, and it was hard for them to look at themselves and see that they were becoming extinct. The second problem was that I brought a five-foot-long, blow-up dinosaur. Ten minutes before the speech, I stood in the bathroom, my mouth affixed to the dinosaur, and blew it up. I marched into the conference room, inflated dinosaur in tow. I got up to deliver the speech desperately out of breath.

Soon thereafter my ad agency merged with a more traditional firm that had been in business for decades. I had two new partners. We focused only on general advertising. Each year, we worked harder and harder building revenues. But my theory about the future of small agencies was true. We were becoming dinosaurs. Even though revenue was growing a little bit each year, profits were not.

I continued studying the industry, and finally I thought I had found the Holy Grail. I threw all my energy into learning more about this new field. I knew it would soon be the answer to every marketing director's dream. The answer of course was database marketing—using a company's database to build customer profiles and mine the information to attract new customers and generate more profits out of existing ones.

With my wife pregnant, and in the middle of a house remodel, I left the ad agency to start a business focused on database marketing. We would help clients design database marketing strategies and then deliver them. This time, I had my fingers crossed that I wouldn't end up delivering pizzas at night.

The Grand Opening

On an unusual Seattle day in February (it was pouring rain), I opened my new database marketing company. I stood in my office, the drizzle dancing down the windowpane. I started to wonder if I was out of my mind. I was making decent money at the ad agency. Here, at my new company, I had no customers and no prospects. My wife and I were back to eating peanut butter and jelly sandwiches for dinner.

So I began to venture forth, selling my new company. On new business calls, I showed a simple-to-understand presentation demonstrating the power of database marketing. At least, I thought it was simple to understand. Back then, most of the businesses I presented it to didn't have a clue to what I was talking about. I droned on about database marketing, customer segmentation, and lifetime value, and they stared at me with blank eyes, nodding their heads politely but not understanding.

The General Store: Generating Profits One Cowboy at a Time

Right after I started the company, an acquaintance insisted that I stop in to see something extremely cool. I went over to his house, and he launched an application on his computer named Mosaic. He started searching what he referred to as the World Wide Web. He pulled up academic sites from Australia. He showed me odd applications named Archie and Jughead. While I was driving away from his house, my head was reeling at the possibilities the Internet could bring. At that time, I didn't fully understand what I saw, but I instantly knew it would revolutionize our lives.

Over the next year, I couldn't stop thinking about the Internet. I needed to learn everything about it. I went to a couple of bookstores, and I couldn't find any books on the subject. I knew it could be a fabulous marketing tool, but I had to learn how to use it, which meant learning UNIX. I signed up for an account with the only Internet Service Provider in the Pacific Northwest. It took me weeks to configure my computer to connect since there weren't any instructions—anywhere. I started to learn more, and soon we had *http://www.fine.com* on the Web. Shortly thereafter, we changed our company name from Fine Marketing Communications to fine.com.

Marketing-Focused Web Pioneers

The fun soon began. The process of trying to find companies that would stick their necks out and hire us to build a Web presence for them was daunting. Most prospects just said, "Huh?" Eventually, I found a few pioneers willing to experiment. The first was Fred Schumacher, who at that time was general manager of KMPS, a radio station in Seattle. He'd already been a leader with a customer loyalty program. I convinced him to put up a Web site instead of a bulletin board system. In the fall of 1994, KMPS was the first major commercial station on the Web with a comprehensive marketing site. The site had advertising and even allowed customers to shop on line. KMPS still features an extremely successful site. (See Figure 6-1 on the following page.)

Figure 6-1
KMPS was an early adopter of Web-based marketing that placed a commercial radio station site on the Web. They added ad banners and commerce in late 1994.

Next up was Seattle FilmWorks, which processes high-quality film. Bruce Ericson, their vice president of marketing, is a leader in understanding the core of direct marketing. He hired us to build a site that would distribute a software product called PhotoWorks. Seattle FilmWorks gives customers their pictures back on a computer disk for a very low cost, but they need the free PhotoWorks software to view them. Seattle FilmWorks was incurring a considerable amount of out-of-pocket expense distributing the software, so we created the Web site for customers to download the code at no expense. (See Figure 6-2.) To encourage usage, we included lots of examples of how consumers could use this service. We even had a photo contest for those who submitted their digital images.

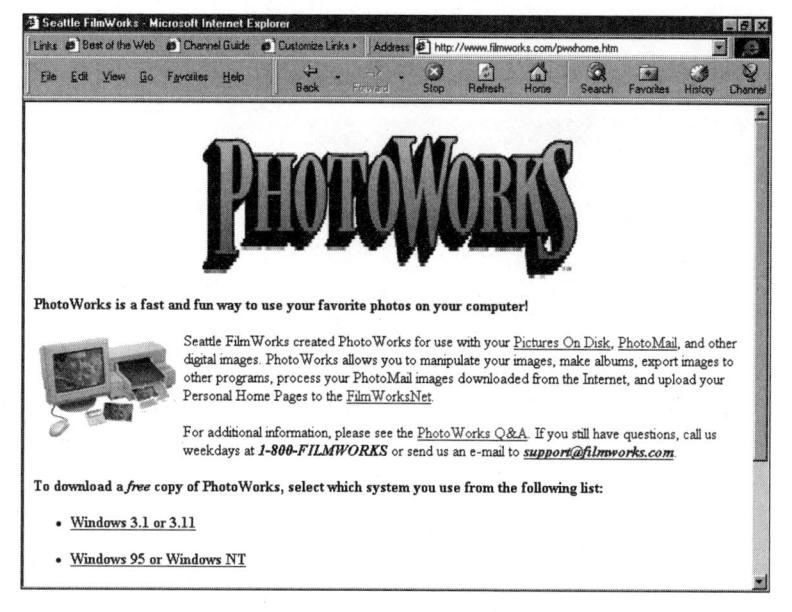

The General Store: Generating Profits One Cowboy at a Time

Figure 6-2
Seattle FilmWorks was already an expert database marketer when they extended their reach and launched their Web site in late 1994.

Near the end of 1994, Brian Allen, co-president of Windermere Real Estate, the leading real estate company in the Pacific Northwest, asked us to build an intranet for them. The term hadn't been coined yet, but the need was there. The Windermere intranet connects their 150 offices and 3,500 agents. They also insisted on having an Internet site, *http://www.windermere.com*. (See Figure 6-3 on the following page.) But as typical market leaders, Windermere wanted more. They wanted to have all their listings downloaded from the many mainframe-based multiple listing services they belonged to, sucked into a database, and then displayed on the Internet with photos.

Our early attempts at doing this with a Sun Microsystems server failed. So this became our first effort using Microsoft technology for the Internet. Up to that point, we had been using a combination of Solaris, Silicon Graphics, and Linux to run our sites. To reduce our training expenses and to speed the development cycle, we wanted to focus on one platform. We wanted something easy and affordable. We went to work connecting Microsoft Windows NT and SQL Server to the Web. We were able to build a system that worked, and life at Windermere has never been the same.

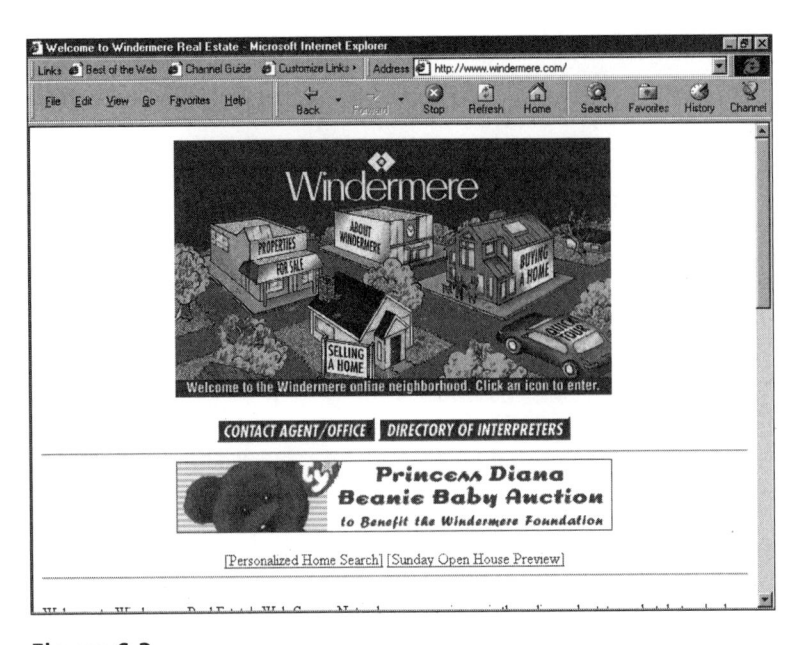

Figure 6-3
Windermere Real Estate was the first real estate company to discover the power of having a database-driven site connecting their properties to the Web.

Turning Your Web Site into a Gold Mine

Since I am a dream machine, I'll use my powers to magically place a proprietor of a general store from the late 1800s in the same room with another proprietor of an Internet store. Imagine the conversation! The opportunities and challenges facing both are probably similar. General store owners of the late 1800s had a lot to learn, and they were early pioneers in retailing. Those setting up shop on the World Wide Web are also early pioneers and have a lot to learn. Many of us can go on line and observe the efforts in place. Truthfully, they have a long way to go. Luckily, we have the advantage of observing and learning from similar industries, such as the catalog and direct marketing industry.

The General Store: Generating Profits One Cowboy at a Time

Both the general store and the Internet store face the issues of inventory, delivery, quality of goods, advertising, merchandising, credit, competition, and service. In our imaginary conversation between the proprietors, the Internet manager whines about how she had to add push technology to attract customers. The general store manager complains that he had to have a telephone installed to attract customers. They might spend some time talking about how to keep customers in the store longer, how to get them to spend more money, or even how to get more bang for their advertising buck.

Designing a Site to Last into the Next Century

Unfortunately, the majority of Web sites have more in common with the general stores of the Wild West than their proprietors are willing to admit. They lack the sophisticated marketing that companies such as American Express, USAA Life Insurance, Eddie Bauer, and Land's End have mastered. Consider some of the reasons people choose to order on line—reasons that go beyond the typical consumer purchase cycle. The successful commerce sites tap into these reasons and give the customer a rewarding experience. A few of the reasons consumers purchase goods on line are as follows:

- **Immediacy.** I want it now, now, now! I'll just Alt-Tab over from my spreadsheet, place the order, and Alt-Tab back to what I was doing before anyone notices I was goofing off.

- **Anonymity.** If I'm going to order a ButtMaster 2000, I don't want to talk to their phone people about it or tell them how my rear end needs this.

- **Coolness.** I'm hip. I'm with it. I order on line.

- **Completeness.** I have all the information in the world about this product at my fingertips. I'm not overlooking anything. Every little option is set out in front of me—every little accessory part is also available. I am tapped into an enormous warehouse, and I can get whatever I want. This company's paper catalog is a mere subset of what I have available before me now.

Consider setting the foundation of your Web site so that it will last you into the next century, not the previous one.

Introducing the Silver Bullet

When we wrote the business plan for fine.com, we wanted to make sure we didn't *just* build Web sites like the zillion other developers. We wanted a silver bullet, so we developed Interactive Response Marketing (IRM). *IRM* focuses on developing marketing strategies specifically for online interactive communications, with the goal of maximizing the lifetime value of a customer while lowering the cost of acquiring one. It combines integrated marketing communications with database marketing and unleashes the combination using interactive technologies. Both integrated marketing communications and database marketing have existed for some time, but not many companies have used them effectively. The problem is that, up until now, it has been costly to accumulate the information, process it, and then do something with it. Companies have had to deal with data input, developing creative communication pieces, printing them, and licking a lot of stamps. Most companies have started collecting the customer data but have done little more than look at it. IRM changes that by shifting the data input to the prospect and customer. Also, using database technology, tied in with electronic communication, there are no more printing or delivery costs. To help understand, here are some definitions:

- ***Integrated marketing communications*** means using all your media and communication vehicles together. In other words, you orchestrate your advertising and marketing and fine-tune them so you get the maximum result.

- ***Database marketing*** involves using cheap computer storage and processing power to analyze and act on prospect and customer demographics and purchasing behavior to gain greater share of customer. The information stores are gleaned and used to sell more to your current customers. And, the information about current customers is used to profile and convert prospects into customers.

- ***Interactive technologies*** involve the new media that allows prospects and customers to interact, or communicate, in a two-way manner. Instead of traditional "push" communication like mass media (television, radio, newspaper), interactive media uses a *pull* method. In other words, prospects or customers are in the driver seats pulling the information they want to see, when they want to see it. Interactive technologies include the Internet, interactive television, fax-on-demand, interactive voice response systems, interactive kiosks, and other online networks.

- ***Customer acquisition cost*** means not all customers cost the same amount of resource to acquire. Some customers are worth more than others, depending on their lifetime value. If a customer has a high lifetime value, you might be able to lose money on the initial sale to acquire a high-value customer. You've heard the old adage, "It costs five times as much to get a new customer as it does to keep a current one." Yet, most companies spend 95 percent of their marketing budgets on customer acquisition. If you're going to chase new blood, you need to do it more efficiently. This is why it is important to look at your customer acquisition cost and use IRM to lower it.

- ***Lifetime value (LTV)*** is the dollar volume of an individual customer over his or her "lifetime" as a customer. Naturally, if you provide good customer service and values and communicate with the customer at the appropriate times, you can maximize this lifetime value. It's all about building a strong relationship with the customer and maintaining it. Positive relationships increase customer loyalty.

The IRM methodology we developed at fine.com is used to maximize customer lifetime value by developing database response systems that allow a "real time," two-way communication and a relationship with a single customer via interactive media (for example, Internet, World Wide Web, online providers, interactive television, interactive voice response, fax-on-demand, extranets, and intranets). IRM builds on these methodologies by focusing on the real-time nature of interactive media and the opportunity they create for companies to provide instantaneous response to customer requests and online marketing activities.

The ability to use information as an asset makes it possible to go beyond a monologue with the customer to a dialogue with the customer. It is not just about refining the offer; it is really about refining the product with the help of the customer. This process begins to tie in with the concept of mass customization. Online communications, by definition, are two way. That is, they are interactive and differ substantially from mass media. The beauty of interactive media is that, compared with conventional media, it lets you present far more information in much greater detail and depth for a fraction of the cost. This represents a great medium for conveying complex messages because you get more space for your message and more time with your target audience. Just as interactive media differ from mass media, Interactive Response Marketing differs from traditional marketing methods. Interactive marketing is about delving more deeply into the sale.

Developing a finely tuned database and marketing strategy is the key to IRM. The information you gather drives appropriate actions from your business to each customer. With this data, you can seamlessly move contacts through the life cycle from prospect to advocate and begin to use this intelligence to cross-sell, up-sell, and increase referrals, significantly lowering the cost of acquiring customers. If you start building the database now, what kind of information will you have at your fingertips in a few years?

If you want a Web site that will start to churn profits, you need a clear set of response-driven objectives and strategies. IRM is based on establishing a clear set of metrics that allows businesses to measure online consumer activity, sales transactions, and database efficiencies, as well as track customer behaviors so businesses can make decisions based on actual behavior rather than attitudes and intentions.

To apply Interactive Response Marketing to your Web site, you need to mix the way business was conducted in the days of the Wild West general store along with the newer, scientific direct marketing techniques. In the days of the general store, the proprietor knew the name of all his customers, what their purchasing habits were, and how to keep them as *his* customers. The general store was the center of the community. People met there to just talk. It's where gossip started. People traded goods. Customers discussed farming, blacksmithing, and saloon keeping with the store owner. The store owner was expected to be educated in their businesses and to provide the right supplies for them. You need to have the same qualities but all with interactive technologies. You'll need to develop creative strategies using technology to get closer to your customers.

From Cowboy to Customer

Most companies have a common customer life cycle. And, many consumers are at different stages of this life cycle. The life cycle consists of suspects, prospects, customers, repeat customers, and advocates. Figure 6-4 displays the five stages of a customer life cycle.

Suspect   Prospect   Customer   Repeat customer   Advocate

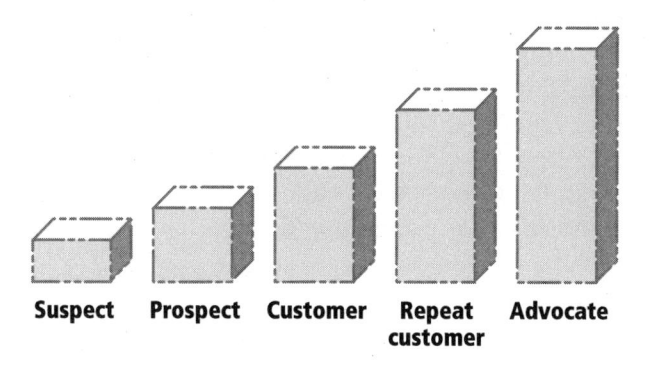

Figure 6.4

A consumer progresses through five stages of the customer life cycle: Suspect, Prospect, Customer, Repeat customer, and Advocate.

- **Suspect.** Someone comes to your Web site, and you have no idea whether they are interested in or capable of purchasing from you.
- **Prospect.** Using carefully placed questions and sophisticated reporting tools on the Web site, you can qualify Suspects and see if they are good enough to be Prospects for your services or goods.
- **Customer.** If your Web site is smart enough and transactional, you can take good Prospects and move them to be Customers.
- **Repeat customer.** Using Interactive Response Marketing and stored procedures, you can keep customers coming back again and again. You can also increase the amount of their purchases through personalization and other techniques.
- **Advocate.** The best type of advertising is word-of-mouth. Using traditional advocacy programs, but marrying them to interactive technologies, can be a powerful strategy to replicate your best customers by making them advocates for your business.

Building Lasting Relationships with Your Cowboys

Some concepts that can help you to create relationships, lower customer acquisition costs, and increase lifetime value by using Interactive Response Marketing follow:

- **Establish frequent buyer or viewer programs.** The airlines have this program down. I specify to my travel agent which airline I want to fly. She knows she has to make this airline work for me because I'm building frequent flyer points. This frequency program even works at my local coffee stand. I get a punch in my card every time I buy a latté. After buying ten lattés, I get a free one. It's easy to build a frequency program for your company that rewards customers for using your Web site and purchasing from you.

- **Generate reminder messages.** If a customer hasn't purchased from you or visited your site in a while, the database can automatically send a message as an incentive to act. The database can also be set up to remind the customer of significant events, such as getting his oil changed, sending flowers on an anniversary or birthday, or even resupplying him with printer toner.

- **Acquire instant research.** Use the customers in your database to give you feedback. At a moment's notice, you can segment customers and send out a questionnaire via e-mail—all at no cost. Customers feel important and more loyal when you ask them for their opinion, listen to them, and act on their advice. You can also collect information about prospects and customers when they visit your Web site. Of course, there has to be some reward or incentive for providing you with this information.

If you visit the site that fine.com built for Twentieth Century Fox Home Entertainment International's *Independence Day*, you'll notice how we collect information to use for future video sales. (See Figure 6-5.) Visitors tell us what countries they are from, give us their e-mail address, and are encouraged to provide a friend's e-mail. This information can help target science fiction video customers for future titles, such as *Aliens Trilogy*, and move them towards purchase.

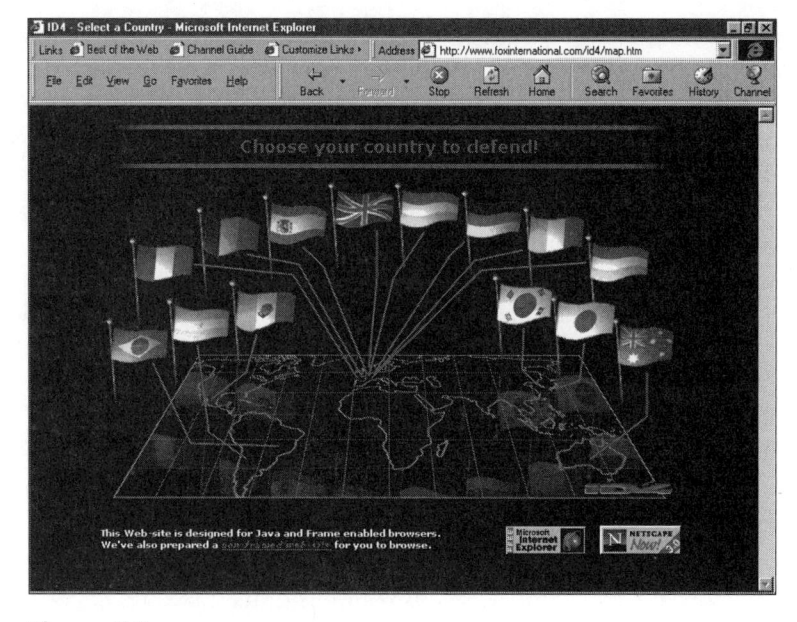

The General Store: Generating Profits One Cowboy at a Time

Figure 6.5
Twentieth Century Fox Home Entertainment International built this site with an eye to the future using Interactive Response Marketing.

- **Predict customers' behavior.** Building a database that captures and analyzes customer behavior will allow you to predict future actions. Being able to predict future purchasing behavior helps you to control inventories and maximizes profits. It can also help you predict when you might lose a customer so you can take corrective action.

- **Save your customers time and trouble.** Some companies make it difficult for customers to retrieve information. They might have to call a toll-free number and then wait four to six weeks for the brochure to arrive. Many times, companies send useless information, wasting paper, ink, and postage. Using the information customers give you can save your customers time and trouble. For example, every month I get a woman's catalog from a local department store. Last time I checked, I was still a man and was not wearing any frilly undergarments. (They might know something I don't.) They're wasting their postage, printing, and handling costs, and more important, my time. You can use the database to segment your customers and then provide valuable messages to the right people at the right time using personalization techniques.

Microsoft Corporation even provides a Personalization Server as a component of its Site Server suite. Imagine sending me e-mail reminders of my wife's upcoming birthday, with suggestions of what to purchase based on her buying behaviors. That would save me time and trouble and increase my customer satisfaction. And I could buy her frilly undergarments without the embarrassment of purchasing them in the store.

- **Reward your best customers.** Make examples of your best customers for your other customers and show them how easy it is to get treated like royalty. Reward your best customers by offering them a discount for their loyalty and purchasing more than usual. Profile and segment your customer base and encourage the not-so-good customers to become better. A simple way to segment them is to use the RFM formula. RFM stands for recency, frequency, and monetary. Recency looks at the last time a customer purchased from you. Frequency looks at how often a customer buys from you. Monetary examines how much a customer spends with you. By putting this into a computer model, you can segment your customers from worse to best.

- **Create multiple entry paths.** Unbelievable as it might seem, not everyone is on the Internet. You should build different ways for customers to interact with you. Some of your customers are more comfortable with a telephone, some with fax, some with in-store kiosks. When you build your interactive site, use a single-source database. Storing content in a single-source database allows you to save money by retargeting information for catalogs, fax-on-demand, interactive voice response, Web, and interactive television. It also makes it easier to keep your product and customer information up-to-date.

The General Store: Generating Profits One Cowboy at a Time

- **Remember Paretta's Law.** This law says that approximately 20 percent of your customers will account for 80 percent of your sales or profits. By collecting this customer information in a database, you find out who these customers are and make strategies so you don't lose them. You can help create a better relationship with them by providing a special site only for them. For example, the NASDAQ Stock Exchange has created NASDAQ Online for the CEOs and CFOs of companies that trade on their exchange. (See Figure 6-6.) This site provides information they can't get anywhere else in real time. In addition, it delivers information that NASDAQ used to have to print, bind, and ship. Delivering this information through a secure extranet has reduced the amount of time and money it takes to get the information into the hands of the people who need it.

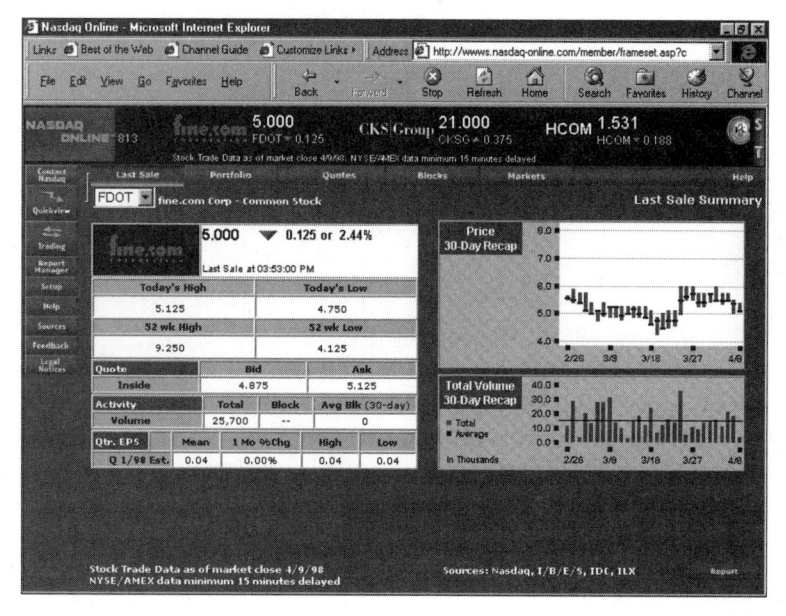

Figure 6.6
The NASDAQ Stock Exchange created this extranet to get closer to the top executives of the companies that trade on its exchange.

- **Bring people together with a sense of community.** Building a sense of community can create a stronger bond between customers and companies. I have been with a number of companies who are afraid to do this because they believe a couple of rabble rousers will turn everyone against them in their own site. Our experience has been quite the opposite. Usually, the rest of the community gangs up on the rabble rousers and runs them out of Dodge. Evan Schwartz said, "This is one of the most surprising facts of the Web: People are looking for more than just information when they go on line. They treat the Web as a place in which they can interact with other people."

- **Create co-marketing opportunities.** Seek out partners that can work on cooperative online marketing programs with you. For example, if you are a hardware manufacturer, find a software partner. By finding a noncompetitive, complementary product or service, you can create opportunities that make sense for their customers and yours. In addition, by sharing the risk and the cost, you minimize your exposure.

- **Merchandise your store.** Collecting information in the database allows you to monitor traffic flow through the site and how it correlates to purchasing behavior. By monitoring this flow and developing tactics to merchandise your store, you can create additional sales and profits. For example, fine.com developed the Developer Store in cooperation with Microsoft Corporation. The URL is *http://www.developerstore.com*. Based on past purchasing and the path a customer takes in the store, she receives related up-sell messages. If a customer has placed Microsoft Visual InterDev in her shopping basket, she will receive a message encouraging her to buy a CD-ROM training program on mastering Visual InterDev.

    By measuring traffic patterns in your site, you can merchandise the site to increase the duration of visits and maximize your customers' purchasing behavior. When interested prospects come to your site, they expect to find comprehensive information about your products and services.

CHAPTER 6
The General Store: Generating Profits One Cowboy at a Time

If you're planning a site to generate profits on the Internet, you need Interactive Response Marketing. IRM can help you meet customers' needs, become transactional, and build stronger, positive relationships. Regis McKenna, president of Regis McKenna, Inc., one of the country's leading technology marketing and public relations firms, said, "Marketing is a learning process. It is not something that you do; it is not simply a transaction in which you're doing all the action. You're not marketing at people. It becomes a learning process so that everything you do, you're gaining knowledge in order to enhance, to build, to change, and to incrementally improve what you do. And everything in the future is going to be integrated with a service. Every product is going to become more servicelike. Because, again, the way to differentiate yourself is no longer through the technology itself but in the use of the technology to create a tool for improving service."

Now that you understand the methodology of how to construct a site, it's time to start planning.

Getting Buy-In from the Sheriff

Setting up any company's Internet site provides a new challenge. To really make an impact, your site has to cut across almost every department in the company. It needs to touch marketing, operations, human resources, finance, and information services. But who should be in charge of the effort? Should this responsibility fall into the hands of the marketing department? Probably not. After all, what experience do they have in building world-class, scalable software applications that tie into legacy systems? Should information services be in charge? I don't think so. What experience does information services have in scripting an innovative and creative site that enhances the brand and moves the prospect through the customer life cycle? I believe that the Internet effort should fall onto the chief operations officer's shoulders. The COO has the authority to orchestrate the efforts of all the departments.

Upper management has to appoint someone to the task that can delve into all the departments of the company and get the cooperation they need. This can only happen if the chief executive officer understands and believes that the Internet can save money and make money for the company. Therefore, the first step in building a world-class site is to educate the senior management of the company in order to get the budget, time, and authority necessary to build a meaningful site.

To get management's approval to proceed, you need to prepare a solid business case. There are many reasons to build a top-notch Web site besides keeping up with your competition. You need to convince management that it's time to capitalize on this online, real time, multimedia exposure by integrating the company's Web site with its customer and operational databases. By doing this, you can truly personalize a customer's experience to get the desired response.

To help you build your proposal, I've listed some of the reasons organizations have adopted interactive technology:

- **Expanding sales.** To establish a new sales channel and generate increased sales and profits. This happens by finding new customers, expanding your geographic sales area, and lowering your cost of sales.

- **24-x-7 communication.** Provide secure interactive communication between customers and your business 24 hours a day, 7 days a week, and 365 days a year on a global basis. Giving customers this kind of response improves communication and your relationship with them.

- **Just-in-time communication.** Enhance on-demand communication and information distribution capabilities. This means that prospects can get information when they need it, not when you decide to send it. Instead of "push" communication, it becomes "pull," which gets the customer more involved with you.

- **Save money.** Reduce costs associated with internal and external business transactions. Automating transactions on your end reduces the cost of processing orders and lowers the chance of keypunch errors.

- **Streamline processes.** Allow the end user to enter information for report generation, ordering, fulfillment, and personnel information. Reengineering these systems into database technology allows management to review information in real time from anywhere in the world over the Internet while reducing entry error.

The General Store: Generating Profits One Cowboy at a Time

- **Build a strategic weapon.** Differentiate yourself from your competitors and build a long-term competitive weapon with database marketing. If you make it easier for your customers to do business with you, they will. Think of the competitive advantage you will have in just a few short years if you start building a database of customers' demographics and purchasing behaviors now.

- **Lock in customers for life.** Improve customer satisfaction, retention, and growth. Many businesses don't focus on this as much as they should. The key to a successful business is happy customers that continue their relationships with your company and spend more. You can use the Internet to help reduce the costs of generating additional business out of your customer base.

Preparing a sharp, concise proposal to management and educating them on the benefits is your first step to building a profitable Web site. In many cases, we discovered that upper management does not understand the Internet or the benefits it can bring to a company. Usually someone lower in the ranks attempts to introduce it into the company. In several of these cases, we've referred an outside consultant to come in and educate upper management. This consultant teaches them about the basics of the Internet and how a company can use it to their advantage. Each week, he gives a different homework assignment to the executives to think about how the Internet can affect their company in a positive manner. In addition, he helps them build a plan of how to phase in this technology throughout the organization.

Having an educator lead the way works extremely well. In the case of Continental Savings Bank, an outside consultant, Ken Mays, paved the way for a truly effective Internet strategy. He spent months holding seminars for the upper management and helped them establish their strategy. Once top management buys into the Internet and sees what it can do for the company, the rest of the job becomes much easier.

Putting Your Team Together

If you've convinced management that you're the appropriate person to lead the Internet effort, your next task is to assemble a competent team. You cannot do this by yourself. You need all kinds of talents, and I guarantee you they don't all reside in one person. To get this accomplished quickly, you'll want to stay nimble, so you don't want to pull in too many people. However, building an interactive Web site that compels customers to buy and that ties into legacy systems is no small undertaking. You'll need to pull expertise from the following areas:

- **Infrastructure.** A person from your information services department that knows what computer systems exist and how to get information in and out of them.

- **Graphics.** A representative from your graphics department to help ensure consistency between your corporate look and feel and the Web site.

- **Marketing.** A marketing strategist to help with building tactics for capturing prospects and moving them through the customer life cycle (Suspect to Prospect to Customer to Repeat Customer to Advocate). It would be helpful for this person to have a background in database marketing.

- **Analyst.** An analyst who can help build the reporting features of the site and generate return-on-investment scenarios.

- **Outside strategists and developers.** A terrific development company with experience in building world-class, transactional Web sites. This means a company that understands interactive response marketing, tying into legacy systems, translating the site into a global effort, and how to work with multiple departments and outside partners, such as advertising agencies.

Your team won't do you any good unless they have the time assigned away from their day-to-day jobs to devote to building the site. They need approval from their supervisors to dedicate sufficient time and energy to their new task. Once you have your experts in place, you need to involve them throughout all the steps, from planning the site to launch.

Plan the Work, Then Work the Plan

Why write a plan when you can start laying code? When I've surveyed companies about their Web efforts, the ones that have unprofitable sites are the ones that skipped the planning phase. I consider building a Web site to be similar to constructing a house. When building a house, you provide the builder with a detailed specification prepared by a professional architect. When building a Web site, you start by preparing the detailed specification, or what I call the blueprint.

The basic elements of building a Web plan that returns a profit are as follows:

- Objectives and strategies
- Measurement and research
- Creativity
- Computing environment
- Project resources, budget, and timeline
- Fulfillment and customer interaction
- Promotion and site maintenance

Objectives and Strategies

- **Overview and management summary.** This section summarizes the overall plan of the site. Upper management should read this section and get a good idea of what you're trying to accomplish without having to delve into the nitty gritty.
- **Business and strategic objectives.** A good Internet effort will be consistent with your company's overall business and strategic objectives. A good way to make your Web efforts dovetail nicely with the company's objectives is to list these.
- **Site objectives and strategies.** Here you will describe the overall goals and tactics you wish to achieve with your Internet effort.
- **Global and other geographic marketing objectives.** If you work for a global company or one that wants to expand globally, this is the place to state what you are trying to accomplish outside your home country.

- **Targeted end users.** Describe the audience you are trying to attract to this site. This might or might not align with your traditional target audience.
- **Risk assessment.** Summarizes the risk factors associated with the successful completion of this project. These can come from all over and could be technical challenges, budgetary constraints, scheduling difficulties, content creation issues, and even political challenges within your organization.

Measurement and Research

- **Competitive review.** A simple review of your online competitors should be listed here, along with the objectives, strategies, and tactics of their sites. You might want to include other sites that you use as a point of reference.
- **Measurable results.** Here you should list what you expect to achieve with this site. In the reporting section, you should list how you are going to measure the results.
- **Report overview.** Details the documents that will be generated to report site results. Some of the reports could include: Usage Reports that provide statistics such as hits per day, week, and month, hits on each day of the week, and hits for each hour of the day; Visitor Reports that list most common cities, organizations, and organization types (government, business, and so on) of visitors to your site; Request Reports that list the most-requested and least-requested pages, most common entry and exit pages, and most common referring URLs; Browser Reports that list the types and versions of browsers used by visitors; and finally, Bandwidth Reports that show the number of bytes transferred per day, day of week, and hour of day.
- **User research.** How will you find out about your customers' needs and desires? Will you do this through focus groups, specific reporting on the site, or customer questionnaires? Before you launch, you will need to conduct research on the user interface and adapt your site. How many clicks are required to get through to desired material? When a user clicks on a button, does she get what she expected?

- **Bug testing.** Most companies will not release a product until it has been thoroughly tested. Your Web site is a representation of your company, and it should also be tested from front to back. Testing includes documenting bugs and accessing the site from multiple platforms, with multiple browsers, on multiple operating systems, and coming in at different access speeds. It even includes proofreading.

Creativity

- **Site key messages.** Just as good advertising pushes only a few key messages, so should a good Web site. On your home page, the first thing a user should see is the benefit of using your site or your company. Take a look on the Internet. Many of the sites you see have a third of the screen taken up with their logo as the first thing you see. Then look through a magazine at ads. You'll see mostly a benefit or image that conveys the unique selling proposition of the company or product. Why should your Web site be any different?

- **Content analysis.** Describes the overall content and tentative structure of the site. Describe the content of the site, links to the site, and navigation of the site. Include the objectives of the home page. Describe any planned client-side technologies. Will there be any cookies, scripting, plug-ins, ActiveX controls, security required, persistent data connections, and push technology? Where will the content come from? If it doesn't exist, who is going to create it?

- **User experience.** What the user experience is, from their point of view, when they first enter the site. Make it easy for the prospect or customer to learn about your company. I use a two-click navigation rule. The user should be no more than two clicks away from anything on the site. Most commerce sites commit the ultimate capitalistic sin: they make it difficult for me to give them my money. I've come to the site, I've read the pitch, I've made the decision to purchase. But how do I do it? Why do I need to weave through 12 more screens? Why do I have to call a 1-800 number; why can't I order right here and now? Make it easy for the prospect to order. If they come to your site and want to buy, and you add unnecessary steps, most of them won't. They should visit your site, find the product they want, and click to order it. Finished.

- **Graphic design.** What are the graphic standards for the Web site? As the site continues on after the initial build, how will you maintain consistency? Remember, when designing the home page, the viewer will make a decision within two to five seconds to click the back button or to stay with your site.
- **Detailed content tree.** Using a graphical representation, detail what the structure of the site will be and the flow from link to link.

Computing Environment

- **Computing environment.** What is the computing environment with which your end users will access your site? What operating system, word processing or spreadsheet application, presentation package, e-mail client, and browser do they use? Tell us how you will coordinate with these factors to make it an effortless and painless experience.
- **Limitations.** Are there any limitations that would significantly affect the architecture and feature set of the site?
- **System specification.** Describes the function and performance of the proposed site and the constraints that will govern its development. This includes a summary of the site architecture, security, and browser support.
- **Architecture Context Diagram (ACD).** The ACD defines all external producers of information used by the system, all external consumers of information created by the system, and all entities that communicate through the interface or perform maintenance and administration.
- **Project development environment and migration path.** Here you can discuss what sort of technical environment the site will be developed on and how it will eventually be transferred to its final hosting farm. This can be crucial information if you are planning on replicating or localizing content in different countries.

- **Technical implications of browser versions.** To minimize difficulties experienced by your users, you will want to discuss what client-side components you are willing to use in the initial release of your site (Java, JavaScript, ActiveX, and so on).

- **Hosting.** No site would be complete without the proper hosting environment. In many cases these days, the Internet is becoming a crucial part of doing business. This means that you should develop a true hosting environment in your plan, which includes high-speed access, redundant systems, back-up power generators, and data backup. In the case of global delivery, you should develop a plan that includes content replication and hosting in strategic countries overseas.

- **Server platform and development tools.** Here you detail what hardware and software will be used to serve up the Web site and to provide access to legacy systems. This includes but is not limited to the operating system, database, Web server, search and indexing software, and proxy server. At fine.com, I decided several years ago to focus on one set of software so we could make it faster to develop and easier to maintain. This has proven to be a major competitive advantage. Focusing on a limited set of software, our developers garner more expertise in the selected set, and it reduces our training costs. At fine.com, our focus is on Windows NT, Internet Information Server, Index Server, Visual InterDev, SQL Server, Visual Basic, and ActiveX.

- **Detailed specifications analysis.** Here is where you can document all the databases, database fields, legacy systems, import/export requirements, updating requirements, security firewalls, routers, software and hardware requirements, and other technical information.

Project Resources, Budget, and Timeline

- **Project resources and responsibilities.** Outlines the roles and responsibilities of the organizations and identifies individual team members. Describe the process through which this site/application will be approved within your organization. Describe the roles and responsibilities of the Web development company, your company, and any other partner in this site/application.

- **Projected budget.** Presents the specific investment necessary to complete the detailed specifications analysis (blueprint) and costs to complete development, testing, and maintenance. Note: in some cases, maintenance can cost as much as development.

- **Return on investment.** Your upper management will appreciate this section. Here you use sophisticated financial analysis to discover what cost savings and profit generation activity you will be initiating for the company.

- **Projected timeline.** Provide a detailed timeline for the completion of each task of site development. This is best accomplished using project management software, such as Microsoft Project 98, to manage the overall process, monitor resource availability, and provide up-to-date status reports and financial commitment information.

Fulfillment and Customer Interaction

- **Customer service.** As customers and prospects interact with your site, they will send you messages—a lot of messages. You need to be ready to communicate with these buyers. You can set up an e-mail auto responder to send a message back immediately, but you will have to send a personalized message shortly after. How will you integrate this into your customer service department? Or will you hire an e-mail service firm to handle this for you? You will want to create a database to log these e-mails, and you'll want to read them and help prepare preapproved copy blocks. In addition, you will want to use this information for research purposes. It can help tell you about service levels, product information, and customer satisfaction.

The General Store: Generating Profits One Cowboy at a Time

- **Delivery and fulfillment.** If you offer e-commerce, product literature, or research reports, you need to make sure that you can deliver it. Whether or not you use an outside fulfillment service, your Web site should map directly to the system used by the service. This eliminates double entry and reduces keystroke mistakes.

Promotion and Site Maintenance

- **Maintenance.** You will need to document how you will keep the site fresh and get information entered on a timely basis. What is the process for doing this? Will departments be responsible for their own maintenance, or will you provide a funnel for this activity to occur?

- **Promotion.** Contrary to what most executives believe, if you build it, they will not come. As with any good product, you need to tell folks about it and convince them that it is worth the time and effort to go there. In the plan, you need to detail how you will promote this site. What specific online and offline advertising, public relations, and promotions will occur to bring people to your site and keep them coming back? There are many ways of telling people about your site. The first and most expensive is to create specific ads about the site, or you can include it in your current advertising promotion. One of our clients, the NASDAQ Stock Exchange, has done this very successfully. They have high-impact television spots promoting *http://www.nasdaq.com*. The results: seven million hits a day. Another client, Safeway Inc., has even had its Web address put into the tiles on the floor of the grocery stores. Another beneficial method for promoting your site is to purchase advertising banners or links at other sites. Using click-thru, content testing, and measurement techniques, you can fine-tune these efforts so that you have an effective campaign. You can also draw folks to your site by creating an event or unique content that garners press coverage.

With your plan in place, you can move into development of your site. I generally allocate six to eight weeks to getting the team together and preparing the plan. Having a plan in hand cuts your development time and cost extensively.

Start Using Your Gold Mine

With over four years of experience planning and building sophisticated Web sites for Fortune 1000 companies, I've learned a lot about constructing a winning site. My expertise comes not just in the process of building a site, or even in the technology, but in the underlying philosophy of what makes a site profitable for the sponsoring company and appealing for the consumer. Like my daydreams of building the perfect general store in the Wild West, I fantasize about building the perfect store on the wild, wild Web.

The easiest part of Interactive Response Marketing is collecting the data. The most important part of IRM is using the data that you've collected. Turn it into a strategic weapon. If you started now, what kind of database would you have in six years? Will your competitors have this powerful weapon? The manager of the Wild West general store never had to face this problem. The database he relied on was in his brain.

Strategic marketing Web sites that utilize Interactive Response Marketing accomplish four basic objectives:

- They promote products and services for the company.
- They support the company's sales processes.
- They generate specific customer responses.
- They move customers and prospects through the life cycle while at the same time building brand loyalty.

Using a smart Internet site, you can collect important customer information through interactive marketing and proactively use this valuable database. With this information, you can set up the database to automatically deliver the right messages:

- To the right people
- At the right time
- Through the right communication vehicle

The General Store: Generating Profits One Cowboy at a Time

The beautiful part of this is that it improves customer satisfaction and increases revenue and profit, all without buying expensive television time or licking thousands and thousands of stamps. The objective of Interactive Response Marketing is to have marketing information systems that provide a response in real time. The key difference between the IRM approach and traditional direct marketing is the timely, customized response via online communications. This nearly instantaneous response system is the wave of the future for marketing-savvy businesses.

The Internet has again poised us on the edge of a new frontier. Jeff Bezos from Amazon.com said, "the sudden arrival of the World Wide Web over the past few years can be compared to the first ten seconds of the big bang. So much has happened in a very short time frame." The businessmen of the Wild West faced a similar opportunity. The future was theirs for the taking. Some of them continued in their old ways and faded into oblivion. Others, such as Sears, Roebuck and Co. and Levi Strauss & Co., used their intelligence and a little bit of guts, invested in the future, and became billion dollar empires.

So remember, a little bit of planning, an understanding of how to merge business savvy with direct marketing science, and interactive technologies can take your company to the next frontier. After all, if you don't make dust, you'll eat dust.

About the Author

Dan Fine is the chief executive officer of fine.com International when he isn't daydreaming. He started his Internet business in 1994 and took the company public on NASDAQ in 1997. Fine.com's clients include Microsoft, Marriott, Twentieth Century Fox Home Entertainment International, Safeway, Amway, and Optiva. With offices in Seattle, Los Angeles, Washington, Tokyo, and London, Dan has enough frequent flyer points to upgrade from the baggage compartment. Prior to founding fine.com, Dan was a vice president and principal in an advertising agency. Dan's father, mother, and brother are all in the advertising business. It's a genetic defect in the Fine family that he hopes won't affect his two daughters.

"If you want them to come, you'd better damn well tell them where the house is."

Bryan McCormick

CHAPTER 7

Pioneers Have Arrows in Their Backs

"I got stuck with the lemon chapter of the book." This dark thought came to me on my way to Redmond to talk about writing this chapter. Why would I think such a thought? If I was going to write anything about content and how it has evolved from CD-ROM to the Web, I was going to need to say outright that it was a net loss venture that deserved to fail. This isn't the kind of thing people fall over themselves to say in this field. How was I going to do it? Should I just let the hype balloon inflate or be a much-needed boy with the needle?

I called a close friend of mine who works in television. If anyone could help me through this, it was someone who lived in even slimier trenches than I. His response, sensibly, was something like this: "It's not like any of this is going to be a shock to anyone who has had their eyes open, and it's your obligation to wake up anyone who might have been napping and missed it. Remember: No prisoners. Name names."

Usually this is the kind of advice that I would disregard, recognizing it for the career killer that it is. Despite that, I'm heeding it. So here we go.

Having the opportunity to write this chapter has forced me to do something that few involved in creating content in the multimedia world have had a chance to do: reflect on where we have been, where we were supposed to go, and why we never got there. The last bit is particularly important, and it needs to be said, especially given the amazing ability of people in this business to generate reality distortions. By some current accounts, particularly those that you might encounter at an electronic entertainment exposition and other such confabs, you get the impression that gold is just bugging out of the ground and that the content biz is alive and well on the Web. Hint: it ain't so.

Rule One: *The amount of truth, wisdom, or valuable information that can be derived at any trade show is an inverse function of the show's noise level.*

I imagine it will surprise you to know that the following remarks come from someone who, by many measures, actually succeeded in this industry. Why then am I going to spend a lot of time here mapping out sins, omissions, and ill deeds? For one reason—because we are on the cusp of yet another dramatic change in this industry. Call it broadband Internet, or Internet-enabled television—that's the stuff of another chapter. If history repeats itself, we will end up blowing it as we did with laserdisc, CD-ROM, Enhanced CD, and the Web. Now, I don't say this because I'm an expert in this area or because I'm smarter than anyone else in the field—I've just made more mistakes than anyone I know. Unlike others, I've tried to learn from them.

Rule Two: *Listen only to people who have made a lot of mistakes. Study them carefully, and do the opposite of what they have done.*

We should be clear that when I discuss content, I am not talking about games, kids' products, or the kind of stuff we might think of as content. I am simply talking about "data." My experiences for the most part have dealt with entertainment, both in CD-ROM and on the Web, so naturally that's where I'm turning my attention.

The truth is, from laserdisc to the Internet, almost all ventures into content failed to find enough of an audience to make them worth doing. A lot of what was produced was just embarrassingly bad. CD-ROMs for the most part were "shovelware." Enhanced CDs missed the point that people don't sit in front of a computer when listening to music, and much of what is on the Web as "entertainment" is amateurish, sloppy, and soporific. The vast majority of developers, producers, and distributors of interactive multimedia content have gone, are going, or will go broke; and why? Because people vote with their feet. That's right. I'm saying we deserved to get kicked. Moreover, if we don't change our ways, we will deserve it all over again soon.

>**Rule Three:** *Never assume that you can get it right on the second try with an audience. If people didn't like it the first time, they aren't coming back—ever.*

Don't get me wrong. I do not believe that the industry then or now was bereft of talent or good ideas. Far from it; a lot of great work happened over the last several years. However, aside from a few notable exceptions, most of you have never seen the good stuff that was made.

The Method to My Madness

Let me tell you up front that I don't quote from expensive surveys or use other people's projections of the marketplace except when it shows how such advice helped us smack into a brick wall. Why? Because a blind faith in those numbers and a lack of common sense led a lot of people down the path to ruin.

>**Rule Four:** *Never believe anything that sounds too good to be true—especially a projection—because it is too good to be true.*

To make sure that you learn something about how we got ourselves into the position of almost always making a silk purse into a sow's ear, I will map out a very brief history of commercial multimedia, tell a few stories in between about my experiences, share observations about those experiences, and conclude with a note on where content may go next.

To get you to that point, I talk about a bunch of truths (some technical, some human) that need to be reiterated. I want to make sure though that by the time you have finished this chapter you will have a built-in, shock-proof, crap detector for content in new media. Reading this chapter will also make you rich and thin. (See Rule Four.)

Where Multimedia Started for Me

I did not come clean to the Web but in fact lived through the three previous incarnations of interactive multimedia, each of which were the next great thing in their time (laserdisc, CD-ROM, and Enhanced CD). They came, and went, within a few short years. Don't feel sorry for me, by the way. As a developer who often did a lot of work for hire, such a situation actually benefited me greatly. Change is opportunity. I'll talk more about that, because people like me also helped make things happen (because we could make money doing so) in the industry that probably shouldn't have happened.

Some 10 Years Ago

When I first became interested in multimedia 10 years ago, it hadn't filtered down to the consumer level. Most of it went on at academic research institutions or was confined to the then-hot promise of the day, interactive laserdisc and hypertext systems available to a small elite. Given that laserdiscs and hypertext systems were about as popular and well-known at the time as sashimi salad, people weren't likely to run into multimedia except by extreme accident.

I came to multimedia entirely through dumb luck and timing. I didn't see the future coming; I wasn't that clever. In 1987 I bought a Macintosh 512K, a computer with a small nine-inch black-and-white screen with a friendly, warm, and graphically oriented operating system (its display looking more like paper than the green-and-black screen of my illegal, Canadian-made Apple II clone). This worked for me, as I was working toward a doctorate in art history and was a sucker for anything that was well designed and wouldn't eat years of dissertation research.

Why am I starting back here? I want you to understand how far technology has come. The state of the art of that time saw few computers with hard drives, color was just being introduced, and CD-ROM drives did not exist. Primitive stuff indeed. Nonetheless, something very cool was about to happen that would get a lot of people interested in computers for the first time. It was the beginning of multimedia as we know it today.

The momentous event was Apple's launch of HyperCard. I remember sitting on the edge of a couch, watching the Computer Chronicles. The program was showing some of the great things HyperCard could do. For the first time there was simple-to-use software that let you put together information of all types (graphics, sound, and text), and you could link them together anyway you chose. Crude as it was, it was impressive—I knew I was seeing a key to the future.

I was hardly alone in this feeling. At the time the buzz and aura surrounding HyperCard was every bit as big as that surrounding the Web today. Of course, that should be scary considering that about six years later it had sunk to near obscurity, replaced by software that could deliver better graphics and sound.

About five months after seeing HyperCard and making a pilgrimage to the first multimedia expo out in San Francisco (summer of 1988), I decided to strike out on my own and learn how to use its power. Like many early converts, I had "drunk the juice" and was convinced that education, my hobby horse at the time, would never be the same—we were going to do great things. Think of the possibilities! Hey, I was earnest. Sue me.

I made one phone call to a company I had never heard of that was producing HyperCard software for education. As luck would have it, and given that no respectable programmer would get within a mile of this toy, I was soon talking myself into a job I was barely qualified to do. I had no idea what I was getting myself into. Mind you, my employers didn't either since I "extended" the scope of my scripting abilities to get in the door.

Happily for all, I learned to program quite well. Within a year and a half I was on to ABC News Interactive to work on a series of history discs that they were producing for the school market. By the way, this was the first unit that I know of that a major network made a commitment to multimedia, a fact we will come back to in our discussion of the Internet. The group was spending a lot of money, with a staff of 28 pumping out several titles a year.

Now, you have to grasp how all of this worked to appreciate what we were putting together and what the poor schlub who bought this stuff needed to make it work. At the time, it was the only way to see video in a nonlinear fashion. CD-ROMs were not around, and even if they had been, few computers in schools supported color or were fast enough to display video.

The setup was to hook a laserdisc player to the serial port of the computer and fire off commands to cause the player to go to a given frame number, play, fast forward, or what have you. It was hardly ideal. Let's face it, it was amazing that it worked at all, and many times it didn't. Does that sound familiar? You had to have two screens, a television, and then a separate computer monitor, ideally very close together. The computer screen had the data and controller, and darn sophisticated it was—the television had the cool stuff.

Clearly this Rube Goldberg assemblage was not going to be really popular in the average living room (nor would the 1988 price tag, something along the lines of $4,000 dollars with a computer, a laserdisc player, and a television). This technology was destined to remain at the corporate and school level, given the cost and complexity of setting up the machines. Although laserdisc manufacturers brought out lower-cost machines, most of those did not have a serial port, in order to save the $1.50 in manufacturing costs, and were therefore useless for anything other than straight playback. I recall the torrents of cusswords that erupted out of our president's mouth when this fact was announced by the then-largest supplier of players. He was unhappy for good reason.

By now it was painfully clear that the mass market for laserdiscs that the pundits assured us was "just around the corner, with sales expected to rise 150 percent or more each year" was never going to happen.

> **Rule Five:** *A market's value that is otherwise too small to publish in dollars is always referred to by percentages to avoid drawing unwanted attention to said fact. The larger the percentage value, the smaller the market's true size and value.*

Everyone knew it except the schools that had just blown their technology budgets for the next several years. And we all know what happens to platforms that don't grow—they become roadkill. The decision makers blame it on the vendor and live to make more decisions.

What's the Point?

Why am I wasting time talking about this when I'm supposed to be talking about content? First, when we speak about CD-ROMs, all this will have a familiar ring to it. Second, although level-three laserdiscs (the interactive type) failed to thrive because of manufacturers' short-sightedness and laserdiscs' inherent complexity, the content businesses built around them collapsed because they had no other option for distributing their content except in this format. The two were inextricably linked. In this scenario, if the platform wanes and dies, so too does the content provider's business. This is a lesson we keep failing to learn.

Rule Six: *Make the mistake of tying content to its delivery platform and the content will live or die by the quality of the platform, not by its own value. In the mind of the public, however, the distinction will not matter.*

Beyond the obvious thrashing that content providers took, schools also were seriously injured financially by the failure of laserdisc systems. Although the laserdiscs themselves had a long life, they quickly fell into disuse in schools where their use was not mandated. Believe me, there were lots of audio visual closets with dusty machines and software that had never been opened. The toll? Conservatively speaking, hundreds of millions of dollars for a system that could not afford such a mistake. Total value today: Landfill.

Cue to Enter CD-ROM

Okay, one industry down, and the consumer market lay before us. Now how to get to it? CD-I, a close relative of the CD-ROM, was supposed to arrive at any moment (this was 1990), and we were all bound to be thrown out of our cushy network jobs as soon as someone in the upper echelons figured out that laserdisc was dead.

But it looked like the opportunities were limited in this realm because Philips Electronics N.V., the creator of CD-I, had decided that only a handful of developers were going to be allowed near it. I guess they wanted to keep all those great titles on postage stamps and Victorian paraphernalia strictly in the hands of the chosen few. The great unwashed were going to need to take a look elsewhere. Fortunately, CD-ROM arrived just in time. But there was yet another cool piece of software on the horizon that was going to give a jump-start to multimedia.

Because of a bit of marketing genius on the part of Apple's developer relations group, ABC News was forced to purchase a CD-ROM player. So were most other developers with a conscience and common sense. Why? Because all developer notes and seed releases would from now on come only on CD-ROM. Sure, you could order the floppies and paper documents, but that would put you a month or more behind everyone else. Considering that shipping a product without having this stuff was inadvisable (lots of people did it anyway), we had to have one. Way to go Apple—software does sell hardware!

Rule Seven: *Hardware people really do need software to sell add-ons. Otherwise, no one will pay more for hardware they don't need.*

Beyond the value of reading the notes and annoying our executive producer by playing endless loops of Sonic Youth tunes, the player was about to help open our eyes. At this point, all players were single speed, wheezing along at a data rate of around 90 kps, so doing anything of significance with the disc for multimedia was out of the question. Back then we had no streaming technologies and no real graphics compression. The best we thought we could do was get HyperCard stacks to run on it, and doing that speedily was still going to be tough. The hefty price tag of a player back then (around $700 to $800) meant no consumer was going to buy one anytime soon. That was all about to change.

I remember getting a new developer disc called "Warhol" under a heavy duty nondisclosure agreement from Apple that we were cryptically told had something new that would be of interest to us. Multimedia evangelists were like *Deep Throat* in those days, giving hints without ever telling us what was going on. This new capability depended on a system extension—in real-speak, a neat piece of software that would let the computer do something it had not done before. I did the install, prayed that the machine was not going to honk for the hundredth time that day, and watched as a blurry little smudge of what seemed to be an Apollo launch appeared in the middle of my monitor. I recall telling a producer standing nearby that we had just seen the next great thing—she quietly and quickly returned to her edit suite. She had this nutty idea that quality and legibility mattered. Go figure.

This, by the way, is not only a true story, it has a greater truth to it. Seeing too far ahead is as deadly as not seeing what is in front of you. At that moment, I was seduced by the possibility of what QuickTime would become only several years down the road. What I could not see in front of me, and something too that most of the nascent CD-ROM industry failed to see, was that people like Amy, our video producer, would turn away from a bad approximation of something that was already ubiquitous—television. Not video mind you—video is just data—but whatever the essence of the experience of television is.

Rule Eight: *If it looks like television, and if you say it's like television, it will be compared with television. Be prepared to lose—television wins every time.*

Process Freaks Try to Share the Feeling

Early multimedia developers were consumed by process and the possibilities of what could be done, as opposed to making products. "Enabling" was the mantra in multimedia. We believed fervently that the end user had to have a full range of choices—if we could cut and paste video, they had to be able to cut and paste video. If we could make links, they had to be able to make links. The ability to "respond in kind" and not be a passive spectator was highly valued. We were tool makers in those days as much as we were content creators. A kind of techno-optimism filled the air, an optimism based on a fallacy: everyone in the world wanted to use the technology as much as the people were making it.

Now, as far as education and reference products were concerned, this was the right approach to take—it was what the products were for after all. Static reference works were already available, and there would have been little benefit for users if there hadn't been some way to work with the information and organize it in ways they needed or wanted to. The philosophy we developed at ABC News Interactive was simple. Give people using the product a lot of predefined pathways through the information, with a clear editorial view, but allow them the freedom to make new associations for themselves. And do it all with elegance and style.

Our view of how products should be was strongly influenced by the marketing messages of the major hardware manufacturers—mostly Apple in those days. We were encouraged to build products that would allow users to control and assemble their own experiences. What was so admirable about HyperCard and what had been exciting about QuickTime was what you could do with them; the hands-on quality of both products was great. As many of us already knew, though, in leisure time people want someone else to do the work.

If we skip ahead slightly in time for a moment, we see that the first spate of music-oriented CD-ROMs that were produced in 1993—Peter Gabriel's *Explora* and Todd Rundgren's *No World Order* among them—focused heavily on the idea of letting users remix tracks from songs or music videos, or even to compose their own work out of raw material that the recording artist had provided. People sensed that what you were dealing with as a user was a vast amount of stuff, but little was "immediately obvious." *Explora* tended to ramble quite a bit, often leaving users scratching their heads. It was visually compelling at least, most products were not, but it lacked coherence—was it a game, a music video collection, an audio mixer? It was a "floor wax–dessert topping" conundrum. Of course, we were all breaking new ground at this point, but something about the large real-estate on a CD-ROM confused even the designers.

Rundgren's work was a series of sounds and samples he had created to allow someone to play with them in any way they wanted to. As a musician's plaything it had its moments. But the problem was, as Rundgren would later state when he recanted his approach to music in this early work, that an artist was above all "someone with a point of view," and that's what people were really after when they bought music. The product failed because in many ways there was no one at home. Not everyone could be a composer or a director, no matter how many tools were thrown at them. As much as artists, musicians, and programmers might have liked to hack around with new media, the broader public didn't seem interested. The musicians' presence was profoundly lacking in these products, and you couldn't help feeling they hadn't been that involved.

Let's skip back two years to a time just before the frenzy of activity in CD-ROM. In 1991, Voyager was putting out some interesting, but esoteric, titles on the "new medium of CD-ROM," as the liner notes went on to describe at some length. The products were hardly consumer mainstream, and I am not holding Voyager up as an example of a company that got it right on the business side. In many cases though, the company did the right thing with content.

One title in particular, Pedro Meyer's *I Photograph to Remember,* changed a lot of people's attitudes about multimedia—most certainly my own. It also split the community into two types—those who knew what content was about, and those who didn't get it and never would.

So what was the big deal about this product? After all, it was extremely low-tech. To some it was nothing more than a series of stills, a slide show with a voice-over by the photographer, and a subtle music track. It wasn't of the medium—but it made people cry.

That's right. Without fail everyone whom I dragged in front of the computer to witness this product wept openly—something that until then I imagined people doing only in frustration when the damn box wouldn't work. The importance of content couldn't have been made more clearly and powerfully evident. But many of my compatriots chose to see this work as "lame," lacking the full-on multimedia tool jockey's sense of why CD-ROM was cool.

I think the problem was, and still is, that for many people who were attracted to new media it was all about detaching an editorial view and letting people play with the raw material. This was better than products that were all effect and no substance; at least there was something there—but the human core of it was missing. It's as if many of these products were odes to machines, not works for people to enjoy and experience.

It never seemed to occur to anyone that what Meyer's work accomplished with extreme simplicity of form, and I presume a budget to match, was more powerful than any product out there then or, in many cases, now. It still works today as an experience, because that's where all the effort was placed. Rather than concerning itself with being a penultimate demo of multimedia capabilities, it focused on striking a responsive chord with the viewer.

Rule Nine: *Use everything you need to tell your story, nothing less, nothing more.*

Was this the "killer app" that the nascent multimedia industry was looking for? It should have been one of them. Instead, the industry attached itself to products that exploited this year's new features. There was a constant pressure to do 3-D environments even when it made no sense to—the perception being that 3-D in and of itself sold products. We were often in a tussle with partners who wanted us to make their property into a game, even when it was detrimental to the underlying content. These encounters were often repeated in the horror stories developers shared in the now demised seedy bar section of Silicon Alley.

The subject matter of Meyer's CD-ROM made it difficult to market, and this problem was no more evident than at a trade show where the din of video games and music washed away its effect. It was a highly personal document about one man's painful family history, addressed to you, one-on-one; this didn't play well next to shoot-'em-up games or children's products emitting slide-whistle noises. No one had yet thought to situate individual CD-ROMs in specific niches. They tended to be lumped together instead, and it was the brand of the publisher that was pushed, not the works unto themselves. This was typical of the scattershot marketing approach that publishers, many of whom had come from the book trade, brought with them. Book publishers have a reputation for soft pedalling books to obscurity.

The first exemplar of the feature set–oriented CD-ROMs came in Voyager's repackaging of the Beatles' *A Hard Day's Night*. It was heavily pushed by Apple because it was a great showcase for QuickTime—and it was the Beatles and easily drew attention. The product had its merit, but whatever merit it had came from the movie that was replicated onto the disc, not from the value that was added to it—largely in the form of the transcript of the film's dialog. Beyond that, it soon became apparent that having a postage stamp–size version of the movie on CD-ROM wasn't a great leap forward. It was a pain to watch it, especially since it ran at less than 15 fps. Why was it made then? In addition to the marquee value of the Beatles' name, it had been chosen because the movie was made in black and white—at the time, this was the only way you could get decent playback. Color movies had too much overhead to compress well and started to drift out of sync in minutes. Voyager also had rights to it through the Criterion Collection, Voyager's connoisseur laserdisc series, which was an attempt to give a niche product from another format some legs. But it was a much better demo than it was a compelling product.

Sadly, no one seemed to understand that a work such as *I Photograph to Remember* was a brilliantly simple *adaptation* to the new medium. As such, it was an original in a market that had games at one extreme and licensed videos slapped onto CD-ROM at the other.

A Hard Day's Night was clearly *repurposed*—a product from another medium simply repackaged in a new format. It enjoyed high name recognition, a first then, and the novelty of being the first full-length film on CD-ROM. As you will read in the following sections, it sold reasonably well at first. Unfortunately, it started a wave that was the shape of things to come.

The Business Model for Repurposing

Why did people even think of repurposing? It was supposed to be an issue of economy and branding for most publishers and developers. And it made sense to the extent that it avoided the "single leg" problem that we saw in the case of laserdiscs. If you owned the rights to material that lent itself to interactive, you had just discovered a new revenue stream for it. If you were the buyer though, your problems were just beginning.

Pioneers Have Arrows in Their Backs

We should outline what was going on in the title business in 1992 before we discuss repurposing. The market was barely emerging at this point. CD-ROM drives were only now starting to ship in sufficient quantities for us to believe that by the 1993 Christmas season there might be a respectable market for titles. Analysts really were predicting a doubling of multimedia-enabled computers each year, up to 1998. As it turns out, the unit numbers were pretty close. But in addition to this, forecasts predicted that each multimedia computer user would buy five or six titles a year. I imagine people believed in *horror vaccui* as a market force—that people would feel they had to have something to put into the new drives. Again, the hardware vendors didn't discourage this view. Why should they? For 1992 at least, new media developers were their best customers and allies. By the way, based on the number of computer owners and the CD-ROM market forecasts, the number of titles sold for 1993 was going to be: 5.2 million drives x 6 titles = 31.2 million title units.

That was a very attractive number. There was one problem—no one had any titles, and few publishers had the in-house capability to get them done. At the time, there were only a handful of developers who could do any significant work; even in New York there were only a few hundred people who had any hands-on experience.

The first wave of publishers in the new market came primarily from the book trade, and they were used to aggressively selling-in to stores (getting a large group of titles on the shelves as quickly and cheaply as possible). This was done to spread risk over as many titles as they could manage on small production budgets and author advances, and it served to hold shelf space, a precious commodity when this was the only significant means of getting books into customers' hands. CD-ROM followed this model as a result.

At that time, many publishers were undergoing heavy aggregation, as in the case of the acquisition by Viacom of Paramount and its large holding of publishing companies (once again on the auction block). There was a huge amount of content sitting in the back catalogs that looked like promising candidates for repurposing. There were also new relationships to be made with the media arms of the new parent companies, which suggested the prospect of being able to tap into those assets too. The stage was set—and the process of repurposing on a large scale began in earnest.

The new media business was based to a large extent on repurposing because of the seemingly reasonable cost for rights acquisition as opposed to creating new material (more on that follows). It was also supposed to minimize the risk in creating wholly original works that did not have name-brand recognition, and it was supposed to speed up production. Very few of those benefits were realized, as it turned out.

License deals, favored by game companies, were another means of getting to market with a known quantity. The best and most successful of these in 1993 were Broderbund's series of titles, *Living Books,* based on illustrated books with great marquee value. These were successful because they were well suited to enhancement and adaptation and had great branding. It was also possible to amortize development costs because of the engine developed for the series. Much to its credit, Broderbund marketed them heavily. As of today, however, this series no longer appears on the front pages of Broderbund's Web site—replaced by Riven, Warlords III, and other games. Nonetheless, in the early 1990s, it was a cash cow for the company.

What made it work? For one, the ability to have the "book" read itself to the child with animated text that followed along provided an aid to learning how to read. There were also lots of little surprises buried throughout that made the experience more open-ended. Unlike other products that would gladly wait until the next millennium for you to do something, the series was able to transition on its own, making the product seem truly of the moment. Kids in the targeted age group (four to six) love repetition, and the CD-ROMs made that possible. You could click on things over and over again and hear funny sounds or see surprise animations. It was a great babysitter and, right along with the Disney tapes, an essential tool for parents who needed quiet time. These CD-ROMs were no-brainers, but they were done well.

Not all such licenses work out. Consider the fate of Atari in the 1980s after the disastrous ET game fiasco. The losses nearly buried the company as deeply as the unsold cartridges still rotting away in some landfill. *Johnny Mnemonic,* the CD-ROM, would later suffer a similar fate because of its own flaws and the fact that the movie property it was based on bit the dust. That's the problem with a license. If the original property did well, you had a shot at recovering cost and making some money. If it bombed, or if it was seriously overexposed in the mind of the public, it would head straight for the bottom.

Pioneers Have Arrows in Their Backs

Generally speaking, a license owner has all sorts of rights and interests in what a publisher or developer does with her or his property, including the right to veto ancillary products that could damage its good name and future marketability. The right to veto tends to keep people on their toes and conscious of what they are putting out. Had most deals been like this in the CD-ROM market, we might have avoided some of the issues that repurposing bought.

To me, repurposing is not as rigorous in its quality demands as licensing. It may be easier to illustrate this point by looking at the way repurposed television programs are created and why.

Some repurposing comes from higher quality sources and is usually a "best of series" designed for on-air or the home video market. However, it is often used to create "new" programs at minimal cost and in as little time as possible. This is apparent on cable specialty channels and in syndication. These shows are created by reusing existing assets from network and other programming sources, and re-editing those segments to create a new package. They come complete with a host who ties the segments together, a logo, and a new piece of theme music. The latter three elements are usually the only things created for the show. The acquisition rights for the footage are relatively cheap compared to a high-quality license, since the assets have minimal value to the holder.

Making these shows is essentially done in the editing suite following scripts for the entire run of programs in the series. The host segments are then quickly produced, taped back-to-back over a few days. These shots are then laid into the already assembled shows. This is an incredibly economic way of making a show and filling a slot. It captures enough audience share to be viable. But it doesn't win awards or get people excited. It is decidedly the bottom of the heap in television programming quality. It has its place though in a market that would otherwise be too expensive for a specialty channel to stay afloat in.

The CD-ROM title business got into serious trouble following this model. The first mistake was that repurposed content made up the *basis* for the title business as opposed to being an exception to the rule. The subjects chosen were often of little interest (hence with lower costs for acquisition) and were put together with little care or attention.

To make matters worse, these titles were hardly low-cost to the end user, fetching prices in the early days of well over $50 per title. You can imagine how consumers felt when they picked up a title like this for that kind of money. Of course, since CD-ROM is a returns business, the consumer could always bring it back for a refund—which they did in large numbers.

Despite returns being a regular occurrence that became the bane of distributors, publishers, and retailers, there was little shift in attitude or reduction in the number of titles that were rushed to the shelves. Quality and targeting were still unresolved issues well into 1995, when industry leaders were urging one another to stop pushing "shovelware."

Rule Ten: *People might not mind leftovers at home, but they won't buy them when they eat out.*

Another issue was that the vast majority of titles produced in 1993 and 1994 were done under a work-for-hire model, sometimes called *call production* in television—you call up a production company and offer it a project instead of doing it in-house. These are often very fast turnaround jobs with little creative freedom, money, or fun. Good talent tries to avoid them at all costs.

In 1992 and 1993 came added pressures to get to market quickly. Publishers' perceptions of the potential market that awaited them drove this. It led to short turnarounds on the creative; on average, developers had to get to a sign-off on a design document (an extended treatment and production plan) in no more than six weeks, and sometimes as little as three, after starting preproduction. Clearly, it was going to be a very tough proposition to get a quality title and invent the future on this kind of schedule.

The supposed economy of repurposing often evaporated when it became apparent that a complete title could not be made from the acquired assets alone. For one, the assets were often in a form or of a quality that made repurposing less than useful for multimedia. This is one reason that a large amount of material that ABC News Interactive produced in the laserdisc days was primarily original. Another was that producers thought a better product could be made if they shot with the interactive portion of the project in mind. They were right. Rarely did a lone rights holder have everything that was necessary to bring a project to completion. We had this experience in putting together *Tommy,* which nearly had a large hole in it because of an obstinate rights holder who refused to license interview materials we needed. The only solution was to hop a plane to London to shoot the two interviews. Few CD-ROM productions could afford those kinds of problems and expenses. In the case of *Tommy,* two other production companies had nearly bankrupted themselves trying to bring the title to completion.

Additional graphics production, reshooting, and rewriting were costs that surprised publishers who rushed to repurposing as a production strategy. They naively thought that those costs should be the least of a productions expenses. Often they were, or should have been, equal to or greater than the acquired materials. Numbers like this, though, had clearly not crept into the budget planning of publishers. In their frenzy to acquire footage and other rights, many publishers busted their budgets without ever getting to preproduction.

Yet another hobbling point in this vision of low-cost title production was the intense technical requirements in making a stable cross-platform (Macintosh and PC) CD-ROM. In 1993, this was a tough proposition because the authoring tools typically used to make most CD-ROMs did not allow for seamless porting from one platform to another. Typically, at least a third of the budget and half of a schedule were spent integrating and building the title. This was a costly proposition if it meant doing each title from scratch without being able to reuse code, and in 1993 the benefits of advanced planning were lost on the majority of title publishers. It wasn't possible to lower the costs substantially without frameworks or "engines." And since each title tended to have unique requirements, unless it was part of a series, there were few economies of scale. The tight cycles for engineering did not allow room for changes in creative direction, and so the critically shortened preproduction phase often killed what chance a developer might have had to tweak creativity. Once you were in production and had the interface locked down, it became impractical to reopen the product. Developers who were under the gun to deliver or face penalties couldn't risk it. Schedules for delivery were insane, and many developer studios took on the aura of sweatshops inhabited by techno-peasants who were forced to churn out products with few rewards or thanks. The bottom line is that the priority became the ship date, not the overall quality of the product. As far as most publishers were concerned, there was nothing to suggest yet that people wouldn't buy. Common sense and an instinct for what works might have, but few possessed them.

Considering the trouble involved in repurposing, and the fact that typical budgets for the better projects still ended up being anywhere from $150,000 to $350,000 for production alone, it was surprising that so many CD-ROMs were made. What we as developers didn't realize is that many publishers were leveraging themselves to the hilt, assuming that they would pay down debt on forthcoming revenues. For many it didn't quite work that way.

Remember the number of units projected for 1993?—31.2 million. The actual number shipped according to Software Publishers Association records was 8 million. Now, a lot of these CD-ROMs also included regular applications, not just titles. The exact number of units of entertainment titles is therefore hard to estimate. However, we know that about half of all units sales were to original equipment manufacturers (OEMs) for inclusion in their boxes, and often units sold to OEMs yielded as little as a $1 per unit as opposed to the $15 that could have been expected from retailing a $50 product. (The suggested retail price reduced by 10 percent became the actual selling price, half of which went to the distributor, the rest of which was eaten into by returns allowance and other associated costs.)

By the beginning of 1994, the industry as a whole was already in serious jeopardy (and denial), plagued by quality issues, production problems, and a revenue shortfall for which no one had prepared.

The Popular Perception

The perception of multimedia prior to Christmas 1993 was at radical odds with the reality we saw. As an example, let's consider this brief shining moment in *Jurassic Park* (Universal, 1993), when the hyperbole surrounding CD-ROM was summed up in the scene where the kids are piling into one of the automated trucks—you remember, the sushi boats that were bringing the warm snacks to the dinosaurs. Anyway, the girl is looking at the dashboard of the truck, and there is a small touch-screen with a map display. Here is her line: "It's an interactive CD-ROM! Look! See? You just touch the right part of the screen and it talks about whatever you want."

The public believed that the future of new media was already here—that you could ask anything of it and get it. If only that had been true. The new media press in particular was responsible for allowing tremendous latitude to publishers and developers who would have had you believe that new media manna was falling from heaven. Not only did the public buy into that happy world view, investors did as well.

Imagine their disappointment come 1993, when they discovered that they couldn't get their multimedia upgrade kits to work, or that the CD-ROMs often bundled with upgrade kits or new computers were nothing but boring repurposed products that couldn't have been sold any other way except as nifty halogen light fixtures. Consider how happy the public must have been to waste money at Christmas and to deal with disappointed children who got a lump of polycarbonate instead of the cool CD-ROM they had anticipated.

Rule Eleven: *Never over-promise and under-deliver, especially at Christmas. The bad karma will keep you from prospering.*

Despite the harsh view I've taken so far, the truth is that six years ago even doing something as simple as video on CD-ROM was a miracle. Unfortunately, as miracles go, it was singularly unimpressive—we were impressed that it could be done at all but disappointed that it was done so badly. The title business had shot directly from stock concept to the consumer market without thinking of the consequences of failing to deliver on the promise.

Breaking the Three Q's (Quality, Quality, and Quality)

Poor quality in CD-ROM design and execution was endemic in the industry, partly because this was a relatively new field with few seasoned practitioners. Most had come to new media from other backgrounds and were literally being trained as they were putting together a multimedia title for the first time in their lives. This could have worked if only greater attention and time had been given to creating a few good titles instead of to many low-quality ones.

Usability was not just a hardware problem. In addition to poor asset quality, the structure of products, both from a content and an interface standpoint, was often muddled and confusing. The immersive environment products such as *Highway 61* (Graphix Zone) didn't make any sense from an experiential or documentary perspective. Why make a user navigate around a poorly rendered (and sometimes wildly inaccurate) city of New

York just to hear snippets of Dylan tunes and see fragments of memorabilia? The answer unfortunately is that it could be done and so it was done. The immersive craze in this case was an attempt to cash in on the success of *Myst,* which had popularized the genre. Of course in the case of *Myst* the immersive environment was motivated and integral to the experience, not a gimmick. By the way, *Myst* seldom gets the respect it deserves in terms of its use of sound. Many people believe that *Myst* is much more 3-D than it is. It used transitions between rendered still frames and is really therefore more like two-and-a-half-D, the underscore that runs throughout the product being responsible for that sense of multidimensional space. Have a listen to it sometime.

In contrast to such craft, publishers rarely had the nerve or the will to cut a title from a release schedule no matter how bad it was. Many projects should never have been given the green light because they were in serious creative trouble for one reason or another. Judging from the glut of bad work, I concluded that no one on the publisher's side had the courage to pull the trigger on products that could give them a black eye if released.

Why is this so important? Because so few publishers, or developers for that matter, were capable of knowing or admitting when a title was substandard. As a result, the market was flooded with the mediocre and the substandard. Like all negative experiences, it generated poor word of mouth advertising, not only about specific titles but about the CD-ROM market in general. Publishers, believing they could strike it rich if they scattered enough product on the market, learned that pushing shoddy products did irreparable harm to the industry.

Quality assurance was probably the weakest aspect of production in CD-ROM. Many title producers or publishers skimped on this aspect, and as a result, serious installation and performance problems further damaged the reputation of the platform as a whole. The most spectacular case of this was the original *The Lion King* CD-ROM from Disney. It had an astonishing return rate because of some show-stopping bugs that appeared only after shipping. Only the strength of the Disney franchise enabled the title to do well enough to offset those losses—any other product would have gone down in flames. Many deservedly did so.

Chapter 7: Pioneers Have Arrows in Their Backs

Buyers Stay Away in Droves

Despite the enormous amounts of money that were funneled into CD-ROM production and development by both major and small developers and publishers, few titles sold and only a handful sold enough to be considered hits.

I've covered some of the reasons: poor asset quality, difficulty in set-up, poor usability, lack of editorial quality or depth, and a tendency to produce many titles instead of focusing on a few of high quality. But one fatal error was made over and over again: almost no marketing or advertising to consumers was ever done. The focus instead was on selling the product to stores.

I argue, and I think few can find the evidence to refute it, that no major prelaunch or launch campaigns were created for products and that little beyond trade shows, reviews, and PR were expected to get sales off the ground.

I had to question why a company would spend money like a drunken sailor to get a title developed and then do nothing to sell it to customers. To my knowledge, the only ads for CD-ROMs that ever appeared were in trade magazines, not in mainstream consumer publications. Considering the tens of millions, possibly hundreds of millions, that were spent each year on creating titles, would buying a little ad space have been so out of line given what was at stake?

There were to be sure a lot of guerrilla efforts—attempts to launch a blockbuster movie by standing on a street corner handing out pamphlets. This was still a common practice up to the time that heavily branded products like Mattel's Barbie CD-ROM showed up.

Another staggering oversight was the lack of effort in bringing a taste of the product to consumers before they were expected to pay for it. I remember endless moans and groans from publishers about the lack of preview capability for CD-ROMs. A cynic might think that preview stations were never organized into existence by publishers in order to guarantee that the buying decision would be left largely to chance. This is where good packaging came to be quite useful. The package that attracted the consumers' eyes could hide many flaws in quality.

Considering the effort and expense that some retailers went to establish in-store areas specifically for CD-ROMs (Borders opened 54 such stores within stores), you'd have expected the publishers to have figured out a way for computers to be in these stores and to have staffed the stores adequately to help consumers understand what was available. Game companies had this figured out and managed to get stations of this type set up in many retail stores long ago. Instead, in the CD-ROM industry the problem seemed impossible to solve. Given that the industry was in many respects on the brink of extinction, a little more effort surely was in order.

If demo stations were impossible, preview disks certainly would have been helpful, but few of these ever appeared. Only once in the entire time that ABC New Interactive was producing CD-ROM titles did I encounter a publisher who had the foresight to have a demo or trailer of the product made in *advance* of the product's release. Again, game companies had this one figured out ages ago and were releasing both disks and downloadable samples or hobbled versions of forthcoming products. Id Software was particularly good at making this happen. Considering what little help CD-ROM titles had, it's a miracle that they sold as well as they did.

Rule Twelve: *Products do not leap off of shelves into consumers' baskets. If you want products to sell, you must be prepared to spend as much money marketing them as you did developing them.*

Why is any of this important? Because the gap between where the content business should have been and where it ended up was wide and deep enough for the entire industry to collapse. By the end of 1994, with another dismal Christmas season behind us, the writing was on the wall. Hundreds of millions of dollars had been lost. The potential upside of a market estimated to be between $150 to $350 million per year was easily erased by the unrecouped costs of developers and publishers hungry to get their products to the shelves. Ironically, many never made it that far, and some good products got lost in the 1000 to 2000 titles estimated to have been created for a market that could at best absorb 100.

The Margin Call

The retail prices of CD-ROMs during the first Christmas period that they were sold were very high—high enough to create a temporary impression for prospective investors in CD-ROM companies that impressive sales figures and profit numbers would result. Projections done in 1993, for example, often kept the expected-high selling price to calculate long-term estimates. Oops. Some of the inherent problems in the numbers used for these calculations were: unlike games, prices for other entertainment software were under extreme downward price pressure, which meant these forecasts were science fiction; sales did not really keep pace with installed base growth; and the top 10 titles received the lion's share of sales, in some cases estimated to be as high as 80 percent of totals, with the rest spread among the remaining 20 percent.

What does this mean exactly? In 1993, let's say you were able to get $350,000 to produce a title. By 1994, and certainly in 1995, investors and publishers, looking at where retail title prices were going, wanted the development cost to drop along with anticipated revenues. If revenue was thought to drop by half, publishers and investors wanted to develop the disc for half of what they had spent for a disc the year before.

Needless to say, it became impossible to continue making these discs. The number of conversations we had with publishers who wanted us to "share risk" with them was enough to indicate where the market was headed. A lot of developers had to get out of the business at this point—it was impossible to make titles and remain fiscally sound. Just imagine the utter humiliation of walking into a store and seeing a title you had worked on dangling in one of the five-foot-long plastic sleeves, marked down to the equivalent of $3 a disc. The fact that five-foot-ten packs were better sellers than current products demonstrated what little value the industry placed on itself—we had been remaindered and marked down for a quick buck.

By 1995, it was clear that that Christmas season, possibly even the spring, would indicate when, not if, to bail out of the business. Unlike a process of natural selection and attrition, this went right to the top of the food chain. By mid to late 1995, almost all of the major media companies that had large multimedia units shuttered their multimedia projects for good. In three short years, an industry that was supposed to be the new path to riches was gone.

The Web Arrives Quietly

In June 1994, at Digital World in Los Angeles, before the meltdown of the multimedia industry, something remarkable was going on behind a curtained area of the show floor that was going to be the salvation (or the ruination, depending on how you saw it) of every entertainment content developer exhibiting on the floor that year. A nice but very geeky group of computer science students were showing off an Internet application named Mosaic, and we were told that a total of 1500 World Wide Web servers were now reported to be in use. They seemed very pleased. Immediately I had the impression that this had nothing to do with where the real multimedia business was going. I warned you. I make mistakes.

One quick look at the interface and a review of the media types supported by the interface convinced us that there was nothing here for us. It could handle text, stills, and links. By comparison to what was then possible in CD-ROM, it looked cheap and dull. True, it ran on everything. But I had seen this sort of capability in the late 1980s with products such as Guide. They had failed. Why were the World Wide Web and Mosaic going to be any different?

Internet wasn't part of anyone's vocabulary back then except for those who had Internet mail, browsed newsgroups, and used ftp. I quickly went back to our booth and prepared for a meeting with two reps from Word-Perfect who seemed anxious to talk about a multititle deal. We will come back to the Web after a brief pause to examine yet another standard on the horizon that was sure to re-energize the multimedia market.

Enhanced CD—The Last Refuge of the Truly Desperate

In November 1994, I went out to Redmond for the first time to see what was happening at a special meeting for select developers and a horde of folks from the recording industry. We should have known something was going to go wrong by the early hour of the briefing. Record guys just don't go to 8 A.M. meetings, and they weren't in a receptive mood.

Pioneers Have Arrows in Their Backs

But I did get to see something of immediate interest to me as it harkened back to the first concept demo that I had done and in fact shown at Digital World in June. The idea was simple—put the equivalent of a couple of interviews and music videos on an audio CD with embedded software to run it. Make it hip, easy, and fun.

The revolutionary part of this meeting was that someone had finally thought to build a real standard for doing multimedia-rich audio CDs. This was an essential step, one necessitated by the fact that accidentally playing the data portion of such a disc on some systems could blow out your speakers. (Look at the warning on the Horde tour disc, if you can find it, from 1996). This standard was the inclusion of a book that first and foremost intended to instruct the consumer on how to not blow out their speakers.

On top of that, it seemed like some lightweight tools would be thrown into the mix as well for easy authoring. All in all, not bad. And as a business opportunity, it seemed perfect. Blue book, the proposed new standard, looked like a potential godsend. With the technical inhibitors out of the way, a record company might have a way to resell back catalog titles by releasing them in this new format. For new bands, which had been our thought, it could serve as a way to educate the public about the group and build some following for them.

We knew that everyone was getting nervous about the increasingly high costs of creating CD-ROM products. In truth, no one wanted to take a risk on green-lighting another money-loser at a time when sales shortfalls loomed and résumés were being honed for the inevitable.

We knew that these projects were likely to be considered marketing costs as opposed to product costs, just as music videos were. And we knew the labels were going to shag us over in terms of the price we would get for our labors. The solution, as with all low-margin businesses, was getting large volumes of the work in the door and learning to crank them out as efficiently as possible. Doesn't this sound familiar?

There was just one hitch. There was profound disagreement as to whether the standard was ever going to gain industry ratification. Without that, Enhanced CDs were heading nowhere. A few brave souls proposed moving ahead without the standard, going with the renegade solutions, but that meant it was impossible to put out the multimedia portion of the disc on the shipping audio CD.

Why? For the simple reason that if anything went wrong with that disc as a consequence of a bunch of questionable multimedia being pressed on it, heads would roll. And, from my point of view and the point of view of many others, if it didn't end up going onto the same piece of plastic as the music and becoming a *passive buy,* something you got for free with the disc, there was no way merchants or customers would go for it. Merchants would pass on it because they would not dedicate precious floor space to ancillary versions of products they were already trying to move. And the public would not risk buying something untested, for a much higher price—better to stick with old format, thanks very much.

Although some Enhanced CDs did get made, the labels were not happy with the process. In fact, as of this moment, the only company that has attached major significance to the Enhanced CD is N2K here in New York. The major labels have only modestly and inconsistently dipped in their toes. The last such project I worked on at BIG was for the tenth anniversary reissue of Paul Simon's *Graceland,* and it was one of only a handful put out last year. Those of us who had pinned hopes on the format were told that the labels had other priorities and that Digital Versatile/Video Disk (DVD) was likely to be the time for this to take off. True, if DVD did what it was supposed to do, there would be no need to compromise. It was designed to accommodate just this sort of thing. We also knew that DVD was at least two years away. Time for a new strategy.

At the time this was happening, around late 1995, the CD-ROM business was receding into the distance; Enhanced CDs were for all intents dead, or at a dead end. You could see that from Billboard's prediction that 1996 would be the year of the Enhanced CD. This was clearly spin, just an attempt to keep the life support on long enough for it to die gracefully instead of doing a face plant. Only one other platform was left to us.

Haven't We Been Here Before?

The Web was a disappointment to me from the standpoint of the kind of work we had been doing as a company and that which I was interested in doing. In 1995, there was nothing that could support much more than what you could do on America Online (AOL) or other online services. This seemed like a giant step down from when, after years of struggle, CD-ROM had finally arrived in terms of tools and capabilities. I and many of my cohorts who had been title builders were unhappy campers. How could we possibly go back to doing the "text with pictures" products we had done nearly eight years before? And given that the Web was, and still largely is, text dependent, was creating entertainment even worth the effort? Shouldn't we just accept it as the communications apparatus it is and leave entertainment out until the Next Big Thing?

It would take something as simple as a lame soap opera parody to change my mind, or at least open it a little.

The Webisodics

If you look back at anything written in the trade press about *The Spot* and its brethren, there was only a modicum of cynicism about the possible success of something that was a tongue-in-cheeky parody of television's much despised but heavily watched soaps. Why? After all the show was nothing more than stills of actors and actresses playing "roles" accompanied by diary entries and a few multimedia snippets. What was compelling about that? Not much as it turns out. But the show did something that previous entertainment Web sites had not done. It let the audience participate. It let them choose how to order their experience, whom they would follow, and whom they would not. It was that little germ of an idea that set it apart from what would have been a flat, magazine-like experience.

The serialized aspect of the show—designed so you could get a daily five-minute fix—was a simple but brilliant strategy. Hook the audience and give them a daily destination and you'd have a following that would help drive traffic and justify your ad rates to potential sponsors or advertisers. The show in fact was popular enough to spawn news groups and companion Web sites for the hardcore fans. This show had legs—wobbly, but legs nonetheless.

The Good

Beyond the serial nature of the show was the fact that, for the first time that I know of, there was an opportunity for fans to blur the line between their side of the screen and the show's. By letting users post comments and e-mail, *The Spot* could tailor content according to the whims and remarks of its constituents. Rather than having to guess at what the folks at home were thinking, the show's producers were now able to hear directly from the viewership. This was a foreshadowing of the current mantra or mania—communities of interest are the best arbiters of their own taste, and the least expensive authors. Giving an audience the power (or the appearance of it) to influence the direction of the program could only heighten its sense of involvement and commitment to showing up everyday.

The Spot was also the first Web-based show I know of that dabbled in the idea of product placement—writing in real-world products from advertisers in subtle and not so subtle ways. One character worked for FedEx for example, and in another an advertiser and his product were placed into the show.

By January of 1996, *The Spot* was generating about 160,000 hits a day, quite respectable back then. And, unlike other sites out there, it seemed that the show had a very good chance of snagging advertising at a rate of $16,500 per month to support the ongoing costs of keeping the daily production afloat.

At this point in time, the allusions to television's early days couldn't have been easier to make. *The Spot* was a show that, like early TV, was created and owned by an advertising agency and was used as a vehicle for client products. Of course in time those allusions were seen to be less than skin deep, but nonetheless *The Spot* seemed to point to the possibility of how shows on the Web could be supported, possibly even how they might become profitable. There were also rumors flying at one point that the creators of the show were in discussion with NBC about bringing *The Spot,* or something *Spot*-like, to television. Heady stuff indeed.

The Bad

All of those plans were soon over. In June of 1997, *The Spot* was removed from the Web. It perished in much the same way that CD-ROMs had, from the overreaching ambition of its creators who had tried to build a mini empire on its back alone—one show does not a network make. After having poured a substantial amount of money, some say millions, into the venture the experiment was over. In its wake, there were nothing but doubts as to how entertainment might find a successful niche in an otherwise information-driven medium. The other soaps that survived did so by staying cheap and low in expectations, but all to my knowledge have faded slowly into obscurity.

The Ugly

The reasons for *The Spot* failing on the Web are plentiful, and we will focus on just two important ones. Perhaps the single greatest mistake, and it is one that continually gets made where content is concerned in new media in general, was in failing to estimate the size of viewership or users necessary to keep the engine running. It wasn't simply that the numbers needed to be somewhat better, they needed to be better by orders of magnitude in order to justify the investment by an advertiser in the program and the outlay of cash for production. The very essence of the show for users and advertisers, "made fresh daily," condemned the producers from the beginning to a burdensome overhead for talent and production. Moreover, the mistake of seeing the show's modest potential as something that would grow exponentially by month was a terrible miscalculation. The spending on *The Spot* and other programs in development was nonsustainable except under the most rosy of possible outcomes. If you spend money on a show as you would with television, you are going to need television-like revenues to make it worth doing. Unfortunately, interactive projects are inherently expensive to make—but their revenue potential is far below that of a niche magazine. Bear in mind that without a fee directly from the end user, you are removing a huge element of cost recovery and putting the burden on advertisers. Advertising alone cannot sustain even a small e-zine, as we have seen in the demise of online publications in just the last few months as this is being written.

Another reason for failure was that *The Spot,* formerly a unique entity, soon had many competitors of a similar type—the novelty had simply worn off and there was a lot more "on" than there had been when the show first launched. Fragmentation on the Web—the fact that there are literally tens of thousands of other things to do, see, or go to—makes a TV show's problems seem trivial. As a worst case scenario, in TV a show might have 100 channels to do battle with, and it has the help of a network or channel to push, promote, and advertise the bejeezus out of it. *The Spot* had no such friends to help gather the audience it needed. Add this to the fact that the number of Web-connected households were relatively scarce at the time and the disaster was inevitable.

Networks—umbrella companies that serve as the marketing vehicles for programming on the system—were entirely absent from the Web in those early days. Only the proprietary online services such as AOL had that capability. But at the time the Web capabilities of those systems were poor to say the least. Going it alone on the Web was the only chance one had, and it wasn't a good one. Without the ability to push viewers, aggregate revenues from sponsors and advertisers, et al, *The Spot* and its brethren were doomed. In the early wild and woolly days on the Web, the desire to be the lone maverick seemed to outweigh common business sense. A show after all, no matter how powerful, is just one show. And in a market hungry for people's precious spare time, this was simply not good enough. The essential step of having built the network infrastructure to hold shows and viewers together had been ignored in the belief that sites, shows, what have you, simply didn't need them. Well, unless anyone has been asleep out there for the last year or so, I think we have seen the fallacy of that belief. And in the end, we still do not have a platform out there that can reasonably support the kind of programming that people such as I wanted to produce and did in fact produce. Much more on that below, with one last necessary diversion back to conventional media and its use of the Web for just one moment.

The Networks on the Web

To be sure, the major networks have moved into the Web on both a community and affiliate level and have ambitious plans for building communities of interest. Only one company, NBC, has invested substantially in developing entertainment content for the Web. Its approach has been to tie and extend its on-air programming, such as *The Pretender,* into the Web space. By all accounts, to date the numbers have been modest—about 30,000 fans, I last heard, take part on a regular basis at *The Pretender* site. And, this extension into the Web has resulted in one character created for the *Homicide* Web site crossing over to on-air definitely a first. But it seems clear which is the tail and which is the dog in this instance. The sites for these programs serve the principal goals of direct viewer response, retention of viewers, and experiments into plot and character development for the on-air use. In many respects, this is the better part of repurposing, and it succeeds where the CD-ROM model failed. As we see more devices like Web-TV Plus come into use, undoubtedly this use of the Web, as an extension or support for broadcast and cable shows, will be more common than the stand-alone site. The potential of those sites to draw users and hold them is great, and the potential revenue stream from additional ad buys, commerce functions, and so forth, is promising. However, I don't believe that anyone in the entertainment industry thinks that the Web can or should be anything more than that sort of extension.

What Television Is

Since people are so fond of television analogies for the Web, let's look back very briefly at the way programming started in the 1940s and 1950s. For one, advertisers owned shows back then, and unlike today they paid networks to carry those programs. The other principal sponsors of programming were manufacturers of TV sets. Advertising companies even supported and underwrote the cost of producing sets in the early days—it meant a lot to them clearly. The purpose of one nicely served the other, for it was in everyone's best interest to get as many TVs into as many homes as possible, and as quickly as possible. Was this done because it was cool? So people had something to watch? No, it was designed and implemented from the beginning to serve the interests of advertising, not the public, and certainly not the creative community. Of course, everyone knew you had to put something on, otherwise the ads would just keep bumping together. Manufacturers needed something to be on in order to sell the need for a television to the consumer. The business model was in place, although it took until 1953 for NBC to make a profit at it, fully five years after the first broadcasts started. The talent was drawn to television for the creative latitude and the opportunities to make wholly original content on a regular basis, something that film and theater didn't offer.

Why the Web Isn't Television

Contrast that with where we are today with Internet-based entertainment content. What we have had to date is the equivalent of someone standing out on the street corner giving away a comic book for free and then running to an advertiser to try to get it to buy an ad because a thousand people read it today. Without a means to sustain and grow programming, properties that make themselves freely available disappear quickly.

So why can't we make entertainment work on the Web as it does on TV? For one, television is single-minded and one way. It has certainly evolved and changed over the years, but it was designed for one purpose—

an advertising appliance. The Internet is just the opposite—it's potentially anything we wish to make of it. And it's this very lack of focus that makes it inappropriate for the type of mass consumer entertainment that television was made for.

The Internet isn't like cable, nor is it like broadcasting—in its current form, it never will be able to match the ability of television to deliver shared moments simultaneously. In fact, even with multicasting technologies, the commercial Web as it exists now is radically inadequate for the needs of broadband content on a mass scale. Consider television and audience sizes, where 6 or 7 million viewers for a broadcast show is a mediocre draw. Right now, the vast majority of home access is dial-up based. In this scenario, only about one-fifth of all users can simultaneously connect through an ISP due to the ratio of available ports to users. If we consider that prospect, the 40 million users claimed to have Web access immediately reduces down to 8 million concurrent users, and that's being generous given outages, busy signals, and so on.

Moreover, there is simply no ability to limit the Web to a relative handful of destinations. As it is now, TV works because the amount of real-estate available is artificially constrained by regulation. The Web has no regulatory bounds within or outside this country that would limit the number of sites that can exist out there. Without those bounds, the level of fragmentation on the Web is much greater than that of magazines—tens of thousands compete for a finite readership, and hence many struggle, falter, and disappear. Only those that can bring the clout of a major brand name and strong distribution and marketing have a shot at doing better. For the Web, even being backed by a major entertainment company has not guaranteed success.

To be sure, we have seen networks of sorts built to try to bring an advantage to Web content. Let's discuss how well that has worked in the past.

MSN Builds—No One Comes

In mid 1995, MSN was looking for new ideas for the re-launch of MSN. It was to be a new way to look at and explore the Web. No more boring content—instead we were being asked to create work that was "entirely of the medium," that pushed the boundaries and limits of the technology and of what a "site" was all about. In fact, sites would not really exist on the new MSN, but instead we would see shows, on channels, that had been geared to specific interest and demographic groups.

CHAPTER 7
Pioneers Have Arrows in Their Backs

This sounded right on the money. Finally, we'd be dealing with a large corporate partner with the ability to manage both the infrastructure and marketing aspects of running a network and allow us to potentially benefit from the aggregate of shows. Needless to say we were pumped—finally someone "got it" and we were chosen from a relatively small group to do exactly the kind of program that we wanted to do, without limits. Our company, in conjunction with Broadway Video Entertainment, created *This Is Not a Test*—a live comedy show that was broadcast from *Catch a Rising Star* in New York City.

I must say, we blew out the stops on this one, and we managed to create a show using NetShow and various other technologies that actually worked for a home user on a 28.8 modem. Trust me, this wasn't easy, especially considering that the code we were dealing with was still in development. In many respects it was a miracle that we were able to pull it off at all, let alone surpass everyone's expectations.

How could this fail after all? We had a great team on both the technical and creative side, stars of a caliber you would have expected only from television or film: Janeane Garofalo, Conan O'Brien, Phil Hartman, and many more. We had a great talent as emcee, Marc Maron, who was able to keep the show going even in the darkest moments when the technology didn't quite get us there. We had real-time polling, chat rooms, cool interstitials, and amazing guest acts that blew us away. All of this was rolled into a hip interface that gave you more of a feeling that you were watching TV rather than using a browser—full-screen, no menus, all custom—it was cutting-edge. Moreover, we were well received, we got great press and a lot of it—more than any other show on the network. And?

No one saw it. Okay, a few hundred people saw it, most of whom were sitting in the live audience in New York.

How could this be? Simply this: there was no advertising of the program itself, other than the PR. And, as I hope I've been able to make clear to you along the way, without telling people, long and loud, all about what you have to sell, you won't get eyeballs, sales, or anything else except tears.

I have to say that personally I was stunned when we discovered how little push the show was going to get. What I could never get my head around, and still cannot, is that all of the money that went into our show, the MSN network itself, was for all intents and purposes "burnt." There was an air of unreality about how MSN was proceeding, as if this were all an experiment without consequence as opposed to a real business. After a year and a half of effort, we produced 13 episodes and were then canceled, along with most of the other shows on MSN.

Now, beyond the very personal loss that we all took in making this show happen, it was clear too that there was very little sense of guidance as to where this was all supposed to be heading. And this I think is the very point I've been trying to make all along. Perhaps it is as easy and straightforward as this: without a plan, all of the efforts spent are so much fretting and strutting—signifying bankruptcy.

The solution I'm suggesting is that we get off the high plains and down to making the next generation of content work on more than just a technical or creative level. Despite all that I have had to say here in the negative, I do think that we need to keep trying. Business, my friends, is what the rest of the entertainment world has always been about first, and they've made it work against similar odds. Great things do not happen without real talent, real money, and a real plan. Despite the fact that some of those essential ingredients have sometimes come together to attract our attention on a few occasions, it's the fact that all three of them have never come together that has kept entertainment and new media from succeeding.

About the Author

Bryan McCormick fell into multimedia entirely by accident, abandoning a promising career in art history for the dubious benefits of hacking out a lot of code into the wee hours of the New York night. Of course, since then he has never looked back, moving from techno-peasant to founder of his own company. He is currently contemplating the next big thing, following his move from president and creative director of Broadway Interactive Group to private citizen late last year.

"If there is a bad review, people are going to find it whether your company gives it to them or not, especially on the World Wide Web."

Adam Heneghan

CHAPTER 8

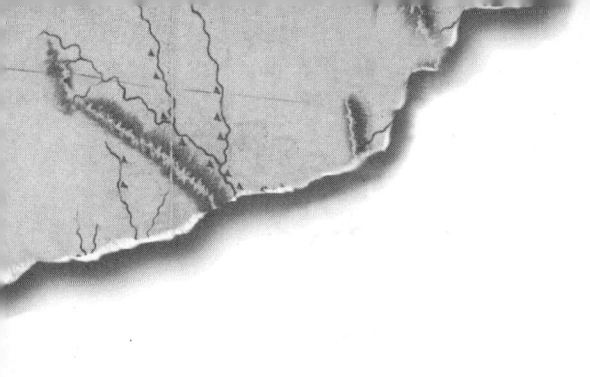

How the Web Was Won

Rounding Up Online Successes

Back in 1990, my brother and I were about to get out of college. We had heard the buzz about multimedia and had seen this kind of crazy guy from California named Joe Sparks who was developing a CD-ROM called *Spaceship Warlock*. At that time, everyone was using CD-ROM as an archival medium to store data. Sparks had taken the CD-ROM and put content on it in the form of a game. It was crazy, and it just blew us away. That was exactly what we wanted to do. We fell in love with it right then and decided to get into this business. So we started out doing CD-ROM development. As the world changed and shifted we were able to take what we had learned about creating rich digital content on CD-ROM and apply it to the work we were starting to do on the Web. We had severely limited bandwidth at our disposal on the Web at that time, but we had learned to deal with this bandwidth issue because the CD-ROMs we had been working on held a limited amount of material. We understood how to make the most of that situation.

We formed Giant Step in 1991 and teamed with Leo Burnett, a Chicago ad agency, in 1994. So we had a couple years under our belt—doing mostly CD-ROM work—when this whole Web thing started to take off. Burnett had large clients who were hearing the buzz about the Internet and its importance. These clients were seeing articles in the media talking about Interactive Television or CD-ROM development and getting very excited about it. Burnett didn't have expertise in that field, so it asked us to come aboard to do consulting and to educate its clients and the agency itself on what these new technologies were about. Eventually, we came up with a model that is very separate from the agency. All it takes from Burnett is the creative oversight. That does not even mean the creative details; it just means the brand positioning. The Burnett team comes in and says, "This is what we're trying to do with Oldsmobile" or, "This is what we're trying to do with Hallmark." Then we take it from there. We develop the whole site, from the concept and the creative details all the way through to deployment.

The diversity of our clients over the past five years has allowed us to see where it does and does not make sense to create a Web-based business solution. One of our first customers was a forward-thinking tire retreader in Iowa. That was one of the cool things about the early days of the Web: companies you would never think of as technology oriented were pushing the envelope. As long as somebody has a sense of empowerment and an idea of what the Web can be, great things can happen.

Chapter Overview

In this chapter, I discuss the elements of successful Web sites in relation to three of Giant Step's clients: United Airlines, Oldsmobile, and Hallmark. I have chosen to focus on these three because, in addition to being successful, they are representative of three common types of business model: service, merchandise, and content. Chances are, your company fits into one of those business models as well. Following the discussion of those three sites, I will look at the Web development technology we use at Giant Step to create successful digital solutions—technologies that could also help your company to thrive on the Internet. The chapter wraps up with a look at where we are today and the direction I see us heading in the near and not too distant future.

First a brief discussion of the elements involved in creating successful online business solutions.

Webbed Victory

One of the biggest questions you will face when you consider taking a business on line is, "What does it take to be successful on the World Wide Web?" Obviously, one measures success on the Web, like success in any endeavor, against the goals a business sets out to achieve. When you are able to show a compelling business reason for building a Web site, and the site you build fulfills those goals, you have a winner.

The Web sites I will discuss—Hallmark, Oldsmobile, and United Airlines—are three success stories on the Web today. These are examples of companies who are using the Web to talk to the right people in the right context. The sites are helping those companies with reducing costs, generating sales, and building loyalty and community, among other things. In the discussion that follows, I will go into detail about the following list of issues:

- **Successful goal setting:** the realistic goals companies set out to achieve by going on the Web
- **The personal touch:** how businesses are able to talk to more people with greater ease and less expense than in the past
- **Focus on solutions:** the functional pieces that translate into practical capabilities for companies and their clients
- **Feedback:** the ways customers make their needs known, including the brand's response
- **Tracking:** looking at Web site usage to create experiences that are more desirable for site visitors
- **Controlling your own content:** ways to take control of your core competencies for increased effectiveness on the World Wide Web

Successful Goal Setting

All media have their strong suits. What types of business goals make the most sense on the Web? Giant Step has worked with major corporations for the past five years building Web sites. In that time, we have had the opportunity to see what works and what does not work in this medium. There are many viable business reasons for taking your business on line. Some of these are listed on the following page.

- Increasing return on investment
- Facilitating effective commerce
- Making customer service more efficient
- Increasing brand awareness
- Facilitating recruiting efforts
- Reducing costs
- Facilitating communication with target audiences
- Increasing revenue
- Selling a product or a service
- Making information more accessible

Right now, reducing the costs of doing business effectively is the single most prevalent goal behind a business deciding to establish a presence on the Web.

The Personal Touch

A year ago, you probably did not hear people talking about ways of creating more individualized experiences on the Web. Now personalization seems to be all the buzz. Everyone is talking about how businesses can make their Web sites more relevant for specific users, more of an individual experience every time people come back.

Companies are scrambling to get a good grasp on who visits their sites to make sure they are catering to each individual client's needs. If a user has never visited a page on your Web site and yet it has always been accessible to her, why should it keep coming up repeatedly as one of the top pages in the site? With the tools that are available now, you are able to start filtering sites so that consumers get the information they want in the way they want it. From a development standpoint, you can build intelligence into your site so that it can learn and change based on consumer usage.

Focus on Solutions

Many corporations, when they decide to build a Web site, believe that people want to come and read about them or see employment opportunities. While that is important, with a service you eventually have to put out the functional pieces. Searching for flights, booking tickets, looking up the price of a car or the location of a dealer, whatever it happens to be—those functional service solutions have to be in the forefront.

Functionality is hot. Right now it is a hugely important element in building successful Web solutions. Because of current bandwidth limitations, creating emotion on line can be very difficult. With the exception of design elements and text, which can be a somewhat emotional experience, people do not see a Web page and react the way they might to a TV or radio commercial.

The Web is becoming much more solution oriented. To be successful, your Web site needs to offer functionality that will make the experience beneficial. That means creating a functional site, which makes some sort of practical solution possible, whether it is a customer solution or a business-to-business solution.

It is important to keep functionality in mind when developing a Web site so that you do not bury the truly substantial elements. Part of the challenge comes from the fact that your company may have a marketing group, a distribution group, and a customer service group—among others—and all of them may think they are the most important. To create a successful Web site, you have to manage that tug-of-war and make sure that what is on the site is the most compelling experience for your consumers.

Feedback

In developing a Web site, it is important to think about how consumers are going to communicate in an effective manner with your brand. Message boards, bulletin boards, and e-mail are a few of the options available. If the answer to customer support needs on line is e-mail, the user needs to get the right response in a timely manner. The response also needs to be consistent with your brand's image. Web sites can generate a lot of e-mail, from requests for specific information and complaints about certain issues to praise for a job well done. You know you cannot afford to waste any opportunity for contact with the consumer. Therefore, even if your company will not actually answer the e-mail, you will need to think about how you are going to deal with the e-mail you receive. You may need to add customer service people. Many of our clients hire outside firms to handle their customer service issues. If you choose that route, you must still be able to look at the data you collect from this important customer touch-point.

Tracking

Tracking is another form of feedback. You will know if your Web site is effective only by studying it over time. If visitors underuse certain sections of your site, is it because the sections are hard to find or because they do not have useful information?

Doing good research and analysis on the traffic and usage patterns of your site is important. That is how you are able to understand what your consumers really want. You will need to understand the use of your Web site from several angles. One angle is what consumers tell you they want. Another is seeing what they actually use. You can learn much from those two perspectives that will help your company build a better, more personalized site.

Controlling Your Own Content

One benefit of having the type of dynamic back end that makes personalization possible is that you are able to go in and add new content without having to rely exclusively on your engineers or programmers to do it for you. That's the beauty of making a site dynamic and serving it out of a database: you can go in and really start to add new content to the site very easily without learning HTML.

Taking control of your own content saves you money, it saves your site builder money, and it puts the core competencies back where they belong. Your site builder is not the best-qualified person to develop content for your site. You are. You have already done it once; your site builder should create automated systems so that your new content props to the Web site without his or her intervention. With the technologies available today, you can go into your site and modify any page or any section of a page. Controlling your own content makes a lot of sense from the maintenance perspective. It allows you a greater degree of flexibility when it comes to creating, maintaining, and modifying the most compelling experience for your customers.

A Passel of Web Success Stories

Now take a look at how these issues come into play in the real world. Service-oriented sites, such as airlines, and high-ticket merchandise, such as cars, make a lot of sense on the Web. A business such as United Airlines, with its focus on service, makes a great transition to the Web because it puts solution-oriented functionality into the customer's hands. That translates into a real return on United's investment. Oldsmobile is enhancing sales of high-ticket merchandise, the type of interaction many people shy away from in the analog world. The Web softens the experience, making it less threatening and more comfortable to shop for a car. Hallmark is a kind of content site. It is one of the few sites where content changes almost daily. Yet Hallmark is more about relationships than about anything else: it is a case study in how to effectively build and nurture an online community.

These three Web sites play important roles for their companies, from providing services and making sales transactions possible to building and extending relationships. Whether it's reducing the costs associated with toll-free calls, minimizing the expense of fulfilling brochure requests by using the Web, selling tickets, or building relationships, these are three successful Web solutions created by Giant Step.

United Airlines: Translating Service to the Web

United Airlines' main goals in building a Web site were to reduce costs that were associated with customer service calls and to provide better access to information about services and membership programs. Another goal was to make use of advanced types of functionality that had not been available before. On the United site (*http://www.ual.com*), a person can quickly find information about flight availability and reservations, get up-to-the-minute information on schedules, and even verify points accumulated for participation in United's loyalty program, Mileage Plus. Putting these functional tools into the hands of their customers has proved to be a compelling benefit that keeps people coming back.

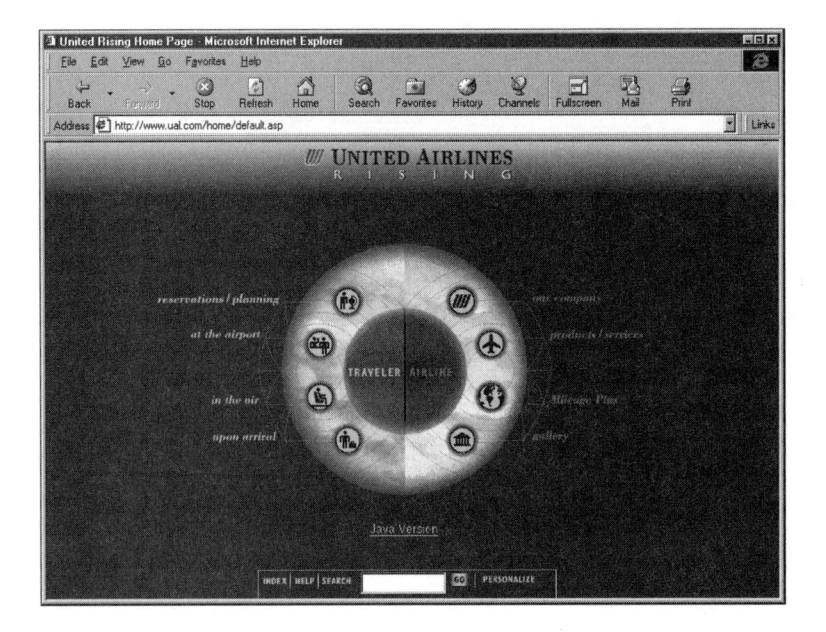

The personal touch

With United, the users are not all equals. The upper echelon customers are the ones responsible for the majority of income. Fifty percent of United's revenue comes from just fifteen percent of the travelers. The folks at United have to be very sensitive about how they communicate with those people. They cannot just go out and talk to everybody in the same way. They have to be very cognizant of who they are talking to.

Giant Step's mission was to make sure that when a person goes into the site, United knows whether she's a member of a loyalty program such as 1K or Executive Premiere so that United can give her the most relevant topics and content. We have relied heavily on the Personalization Server component of the Microsoft Site Server suite of Web development tools to tie into information collected about consumers in order to make their experiences much more targeted. Now, when a 1K or Executive Premiere member enters her program number, United immediately has a lot of information about her.

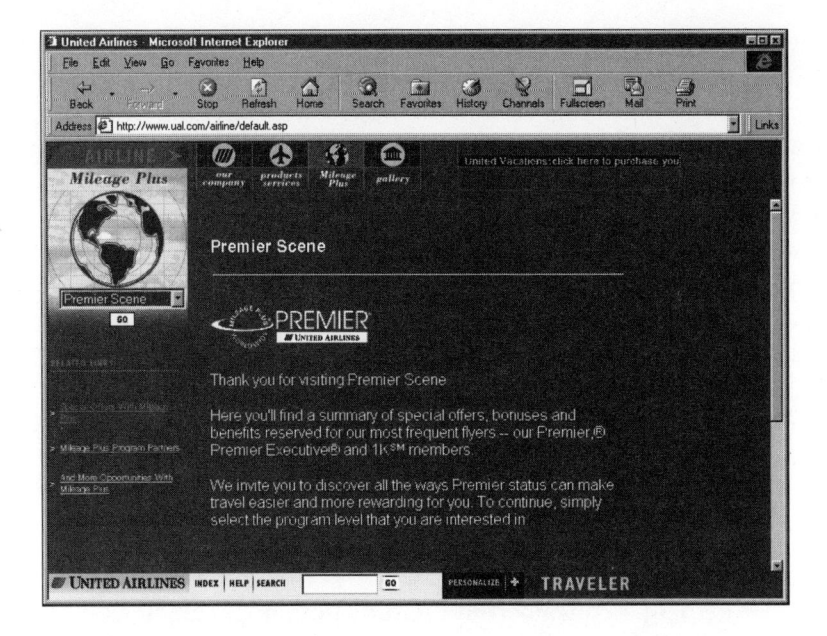

How the Web Was Won: Rounding Up Online Successes

United is starting to collect customer profiles so that the company can build personal relationships based on the way individuals use the site. Using the information contained in consumer profiles, United can create a specific site for a specific individual. It is possible to give consumers sites made up of only one page or sites containing every page, based on personal use profiles.

The United site is customizable, so people do not have to plod through everything to find the things they want or need. By using the Personalization Server, United will be able to go in and say, "We know you're a 1K member. We know you're interested only in flight status or booking and you don't want to hear about our company." The company will be able to give the user exactly what she wants.

United's site is served completely out of a database. The site sits on top of Microsoft SQL Server. Giant Step developed a dynamic back end for the site because of the need for personalization and segmentation. When a request for an Active Server Page comes through, that page looks at the database and makes a query that is appropriate for the individual. Soon, if he is a 1K member and flies to New York all the time, every time he requests a page, his personal information will be sent to the database and will pull back the appropriate information.

United is starting to understand its customers better. When users come in looking for the cheapest flights, United can show them the best fares between cities they have designated in the past. When United knows that a 1K member flies from New York to LA twice a week, it is going to give her information on the status of those flights when she visits the site. United can also give her information about future flights and prices. Again, personalization is about having one-on-one conversations with consumers and placing them into the right segment of the site to give them the most relevant experience.

In addition to personalizing the site for individual users, United is able to gather information with Microsoft Usage Analyst and apply what it learns to more of the categories on the site. For instance, if the majority of 1K members use the functional pieces available on the site, the 1K experience as a whole can evolve into being much more functional overall.

Focus on solutions

You can and should make Web sites useful tools. Whether you are building a brand or helping a consumer find information, it is really making a utility, rather than trying to entertain, that is going to pay off for your company in the end. From the tracking we've done at Giant Step, we've found that people are repeatedly going back to the parts of a site that are the most functional.

Loyalty programs are an excellent example of what works on the World Wide Web. Before, when a member wanted to check her Mileage Plus points, that was a relatively expensive customer service call. In some of our clients' cases, a service call can run a whopping $5 to $10. If you can do the same thing for a few pennies, it becomes very cost-effective. United has tied functionality into its Web site, allowing loyalty program members to review points easily on their own. When it is both easy and cost-effective for a company to share information across the Web, it makes good business sense to do so.

Tracking

If you are going to give a consumer a personalized experience, you have to understand how that person uses the site. You are able to do that using the Usage Analyst component of the Microsoft Site Server suite of Web development tools. It allows your company to analyze specific consumer usage of a Web site and shape your site accordingly.

For example, when a 1K member visits United's site, she gets the 1K look and feel. Then, as she uses the site more and more, the site increasingly caters to her needs. She can go in and say, "I'm interested only in flight status and availability" or, "I want to send e-mail when I have an issue." After that, the site will no longer give her all the other sections about corporate information or traveling abroad. She will get just the things she has asked for. There is no such thing as a "snapshot" of the site because the site is totally dynamic in nature. Some pages might be there for her that are not there for another member, or parts of a page that would be there for another member might not be there for her.

Loyalty programs are also an excellent way for you to create personal consumer profiles. Information collected on your Web site goes a long way toward helping to personalize the interaction you have with your customers.

Oldsmobile: Selling High-Ticket Merchandise On Line

To be successful, Oldsmobile wants to drive more car sales, and whether that is done on line or off, the more car sales made, the more successful the company will be. Keeping current Oldsmobile customers loyal is part of the larger goal behind the company's decision to go on the Web. Oldsmobile wants to make customers feel they are part of a select group and that the company cares about them and wants their business in the future. The Oldsmobile site is an excellent channel for keeping these types of relationships moving ahead.

This site is successful for a variety of reasons. Every time a brochure request comes through, it costs a lot of money for a customer service representative to talk to that person and take the survey information. Now Oldsmobile is able to fulfill brochure requests very easily and inexpensively on the Web. Customer service conversations that the company once handled through an 800 number now happen on the Web, so they have reduced these costs significantly as well. Oldsmobile is also able to keep information about car costs up-to-date, so potential clients can always look at a window sticker on the Web site and know exactly what a car will cost.

On the West Coast, General Motors is actually experimenting with doing sales transactions over the Web. Across the industry, out of 15 million cars purchased last year, 1 million of the purchasers went into the showroom only to pick up the keys. They had already bought their car through a Web site. They had taken care of everything on line, from finding the dealer to getting the loan approved.

The Web site is also helping to pull people into Oldsmobile's showrooms. *Business Week* reported that for 67 percent of car purchases last year, the buyers did their research on line or learned about the car through telemarketing. If they did not have Internet connections of their own, they had relatives or friends who did, and got the information they wanted through them.

The personal touch

Oldsmobile's brand positioning has changed. The company has somewhat negative brand equity. It needs to change consumers' perceptions by getting people to have an open mind. Oldsmobile is trying to achieve this by placing emphasis on how the brands fit the consumer's unique lifestyle and demographic positioning. The company is moving away from making Oldsmobile the focus and is placing it on the individual car brands. Each car is a brand in itself. Each has a demographic of its own. Aurora, Bravada, and Intrigue are the car names and they are "brought to you by Oldsmobile."

With that in mind, Giant Step did two very different things. One was to create Oldsmobile.com, which is the main Web site. It places the user in the correct segment depending on where she is in the purchase cycle. Then we took each car and created a brand site for it by breaking the cars off into independent sites. Each is accessible as a stand-alone site but also plugs into the main Oldsmobile site.

One person may come to the primary site looking to buy an Oldsmobile. Another person may be just learning about Oldsmobile through a car he saw and liked. He may come in from an ad or a banner, go right into the Aurora or Bravada site, and never even know it is an Oldsmobile. He just knows he likes the car. Digging deeper into the information will take him into the main brand site.

How the Web Was Won: Rounding Up Online Successes

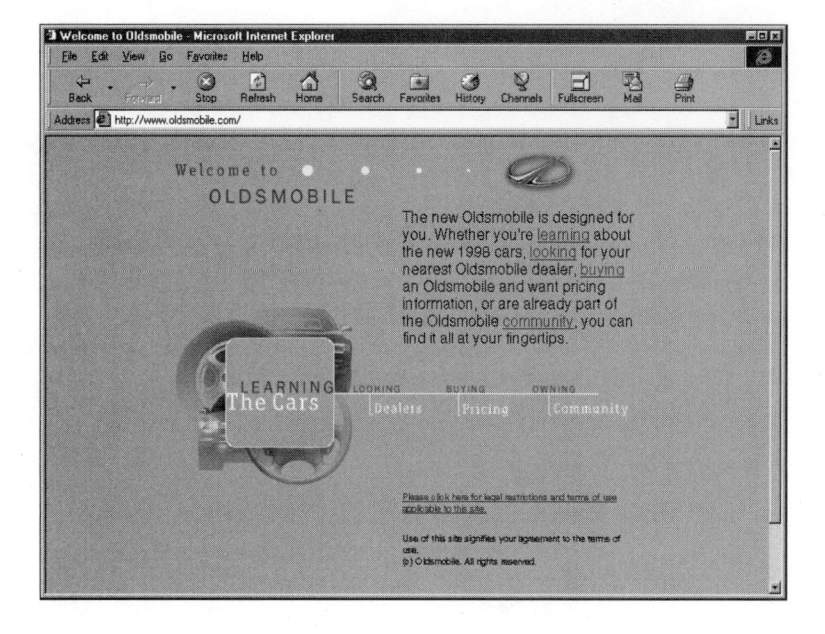

Segmentation

The overriding goal behind the creation of the Oldsmobile Web site is to sell cars. However, in this kind of high-ticket field, a huge part of the battle is getting a consumer's attention so that Oldsmobile can begin to move her toward a sale. Therefore, the Oldsmobile site breaks down into several sections that take the consumer from simply browsing to learning about a car in detail and eventually to locating a dealer to make a purchase.

Giant Step segmented the Oldsmobile site so that when a person comes in he clearly chooses a category for himself depending on where he is in the purchase cycle. If he is just browsing, there is no sense in starting to talk about the window sticker or about where to buy the car. It makes more sense simply to give as much information as possible. When a person is ready to buy, she does not want to read about the car's V6 engine or mileage per gallon. She just wants to find out how much it is going to cost and where she can get it. Using site segmentation, Oldsmobile can quickly and easily place the customer in the right area of the site.

When customers come into the site, Oldsmobile obviously does not know what's on their minds. The company asks people to make a choice by clicking on an image that represents their position in the purchase cycle. Once the visitor has made the decision, Oldsmobile no longer has to worry about what the Web site is serving up to the customer. Once they have made a decision, Oldsmobile caters the rest of the experience to them. The focus of the site is clearly on selling cars, but Oldsmobile segments customers to have a meaningful conversation with them, one that is appropriate to where the customers see themselves in the purchase cycle.

Feedback

Giant Step designed Oldsmobile's site to tell the user everything, good or bad, instead of only what Oldsmobile felt was important. If there is a bad review, people are going to find it whether your company gives it to them or not, especially on the World Wide Web. The idea is to keep them in your site—where at least your company has some input into the conversation—tell them everything, good or bad, and be honest. The Web, after all, is moving more toward being a complete information model. It is a much more honest approach to say, "We're interested in having users see all the news, good and bad, on our site."

Working with these ideas, Oldsmobile put message boards on its site. It is a bold thing for a company to create a forum for people to come in and talk about the company's products. Why let people talk about your product where you cannot hear or be involved? Why not host the discussion on your site, where you can actually be part of the conversation? The same people who are handling Oldsmobile's e-mail customer service are also managing the message boards. If someone posts a message that requires an answer from Oldsmobile, the monitors respond and identify themselves as Oldsmobile's representatives. When a negative issue arises, loyal clients often come to Oldsmobile's defense. Someone will say, "I don't like this car" for whatever reason, and somebody else will come back and say, "I love this car, and here's why." When your company is involved in the conversation, you can step in at any time and say, "He's right" or, "You're right" or, "If we can help you, let us know." People are going to have these discussions whether you are there or not. With message boards on your site, you can be part of the conversation, which is an important advantage. You can even archive contributions to the message board to understand the whole customer contact better.

Tracking

It makes sense that someone is going to go to a Web site to learn more about a car before making a purchase decision. The Oldsmobile site has great tracking built in, so the company knows what influenced a buyer to make a purchase. When a person requests a brochure on the site, Oldsmobile can track that all the way through to the car's vehicle identification number. A large percentage of the people who buy cars from Oldsmobile now have had some influence from the Web site, whether it was going on line to read articles, finding a dealer, or checking the window sticker.

E-mail tracking

Giant Step built a solution on the Oldsmobile site that uses Microsoft SQL Server to log and track customer e-mail when the company receives and answers it. Among other things, the tool lets Oldsmobile know how long it took someone to receive an answer to an e-mail request, how often a user has contacted Oldsmobile through e-mail, and the types of issues that are generating the most e-mail messages. Oldsmobile added these comprehensive customer support solutions to the site to make it as integrated as it can be with all the other tools used, such as Microsoft Windows NT Server and SQL Server.

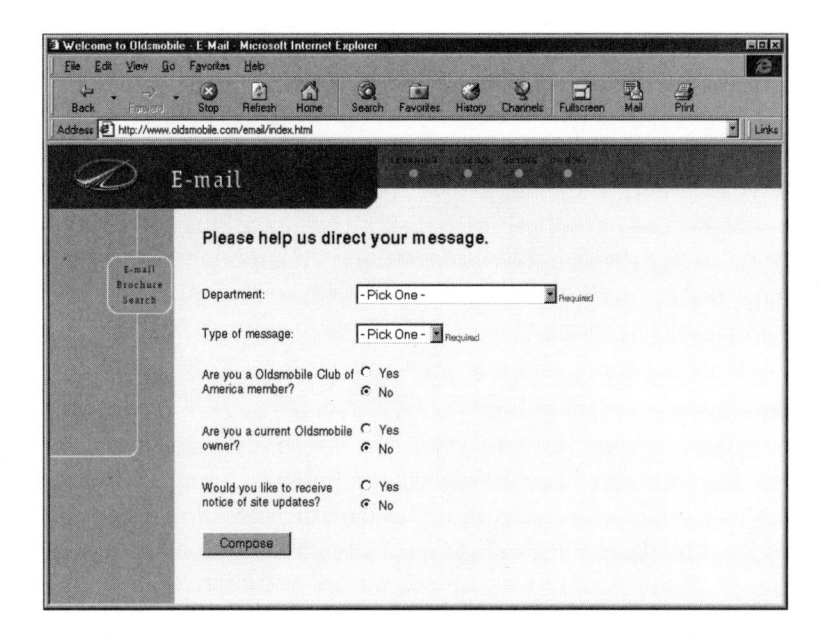

Here's an example of how Oldsmobile was able to put this tool to work. The head of Oldsmobile had been hearing about complaints that one of its new cars had wind noise through the windshield. The engineers told him it wasn't a problem. As soon as they launched the site and e-mail started coming in, some of the first e-mail they received was about the noise coming through the Aurora windshield. The head of the company was able to look at those complaints and see that there obviously was a problem, and he made sure that they fixed it.

Hallmark: Building and Extending Relationships

Hallmark wants to be the place people turn to when they think about relationships and how to communicate with another person. Whether it is a daughter's birthday, Mother's Day, an anniversary, or whatever the occasion happens to be, the company wants people to think of Hallmark as the place to go to do one-stop relationship building. For Hallmark, Web success has meant extending the company's unique ability to build relationships with its customers as well as helping those customers enhance the relationships they are interested in pursuing. Hallmark has been able to do those things by finding new ways to extend and empower its community, by increasing accessibility to its artists, and by giving its customers new and unusual ways to interact and make contact with one another.

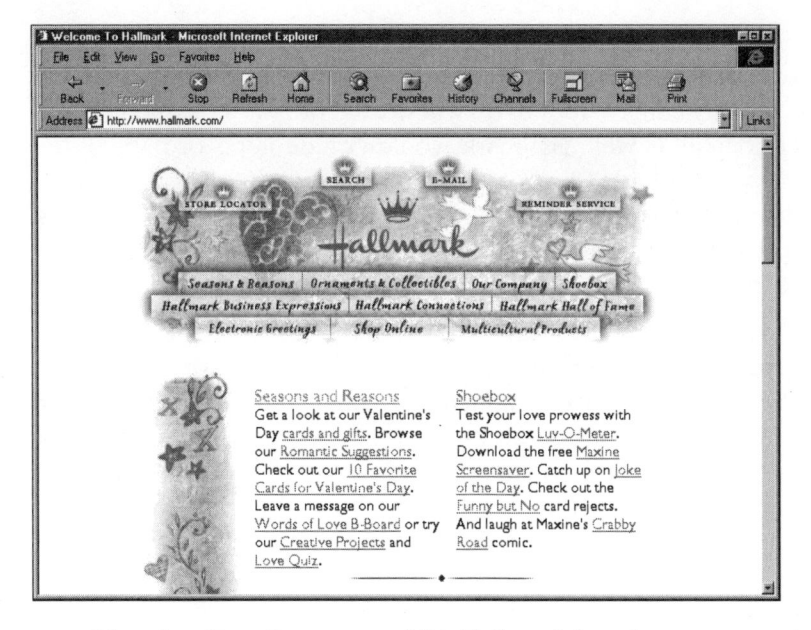

How the Web Was Won: Rounding Up Online Successes

The site Giant Step created for Hallmark lets the company do all that and more. Through personalization, message boards, and dynamic content, Hallmark is able to address effectively the business-related goals it set out to achieve.

The personal touch

By starting to understand how people are using the site over time, we are able to make the Web experience more relevant by giving individuals the experience that is best suited for them. For instance, if a person visits the Hallmark site often and buys mostly ornaments, one of the most prominent things on her site will be the Ornie Message Board. Hallmark is not going to start out showing her the cards.

The goal is to take the site and target who the consumer is, to understand the consumer's relationship with Hallmark. By something as simple as a loyalty program such as Gold Crown, Hallmark actually knows how many cards and ornaments a person bought in the last year, which is pretty powerful from a marketing perspective. The company also knows where the customer is coming from because it knows the member's address. Therefore, it is able to do some regional content as well as doing marketing specific to purchasing habits.

Hallmark can start to give individual site visitors personalized experiences. For example, if a person celebrates a special holiday, each year when that holiday comes around, he will get the proper look and feel and the proper content as well. Hallmark wouldn't hide items or parts of the site that a consumer hadn't expressed an interest in but might move them down in the priority list, start to show things that make more sense for each individual. It is more of a shifting of the popular content to apply to a particular consumer's preferences, shifting popular content toward the upper navigational elements and moving less popular things down further.

Focus on solutions

The Hallmark audience loves Hallmark ornaments and collectibles, the Maxine comic strip, Hallmark Hall of Fame movies, the Gold Crown loyalty program, and even the artists who create the products. Hallmark is interested first and foremost in making sure those passionately loyal fans are happy before trying to build new customers. Hallmark wanted to create an experience to make those people feel like part of a community, make them feel as though they are sharing with each other and with the brand.

One obvious way to encourage that sense of sharing was to include message boards on the site. People enjoy the feeling that Hallmark is communicating directly with them. Then there's a huge interest in all the ornaments and collectibles. Hallmark's site provides ways for people to trade those things, so they are able to develop relationships with one another, not just with the brand. In addition to providing a kind of self-creating content, these are reasons for people to come back to the site frequently and really feel they are a part of it.

Controlling content

Most of the information found on Web sites has been repurposed. Oldsmobile is not going to write specific Web content: the car is the same whether you are on the Web or in the showroom. Hallmark is an exception. They have approximately 700 creatives at Hallmark, so they can use many of those strengths to create specific Web content. Hallmark is also able to repurpose many of the things they have, such as Maxine, which is a daily comic. Whether you re-purpose content or create it specifically for the Web, that daily change can help keep people coming back.

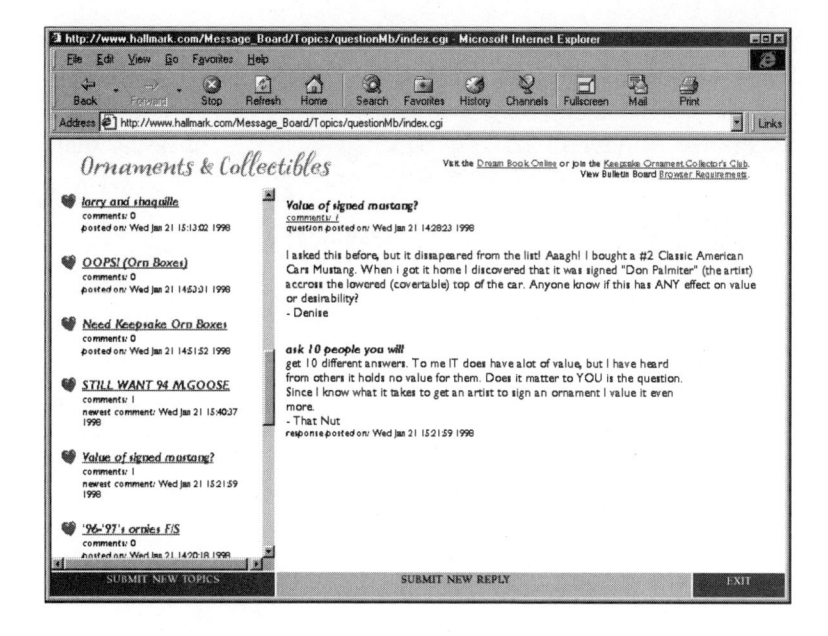

How the Web Was Won: Rounding Up Online Successes

[screenshot of Hallmark Ornaments & Collectibles message board web page]

Hallmark has a variety of Web-specific content. There's a feature called *Funny but No,* which highlights cards that are a little too harsh or over the top. Those things all go up on the Web site, and it's fun for people to come back to see what is new on a daily basis. It has helped create a strong sense of community as the site has evolved.

Hallmark has a lot of information that changes based on seasons. It has to be relatively dynamic—content has to change quickly. If a person comes in on Father's Day, the site looks one way, but when she comes in the next day, it looks different. Once Halloween is over, Hallmark has to change the site for Thanksgiving and Christmas. The company needed a site that would be very dynamic yet inexpensive and easy to change.

We have developed all the Hallmark interfaces using Microsoft's Active Server Pages technology. The interface layer sits in a database so we can go in and tweak it, perhaps change the graphics and immediately swap them out across the site. It saves a lot of money and effort.

With the Hallmark site, the majority of the changes typically happen in the interface, which requires Giant Step to be a part of it. Giant Step handles most of the seasonal changes. It is something we wanted to give to Hallmark, but it really depends on the client's willingness, interest, and resources to do something like that. If Hallmark wanted to, it could certainly come in, take that piece away from us, and move it inside the company. Many companies have creative departments capable of doing that.

Web Development Contraptions

In this section, I will take a look at the Web development tools and underlying architecture that Giant Step uses to create the types of successful digital business solutions we have been discussing.

Tools of the Trade

As far as tools go, everything Giant Step builds uses Microsoft's Active Server Pages technology. We use SQL Server as our back end and run a Microsoft Windows NT 4.0 Server for our hosting environment and serving environment. Our workstations are also Windows NT. We use Microsoft Visual InterDev and Microsoft Visual Studio as our development tools. We are also using the Site Analyst, which allows us to check all the links and images used on a Web site. So we know right away before we send the site out if we have broken links or pages that are not accessible.

The tools we use in Web development have evolved at a rapid pace. We saw things go from relatively simple VI editors on UNIX boxes to suddenly having some elaborately integrated development environments that allow us to do everything from process development to deployment. It is amazing where these tools have come in a very short time, especially for someone who is starting to build Web sites. It is a great time to get into it. Looking back to as recently as 1996, Web development was a painful process. Now, because it has been such an interesting market, there are some amazing tools.

We did not have a good set of tools in 1996, and then suddenly these developing environments came along and allowed us to do development in a way that made sense from a team perspective. Before, we needed to have one programmer work on a site alone because it was just too hard to share. The ability to work effectively as a team will become even more important in the future as these sites start to become more and more complicated and increasingly integrated with systems at the back end.

Before, there was not a good model to understand what Web development did or did not require, whether it was a good team environment, or whether it was more of an isolated environment. Obviously, with the size and scope of today's projects you can no longer have one person or two people working on it. Having the tools that make it possible to develop as a team is very important, even from a process perspective. What happens to a file once a programmer or a designer is done with it? Who's next in the chain, and how do they understand what the next steps are for that particular file?

It is important to get designers involved in the development process. Right now, designers, in some cases, are working on different platforms. They do their work before the programmer. It would be nice to see designers and programmers working more closely together so that designers will know what is and isn't possible.

With today's tools, it is possible for project managers to come in and track a particular task. They are able to say we are on schedule and on budget based on the current state of the Web site as it sits on the server. In time, a single system will tie together all the different aspects of complex digital projects.

We are getting to the point where we have amazing control over the approval process of a file before we prop it on a Web server and index it. If I am done with the file, the editor needs to look at it and then give it to the client for approval. Then, finally, it goes live. That is more of a vision of where this process is going. It is going to be increasingly true as sites become larger and larger and tie into increasingly complex systems.

Currently we are developing using Visual InterDev. By using meta-information in the header of the file, we are able to move it down the process further and further. When somebody approves a file, she adds new meta-information to that effect in the header. That way we know before something goes live that in fact the proper people have approved it. As it sorts through information, the Index Server will not pick up a file if it does not have the proper approvals. The Web server will not display a file if it does not have the proper approvals. Those kinds of concepts are probably what we will see put into place in the near future.

Architecture

From the architecture perspective, Hallmark was actually our first success when it came to Microsoft's Windows NT architecture. Before the Hallmark site, we had been developing nearly everything using typical UNIX tools such as VI editors and some tools that were available from Silicon Graphics and other companies for doing Web development. Then these amazing tools came out of Microsoft. Compaq and others made commitments to Windows NT as a viable server and development platform.

We made the decision to focus on Windows NT as a development and serving platform because of all the tools coming out. That is when the shift started to occur, and we started to develop almost entirely on Windows NT. It was a paradigm shift driven more by the development tools than by the server itself. At that time there were not many tools for development, especially on Windows NT. Microsoft came out with Visual Studio and started working on Web servers, and we started to make the shift. Right away, we saw a dramatic increase in our productivity and in the price/performance ratio of using Windows NT servers.

We had great success with Hallmark. The site gets a ton of traffic, and we realized right away that Windows NT was a price/performance box much greater than we had expected for both development and hosting. Now we use Windows NT across the board. We saw how much traffic Windows NT was handling and how much easier our development cycles were. Getting the product to market on the UNIX platform was much more difficult and time consuming. From a hardware and server perspective, that really was the factor that opened our eyes.

At the same time, we started to have a sense of community with other developers. It was not so much of an isolated environment any longer. In the UNIX world, we did not have good source control tools; we did not have good tools for actually developing these pages in a team environment and for sharing the development process. Now we have been able to integrate with the entire environment. If someone's writing C++ and someone else is writing J++, we're still a development team working on a Web site together—checking in and checking out documents and rolling back versions.

Phased Approach

The Web is at a strange point in its history. Web development technologies are making unbelievably rapid progress, yet expectations can sometimes outstrip what is immediately possible from a practical perspective. Because of that, we need to create Web sites using a phased approach.

Ideally, you would launch a site with every system you can imagine on line and instantly accessible. However, because of the time and effort involved and the speed at which the technology is changing, it is just not feasible to delay the launch of a Web site until every piece is available and working. At Giant Step, we approach the creation of a Web site in phases. Phase 1 is about getting the site operating with some functionality that will achieve a primary goal such as reduction of support costs. For instance, when it comes to customer service, e-mail is much easier and cheaper to answer than a telephone call, so giving a company that functionality is a desirable and achievable primary goal. Later, in phase 2, we can go back and add more and better high-tech functionality, using emerging tools and technologies to increase the effectiveness of the site to achieve its secondary goals.

Where We Stand

The Web development business as a whole is becoming much more vertically integrated than we ever anticipated. At Giant Step, we originally set out to be a kind of agency that also did production. We would come up with the ideas and follow through to the execution of a Web site or a CD-ROM or whatever it happened to be. Slowly but surely, we started adding services because our clients were looking for turnkey solutions. It is much easier for businesses to get their media from the same place where they get their tracking, research, and hosting. Right away, we were getting into types of work we had never anticipated doing. Take hosting, for example. We ended up hosting because it was much more cost-effective to do so, not only for our clients but also for ourselves. It is a big money saver for us, although we do not necessarily turn around and make a lot of money from it.

Since roughly the end of 1996, agencies have decided that they cannot do Web development. Smaller Web shops are more agile and have lower overhead. Therefore, ad agencies have purchased garage shops to do Web development , and Web shops have started to take on some of the characteristics of agencies. Web shops are now offering services they never thought they would be doing to make sure their clients get the most integrated experience possible.

Giant Step is doing everything from strategy through hosting, but only as it relates to the digital world. Typically, the reason that people have not gone to their ad agencies for Web development is that it is a specialized service. Web shops sometimes say vertical integration is bad because of the perceived lack of specialized expertise it implies. They say it is best to separate digital development from print design and integration. Although it should have the same look and feel, different people should do each of those things.

That is exactly the mentality Giant Step went in with—we thought this should be a specialized service. "We do something specific, and we're going to let your ad agency do the rest of it."

We soon realized that we were vertically integrated. We do strategy, marketing, ideation, creative, production, hosting, media, e-customer service and e-commerce, research, and analysis. We have become a mini ad agency. We have a huge list of services that we never anticipated having. That model makes the most sense right now. To separate all those services would be too costly.

Imagine that you hired a separate agency to do each individual piece of a specific job. Integrating those elements is difficult enough when you are dealing with a single shop. It becomes unbelievably complex when you start working with legacy systems and other issues. To have multiple shops working on different pieces of a particular Web site would be nearly impossible.

We have found that it makes the most sense to integrate as much as possible. That way, the research team is tied into the data that's coming off the hosting server and tied back into the strategy that was outlined at the beginning. Then companies end up having full-circle, turnkey solutions.

Giant Step offers an integrated and extensive scope of strategic Internet services. These include strategic and marketing consulting, creative production and visual design, programming and engineering, online media and content partnering, quality control and testing, research and measurement, e-commerce, electronic customer care, and system administration. Our complete package of services allows Giant Step's clients to receive a turnkey solution from a single provider with a single point of accountability.

While Giant Step offers some services, such as research and online media, à la carte to clients, we do not offer creative development or design, engineering, programming, maintenance, or hosting as separate services. We believe that separating these components of the development process is not viable for several reasons:

Communication: When you separate services, communication becomes more difficult because clients must then interact with more than one provider for each service. The result is an increase in cost because you have to take more time to discuss the scope of tasks and project.

Coordination: When you separate services, coordination of tasks becomes more difficult. The result is an increase in cost by all providers and a potential decrease in product quality.

Development and Implementation: Because processes are so tightly integrated, overall development and implementation of the digital solution becomes more costly when you separate services.

Accountability: When you separate services, the client can no longer hold one party accountable for the product.

Web Team Organization

So far, we have been flat organizationally. That is starting to change a little—we are getting so large we have started to think more about hierarchy. One person could run a Web shop, but it would have to be a versatile person. He or she would need to know as much about design as about programming, development, and marketing and have the organizational skills to effectively put them all together. At this stage, we have teams of four leading each project.

Each Giant Step team consists of a lead program manager, a lead engineer, a lead creative designer, and a lead planner, all of whom are responsible and accountable for the quality of the product and service that Giant Step delivers.

One person could perform those roles, but it is somewhat rare to find all four of those skill sets in any single individual. We have always felt that ideally, those four skills would be rolled up together in one person, but the closest thing we have found is taking teams and sitting them so close together that they act as one. We are very team oriented. A successful digital business solution recognizes the equal importance of each skill set. The designer does not necessarily have a monopoly on the visual design. The project manager may see a better way. We weigh input from everyone on the team equally, which ends up being the best for the site.

In the Web By-and-By

Everyone has his or her own idea about where the future of the Internet lies. I think one interesting development is going to be bandwidth. That will be the most significant change. If we get decent, cheap bandwidth at home, that will have huge implications on what we are developing and how we are doing it. WebTV is a good example. It is very integrated into the television experience. That is the sort of integration we will see when bandwidth issues are resolved. There is no reason why we could not have much richer, much more powerful experiences on the Web, much more like CD-ROM experiences. That would be exciting from a development perspective. Limited bandwidth is keeping content from really taking off.

The next wave in personalization involves strategic collaboration among companies to meet more of the consumer's needs on a single Web site. If United knows you travel to New York every week, why not give you a New York–specific site? The site could show you the best places to eat and stay in New York. Looking ahead, we're going to be able to take the site and make it customized and specific based not just on how you travel but where and why you travel. Business travelers are not necessarily looking for the cheapest flight; they just want to get from point A to point B and have the least painful experience possible.

Conclusion

What does it take to be successful on the Web? As in any other endeavor, you need to measure success on the Web against the legitimate goals you set out to achieve. In this chapter, we have looked at three successful Web sites. Some of the goals that drove these businesses to go on line include increasing return on investments, reducing costs, increasing revenue, selling merchandise, and making a wide variety of information more accessible. For United Airlines, Web success is about decreasing the high costs associated with a variety of customer service issues. Oldsmobile is generating car sales with its Web site and building loyalty among current Oldsmobile owners by making them feel that they are part of a select group and that the company cares about them and wants their business in the future. Hallmark has been able to extend its ability to help its customers build important relationships while deepening its own relationship with those customers.

I started out this chapter sharing some background about Giant Step's decision to work on the Web and, following that, went into detail about three of Giant Step's clients. Those clients are representative of three common types of business model found on the Internet today: service, merchandise, and content. The types of successful work those companies are doing on the Web should serve as guidelines for your company to follow. I then discussed the tools we use at Giant Step to achieve the types of successful Web solutions found in this chapter and covered the current state of Web development, especially as we practice it at Giant Step. Finally, I took a brief look at the future of Web development and shared some thoughts on where it is all heading in the months and years ahead. If you take only one thought away from this chapter, it should be this:

Create user-sensitive, business-building digital solutions by combining experience, business focus, marketing expertise, state-of-the-art technology, and creativity.

About the Author

Adam Heneghan cofounded Giant Step with his brother Eric in Iowa in 1991. From cornfields to Chicago, the brothers built the company from a two-person CD-ROM development firm to a highly successful 70+ person full-service digital agency. When not developing Web sites, Adam immerses himself in fine dining and Chimay and in extreme sports such as snowboarding and blading.

"Tread carefully and stay informed."

Tony Leininger

CHAPTER 9

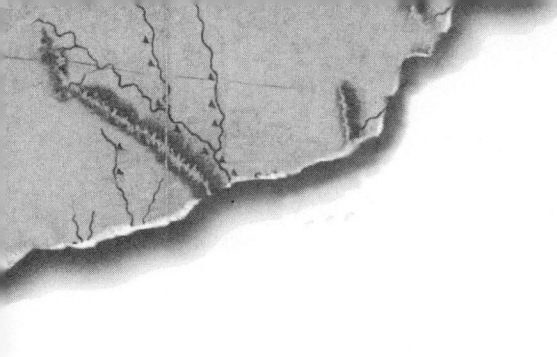

Conquering the Digital Frontier

Seven Issues to Face En Route to Web Success

The idea behind this chapter went through several transformations. In November 1997, when the authors of *How the Web Was Won* first met in Redmond, Washington, the concept was to collect brief quotes from various industry leaders on their visions of where the World Wide Web might be 10 years from now. Another idea we batted around was similar, but it shifted the focus to our own forecasts. With the millennium just around the corner, though, the passion for prophecy has run amok. Views of what the world will be like after the turn of the century abound, making foretelling the future of the Web a dime-a-dozen proposition.

We eventually settled on something much more valuable. We decided to focus on today's real-world issues, questions that you will face if you are interested in creating a digital presence for your company. These are details that could make or break your efforts to successfully do business on the Web, things like planning for globalization, establishing new means of distribution, understanding appliance convergence, and keeping pace with rapid technological change.

At a two-day roundtable discussion in January 1998, the authors met a second time and identified seven specific subjects they felt you would need to address. They carefully divided the issues into pairs of topics and questions in a way that they hoped would put the concerns into perspective. They debated whether they would be able to answer the questions adequately, and they finally decided that more important than providing all-encompassing answers—an impossible task in the scope of a single chapter—was asking the right questions and suggesting some initial answers to help you get the discussion rolling within your own organization. The following debates look at a comprehensive set of concerns that the authors, who are themselves successful business leaders, know your team will have to address if you are going to take your business into the digital age and make it thrive.

In framing the questions that follow and discussing some possible answers, the authors focused on *you*. They assumed that readers of *How the Web Was Won* would be business decision-makers planning to take a company on line. They focused on you as they discussed each topic and concentrated on communicating their combined experiences to steer you past the pitfalls and point you toward the benefits of successfully moving your enterprise to the Web.

There are few rock-solid answers in what follows. More often, you'll find ideas about how you might begin to answer the questions we've raised, and indications of additional issues that could come into play. Occasionally, the authors agreed on certain recommendations. Generally, though, the opinions that emerged were more diverse, representing the variety of successful responses your business might adopt to deal with these kinds of concerns.

Although this chapter comes at the end of the book, think of it as a starting point. These are issues to face when you're in the planning stage, before you choose a digital development company. The questions in this chapter cover many topics and hit upon the following points:

- **Globalization**   and the pitfalls and opportunities that await your business on the Web

- **Convergence**   of computers and other appliances and how this can be turned to your business's advantage

CHAPTER 9

Conquering the Digital Frontier: Seven Issues to Face En Route to Web Success

- **E-commerce** and the paradigm shift that is coming in its wake
- **Technology** and the rapid changes that affect today's businesses
- **Legal issues** that can seriously affect online commerce
- **Distribution** and how the Internet is changing today's workforce
- **Liabilities and accountabilities** that will come into play when your company sets up shop on the World Wide Web

Topic 1: Globalization

Network globalization is creating a world of opportunities. *How will you avoid the pitfalls and seize the opportunities?*

Dan
Is your company prepared to deliver on a global scale? We have clients who are getting requests from all over the world to deliver a product, but they're not prepared to make that happen. When you're dealing in a global economy like the Internet, you have to make sure you're ready to meet the challenges of worldwide distribution. That includes taxation, shipping, dealing with the governments of those local economies, and trying to do it profitably.

Jesse
There are also the issues of finances and currency, which pose a problem.

Adam
Our experience to date has seen companies missing the opportunity to take full advantage of network globalization—which is to create distinct and relevant sites that still tie into a unified data source. Instead, companies are following a fragmented approach, oftentimes creating sites independently with incompatible tools. This approach not only increases development and maintenance costs but also fragments the message to the consumer.

Dan
We found the issue of geographical localization is not as important as cultural localization. For example, we take copy down to San Francisco and get it translated into 17 different languages. That doesn't do anything for the country because someone from Japan may look at that and just say, "This wasn't done here." It immediately turns them off. You have to have some cultural embellishment, and that's why it's almost necessary to have the translation done in that country.

John

We've also had projects where that's created issues. It concerns centralization vs. decentralization of company process. There has to be a certain amount of centralization because a Web site has to have standards as well as coordination. A number of issues have to be coordinated with the foreign offices. That can be very difficult. There are language issues, cultural issues, internal procedure issues. There are also sign-off issues.

Dan

Companies need one central point person. This is a problem with the Internet right now and with global companies. General Motors is in 134 countries. Amway's in 70 countries. To be effective, you need one central person who controls your company's Internet effort for the entire world.

Jesse

Most companies are not equipped to handle the issues John just addressed—sign-off and understanding the local cultures. They come to rely on the developers to do more and more of that. That means it's incumbent on us to be successful in the global economy and the global network. Therefore, it's incumbent on us to go get those skills or to have the strategic alliances in place to be able to do that on behalf of our clients.

John

One of the services we offer is coordination for localization. It's so easy for people to think a Web site is just for America. There's a large market out there. A very large percentage of the people who have computers and who are on the Internet are in European and Asian countries.

Jesse

The real winners are going to be those who come up with robust distribution where they can drop-ship worldwide for anybody.

Dan

You have to be prepared electrically to meet the demands of the European and Asian communities—involve the different electrical standards and codes. A lot of work has to happen. Unfortunately, a lot of smaller companies are so unprepared to deal with this that they rely on us. We're being strained to meet the needs of things we're not used to doing.

Conquering the Digital Frontier: Seven Issues to Face En Route to Web Success

Jesse

Maybe it's incumbent upon us to counsel the clients, where appropriate, that they may need to put off globalization. It's appealing to many companies to open new channels and new revenue streams. But if they're not equipped, it's going to be detrimental to their business in the long run as opposed to going out and doing it right. Maybe we need to be looking for solutions that direct international traffic appropriately.

John

Globalization really introduces a much higher level of complexity into thinking about what type of presence you have on line. Companies really need to examine the payoff vs. the resources it's going to take.

Bryan

Jesse, could you describe for me what the opportunity or pitfall would be for the entertainment industry in this context? In terms of the promotional sites you've done, is globalization an issue?

Jesse

Globalization is always an issue for anyone publishing on the Internet. Many of the studios are set up in such a way that they separate national and international distribution and therefore all of the associated services that aid them in their efforts. That includes separate marketing support, and therefore, many have separate Web sites. While I'm not familiar with international traffic on the international sites, I do know that upwards of 30 percent of traffic on many domestic sites comes from international visitors. My guess would be that the majority of international Web traffic actually goes to the initial U.S. theatrical site. That may be because these sites are primarily where the development money is spent, and therefore where the better sites are. On the flip side, I would also imagine that the international user looking simply for release information is going to go to the appropriate international site for such information.

Bryan

It's not an opportunity for them to be able to do a more coordinated promotion? They don't take advantage of globalization in that way?

Jesse

Some studios do try and take advantage of their international presence and coordinate their globalization efforts.

Dan

The problem is movies are released in the United States way before they're released overseas. There can be some confusion. Which site do you go to? Do you go to the international site? Do you go to the national site? The international folks are struggling with all these countries, all these localization issues, all these different distribution dates happening. When we did the international site for *Independence Day,* we had 17 countries that had 17 different launch dates that had to be coordinated from one site and localization issues built into each portion of it. It was a confusing effort on the part of the studio. That does provide an opportunity at the studio for someone above the international or the national to say, "Let's look at this, and let's start dealing on a world landscape, instead of trying to divide this effort." The United States is not its own world. It's a part of the world. It's shortsighted not to look at it that way.

Bryan

Instead of dividing along traditional geographic zones, having a single point of entry for promotions would allow companies to be more efficient. Have one primary site with versions coordinated from one location.

Dan

Let me give you an example. NASDAQ makes its money on how many trades happen. They found the Internet was an opportunity to create more trades by giving information to individuals so they could be on the same playing field and start trading more, which is better for NASDAQ. Then NASDAQ said, "Wait a minute. If we can do that, why don't we go out and get this information localized and culturalized for each individual country so we can get other countries trading NASDAQ stocks?" The first country my company is doing for them is the United Kingdom. We had to go there, talk to traders and banks, and learn the law so we know how people have to trade stocks there. We had to take a massive amount of information, which is delivered in real time, and change it into their standards. We had to educate people on how they can start trading NASDAQ stocks. The next stops are France, Germany, and Japan. It has to be coordinated centrally, and it has to be done the right way. If they think we're just going to give people in other countries the same information we give everyone in the United States, it will fail.

Tish

One of the issues we're bringing up is the political issue. As you start to go global, who owns what? Our experience has been that there's a pushback from the subsidiaries as far as what they own. That's one angle. But we found the technology supports this very, very nicely. Particularly databases. The way you design the architecture can also support cultural issues. For example, if you think of a Web site as a tree, if it was a linear type of thing, the ability to, once you got into, say, an event component of a certain site in one language to be able to move laterally into the events from Germany to France or something supports the culture, and that's where technology can be used very nicely to augment that. It's been very successful for us in that way. Technology has the ability to deal with many political issues as well as cultural issues. I'd like to see the focus on the development of the technologies and the methodologies that support the business need more. There's a real capability for that to happen more and more.

John

When you're first looking at designing an Internet presence, you have to take globalization as one of the issues. It's imperative that you think about it and you examine it, because you have to design this thing up front. If you don't, it gets very costly and very expensive later to retrofit for the global audience.

Jesse

If you are a global company, you'd better be prepared to deal with this up front. When I produced the original Epson America site, they were not prepared for the fact that Epson is a global company. A large majority of their audience was apparently starved for the technology and the support they were not getting locally and came to look to Epson America for that support. The support mechanism Epson was creating on line opened up the company to this glut of new international visitors the company had not anticipated, and they were forced to address issues for an international audience at their expense.

Tish

It can have so much impact on the brand. You spend so much money and energy figuring out what your brand is going to be and then you blow it over something simple like globalization.

Jesse

Here's another issue. Products are different by country. Products sometimes release much earlier in, say, Japan than in the United States. All of a sudden people in the United States have information on a product that's not available there and wonder why.

Dan

Another thing is, a lot of companies price differently by country. How do you deal with the different pricing issues? One country will be able to see the other country's prices. One of the biggest challenges we've had is the database side of this. One of the strengths of the Internet and going global is the central database. But like Tish mentioned, when you get into Unicode, the Asian markets, you also get into having to set up an SQL database with fields that accept Italian, German, French, Spanish, et cetera. Especially difficult is trying to set up the data fields to accept a different currency. For example, Swedish kronors being in the millions vs. U.S. dollars. These issues need to be well designed into the database before launch.

John

Companies need to try to synthesize some of the things we talked about. Look at this issue from the perspectives of branding and commerce transactions in terms of everything from pricing to the question of are you going to compete or undercut your existing distribution network within a country. These are sensitive issues we have to deal with when we work with other countries. What kind of support will you need to deliver? For example, if you're going to open up your support—e-mail, phone, or whatever—to an international audience, there will be translation issues that have to be faced. You need to think through that process.

Dan

One of the biggest challenges is hosting. If you've ever been overseas and tried to come back to a site in the U.S., it is really brutally slow. You need to be prepared to keep a network of servers up. If you're a CEO and you're looking to expand internationally on the Internet, what do you want to look for in partners when you select them? One of the most important things is, have they done this before and who have they done it for? Make sure they're prepared, that they've been down that road; you're not paying for them to learn on your nickel.

Tish

Make sure the strategy is down before you start embarking on implementation. The topics you need to hit are globalization, localization, internationalization, distribution, education, and support. Make sure you've got a plan in place before you start implementing because it can be very costly. It's an area companies are embarking on very, very quickly because there's incredible opportunity there.

Dan

Just because it's a challenge doesn't mean you shouldn't do it. You should go out there and be prepared to make mistakes, be prepared to learn, but at least go out with some semblance of a plan and strategy and thought.

Jesse

The flip side of this is if you're not prepared, you still need to have a plan.

Tish

Exactly.

Key Recommendations

- Appoint a central coordinator to oversee efforts from a single location.
- Plan your strategy carefully before implementing a Web site to avoid pitfalls.
- Work with site builders who have experience with global issues.

Topic 2: Convergence

Convergence is inevitable. *How will you define it and benefit from it?*

Dan

When I start thinking about convergence, the first thing that usually comes to my mind is convergence of television and the computer. Then I started thinking more of the digital media appliances available today. One of us has a cell phone with liquid crystal display (LCD). That could be communicated with through personal communications services (PCS) networks. I have my little Hewlett-Packard palmtop that can get on the Internet and get e-mail and do Word and Excel. Yesterday we had a pager that had all kinds of interactive messaging. I refer to them as personal digital media assistants or information appliances. The key question for a company is, "How are you going to be able to communicate to people?" Because people will have their preferences. For example, I prefer my palmtop. Some people prefer their laptop. Some people prefer their desktop. Some people will want WebTV. How does a company effectively communicate and pick the right tool to deliver the right message to the right person using these different personal digital media appliances? It's a major challenge because you're going to have to find out what each person's preference is. You're going to have to have a database to store that information. Then you're going to have to pick the right tool to deliver the right information to the right appliance.

Bryan

One of the issues for defining convergence is that it seems as if it's going toward a single point. In fact, what's happening is integration and proliferation of devices. It's really important to understand we're potentially going to be dealing with things in the near future that we can't even imagine right now. In terms of planning, you have to make sure you deal with an open standard that will allow you to take advantage of future innovations. That's one of the most critical things to look at. You could be in serious trouble implementing a solution today that can't scale to take advantage of those things tomorrow.

John

It's almost impossible, though, to plan for this. I define convergence by the distribution of computing technology into many existing appliances. They could be hybrid; they could be specialized products. We do not know what they're going to be. Pilot is a great example. This is a product that came to market and just took the market by storm. Everyone thought the personal digital assistant (PDA) market was dead, but they provided a solution at a price and with the functionality consumers wanted. Within this context, the best you can do is to understand these things will happen, and you may have to retrofit. It's inevitable with this amount of change that no one could predict all the things that are going to come up.

Chapter 9
Conquering the Digital Frontier: Seven Issues to Face En Route to Web Success

Adam

Convergence will fundamentally alter the way a user perceives and interacts with the Internet, as it becomes more accessible and prevalent in the user's everyday life. Messages will resonate across media, providing more relevant and useful experiences for consumers. We have already tested this shift on both WebTV and @Home via online media and have taken convergence into account when developing sites.

Bryan

We tend to think of convergence as meaning things are becoming more media rich. In fact, it could mean the very opposite. It could be text-only delivery. You have to take account of that with pagers or other devices where you're basically dealing with advertising messages.

Jesse

We grow and grow as far as our ability to brand, and we look at the look and feel and similar things becoming important issues on the Web. Now we're looking at information dissemination because we have multiple venues where we can send information to reach people. But the technology is not in place yet, so we're having to go backward with the information we're sending. It becomes much more text-based until the technology can catch up to where we are.

Tish

I'd really like to see nontechnical people making sure we keep the business and communication needs in the forefront and have the devices evolve as a result of the needs.

Jesse

Understanding the demographic audience.

Tish

Correct. It always seems we're just throwing stuff against the wall and seeing what sticks. It would be really neat to see companies be very clear on what their business needs are and communicate that effectively so the convergence can evolve as a result of a business need. That way we could push the limitations of the medium based on needs rather than the other way around.

Bryan

Right. It's important to remember that the Internet doesn't necessarily mean you're dealing with a browser or a Web site. You have to think way beyond that in terms of the potential opportunities for delivery. That's one of the key issues to look at in terms of planning.

Tish

Yeah. What makes sense? If centralization makes sense, then that should be where it goes. If it doesn't, which you're suggesting, then let's drive it. There's an opportunity for business leaders to articulate the business need and for their partners to meet it.

Dan

One of the things I'm most excited about is the convergence of the Web and television. A good example is WebTV. It is such a great product because instead of trying to create something and throwing it against the wall, it brings a product to an audience who're already there but need something simple. My grandfather could plug it in and within three minutes be up and running on the Internet, sending people e-mail, cruising Web sites, and using his television at the same time. It's a great opportunity for businesses to say, "Here's an audience we can deliver to that we've never been able to interactively deliver to before. We've always pushed messages to them. Now we can start having them pull messages and then create a bigger bond with those folks."

Tish

My point, though, is what is the message? We keep falling in love with the technology. We keep getting so preoccupied by the medium. It's important to take one step back, now that we have easy access to this audience and ask, "What the hell are we going to tell them? What do they want to know?" That is part of how this convergence happens. It's part of the evolution.

Bryan

The issue might be more. We're dealing with the world with all these devices, and it touches on issues of personalization to some degree. What's the cost of actually making this happen? Is it worth it? You have to be able to go down to a much finer grain and analyze where that demographic is. Is it worth trying to reach someone who's on WebTV? What's the cost of doing that? If there's a cost-effective way to provide a solution, whether it's technical or communicative, that's potentially a huge win for a company dealing with the right partner.

Tish
Exactly.

Dan
The key is you need to deliver a different message to the WebTV crowd than you do over the Internet or over your Pilot or your HP or your pager. You've got all these different devices, and you have to create a separate message for each one of them. The benefit for the company is that it can finally reach an audience that's large enough to make sense to go do this. It's not just the upper crust or the elite that have Internet capability. It's Middle America now, folks that have television sets. It brings in a big enough audience.

Adam
Convergence will make the transition from advertising messages to product information to purchase seamless. Benefits include messages that are more integrated, personalized messages, and instant purchasing—and that's gratifying for both consumers and companies.

Bryan
The issue becomes: plan for this appropriately and have a very good sense of who you're dealing with as a target audience, regardless of what the form of communication is. It could be advertising. It could be messaging in the form of information. You just take account of both the device and the individual you're dealing with at the other end of that and make sure you can reach him or her. The fact is, if you planned only at the upper level, you'd miss that entire audience range underneath. That's one of the possible things that can happen. If you think about the Web or the Internet in too narrow a sense, you're going to cut out that entire tier that you could have easily reached. That's what this is about.

Tish

I've got a question. Would WebTV really have happened as big as it has so far if it weren't bankrolled? It's not demand that's driving it right now; it's largely subsidized. Are we not seeing other products saturate the market as quickly? That's sort of a supply-and-demand thing. Most of these things cost so much to develop and to distribute, say, Palm Pilot or whatever it is. It's a very valuable tool, but without it being available to the masses and the development costs and the distribution costs being bankrolled by somebody, is it really going to happen, this convergence, as quickly as we think it is?

Bryan

I don't know if it's a question of quickly, but I think what was important about WebTV is that it defined a new type, and that type is going to survive. It's going to evolve and change. It was important to take that stab. Create a device that's very low cost, that's hassle-free for a consumer who doesn't want to deal with the complexity of a computer. That was an important thing to do. I can also envision that we might potentially be dealing with devices that deliver audio messages. If you're dealing with a computer that's small enough to be voice-only, that's something you'd want to take account of in the future. Rather than thinking about the consumer, we think about business people who are carrying devices around—people we aren't reaching or thinking about, because we tend to think of their devices as being communication tools for that individual's use in the other direction. But now we have a down channel that allows us to reach that individual as well.

Dan

The benefit to the company is you have both an *up* and *down* channel, this interactivity that allows you to create a relationship with your customer, which you don't have in the standard mass media.

Tish

Very good point. This is a very exciting time in that if the CEOs are very clear on what their business needs are and they are able to pull away any restrictions or any scarcity of resources or any of those typical things that guide decision making and partner with an Internet partner, they can architect something that could potentially really change the way they do business and really drive that convergence. But it's going to be an evolved thing. The convergence isn't going to happen all at once. There'll be a lot of intermediary steps, but as long as you keep that business need clear, you should be able to deliver on it in an evolving way.

Dan

Convergence is still a ways off, and we're still dealing with today's issues. I don't know if anyone's really prepared yet. If you're a CEO and you're looking for a company to help you with convergence, you might be a little too early. Just concentrate on the basics right now. I met with a company who wanted to set up a Web site. One of my first suggestions was, let's look at your marketing plan, and they didn't have a very good marketing program. I asked them not to do a Web site and just do their marketing right first. I'd like to see companies just get their interactive or their Internet efforts set straight first and their traditional marketing efforts set straight before they start worrying about convergence because that'll come, but it's not here yet.

Jesse

Do you think WebTV is enough of an audience for some of these companies that we need to be addressing it now and in the short term?

Dan

It's 1 percent of America.

Jesse

Again, I ask the question, is it a viable audience for us to address? Do you want to develop for this medium now?

Bryan

It's a good point, Jesse, because the issue is going to be how many people do you want to disappoint by not being able to reach them with the device of their choice. Should you, in fact, start experimenting now at relatively low cost? That really becomes the issue. If you're sitting at home as one of those 250,000 people and you happen to be part of a group that's important to reach and you're not being reached, that's potentially a huge lost opportunity.

Tish

Take an example. Let's say banking. That's a real-life example of something that reaches almost everybody. How would you counsel a bank manager on the effects of convergence and what they should think about?

John

What this ultimately means is that we need to move away from interactivity, a way a consumer interacts with business from a physical base location. That's a big thing. Perhaps in the future you can do your banking with your beeper or with a device that's there. First of all, you separate the physical locality. You don't have to be physically at a certain place. Consumers are going to have much more choice in terms of where and how they get to interact with business. That's a new way of thinking that corporations must start adopting in order to deal with some of the emerging issues.

Jesse

One other thing we need to address, again playing devil's advocate, is that what we have today is a very, very fickle audience. Can you really afford to alienate an empowered audience? They are empowered because everybody can publish on the Internet. Even one person publishing on the Internet can be incredibly detrimental to your businesses reputation and can severely damage it. So often you need to consider the negative potential of not addressing even a small demographic.

Bryan

You have to look at them as a community. There's a whole world that's about WebTV, and that's their access to the Internet. That's what the Web means to them. It's really important to look at it from that side. Not just slice and dice numbers and look at them from the other perspective, but consider what they are all about from a psychographic standpoint.

John

Companies need to move away from traditional demographic analysis. You cannot say I'm going to try to reach people who are in this age group, male and within a certain income bracket mainly because you're seeing communities that are formed by common interests. The actual demographics in terms of the people may be completely different.

It's important to try to reach some of the audience. At the same time, this field is changing rapidly and we don't really have a clear winner. WebTV may win, but, again, there's no guarantee because it is such a small market currently. While it's important to examine this market and the results that may come out of it, it's also important to keep in mind these products may not be here. Many products are going to fail, and you have to recognize that fact and be prepared to deal with that also.

Conquering the Digital Frontier: Seven Issues to Face En Route to Web Success

Bryan

It's rapid evolution, then, as opposed to advance planning.

Jesse

Yes.

Key Recommendations

- Keep business and communication needs in the forefront.
- Think beyond the browser or Web site in terms of potential opportunities for delivering your business message.
- Deal with scalable standards that will allow you to take advantage of future innovations.
- Know your target audience: create a database to track user preferences so you can use the right tool to deliver the right message to the right appliance.

Topic 3: E-Commerce

E-commerce will fundamentally change the way we buy and sell products and services. *How will your company cash in?*

John

This is a huge question. There are a lot of issues that are going to come out of this, everything from moving to a cashless society with electronic commerce to the way this is going to affect corporations in terms of how they order, fulfill, distribute, and market products or services.

Jesse

Legislation and tax issues.

Dan

This Christmas I didn't step into a store. I did all my shopping from my laptop in bed one evening. That fundamentally changed the way I shopped. It was a great experience because I was able to find things for my whole family that I could have spent a week shopping for physically.

Tish

It's important to think about what you bought as well, because it's supported nicely for certain consumer products but not for others.

Dan

That's right. It's not for everyone.

Adam

Our clients see e-commerce as an extension of their businesses. Giant Step has been working with clients to establish business-to-consumer and business-to-business solutions. Some of our clients are using the opportunity to redefine the roles they play in the brick-and-mortar world, while others are greatly enhancing their current offline relationships. We are looking to help our clients manage the transitions and maximize profits and cost savings from their online efforts.

Bryan

What can you realistically sell in this way? I was very surprised General Motors had made the move to car selection through the Web as rapidly as they did. But one thing they did very well was to figure out a way to preserve the relationship they had with their dealers and distributors so they were not cut out of the chain. There's still value for them to add to that process, but it is no longer an issue of direct selling; it's an issue of support. It changes the nature of the dealership.

John

One way we think about e-commerce is in terms of presale, the actual sales transaction, and wholesale support. These are three related yet different aspects of commerce.

Tish

The buying experience on line really sucks. We're dealing with a computer company right now and helping them to rearchitect their buying experience on line. You can do everything on line, but the experience sucks. It's incorrect, it takes too long, et cetera, et cetera. My advice to a CEO right now is not only to think about the philosophical aspects but also try it, see if it's a pleasurable experience. You may have everything on line, and then the experience is so bad you've lost an opportunity. That's very much a here-and-now thing for them to think about.

Bryan

You're basically saying look at the functions of what the middleman did and make sure that experience is translated into what you're doing on line so you don't lose that.

Chapter 9
Conquering the Digital Frontier: Seven Issues to Face En Route to Web Success

Tish

Or enhance it in some way, and that's just in the basics of how the site is built and how you interact with it. For example, suppose you're comparing two PCs on line or something like that and you want to compare price—can you really? That's really fundamental. If you increase RAM, how does the price shake out? In addition to thinking about the middleman and all that sort of thing, what's your site like, and is it really moving you ahead?

Dan

Right. When they build e-commerce sites, a lot of companies take their flat catalog and put it on line. You're doing nothing more than if you were to read a catalog, which is not an exciting experience. A lot of people like to walk into stores, interact with the salesperson, interact with people in the store. Some of the experiments we started this last year tried to use virtual worlds and marry them to e-commerce so consumers can get in and pick an avatar and have other real people in their shop. You have a store person there that they can walk up to, talk to, interact with, interact with other people who have similar tastes to theirs, and get advice just as if they were to walk into a real store.

Tish

That's not at all how we design. We're not trying to simulate an experience.

Dan

No. I'm saying most people go and just put their paper catalogs on line.

Tish

I'm even challenging a design of an avatar experience. The way we design is very different from that. We try to get to the essence of the shopping experience. Are you trying to simulate what a consumer's physical experience will be within a store, or are you getting at the essence of what is it that makes a person buy or not buy? It may be a subjective thing, and perhaps a certain type of client would like that. We don't do it like that; we don't try to simulate that.

Jesse

The Internet is a great research tool. That's what many of us use it for. It's incredible for comparison shopping. But, there's still a fear that people want to see, touch, and feel what they're going to buy. Where the Internet comes into play with that and can override that is if there's an incredible value added, which is typically in cost savings. Here you really need to take into consideration the ability to increase sales by reaching your audience. You're going to need to pass along the reduction in costs. If you don't, they're going to take the extra effort and go to the stores.

Tish

I disagree. It's not always the cost savings. I liked where you were going on the research aspect, the depth of knowledge. When people go into some stores and ask anybody about anything, they don't know. They don't know a thing. It seems to us from our research that it's not necessarily just cost that could potentially create a sale on line but also the depth of information and the comparison and the research tool.

Bryan

We're drifting into issues of convenience for commerce and not focusing on the middleman. You're basically saying in that situation it's going to apply pressure for people who are running retail outlets to better train their staff to be able to be responsive and be more knowledgeable.

John

There are two kinds of shoppers. We can see that especially on line. There are the people who know exactly what they want, and they want to get it with the least amount of trouble. Their purpose is to purchase a specific product they know. The other type is people who browse. In the browsing mode, all that can be replicated on line is most often best done when a person goes to a mall or a physical store. Online commerce for most companies that have existing products will probably be a complementary strategy. None of us are saying this should be your sole distribution medium. But you need to be aware there are always going to be malls and physical stores. In fact, we work with some companies who are looking at creating a physical presence in addition to their online presence.

Bryan

What happens to that physical presence as a consequence of selling on line? How does that affect the real-world situation?

John

In the case of the users who know exactly what they want, they want to shop on line probably because of convenience—possibly lower cost—but mostly they want the convenience, and they don't want to deal with the hassle of driving and dealing with other people.

Conquering the Digital Frontier: Seven Issues to Face En Route to Web Success

Tish

We're focusing a lot on consumer products. One of the things we talked about was cost savings. This is where we really get into the heat of the middleman, the potential to cut that guy out or change what that guy does. There's a tremendous potential for cost savings.

Jesse

Do we need to then open up this discussion to cover extranets as well as business-to-business solutions?

Bryan

Absolutely.

Dan

The question is, how will your business cash in with e-commerce? There are a couple things. Jesse bought a computer on line. If that computer seller provided a pleasurable experience for Jesse, he is more likely to come back. It's building a relationship with Jesse, enticing him to come back. One of the mistakes our clients make is they put in too little information instead of too much. People on the Internet want more information, not less.

Tish

It's not a brochure.

Dan

Put in as much information as possible. Make it a pleasurable experience. You need to create a relationship. You need to promote this site in order to bring Jesse back. Whether it's business to business or business to consumer. Then use that information to enhance your other channels of distribution—your physical store or whatever—to figure out what products people want. How are they buying them? How they are using them? How often are they buying them? What's the motivation for purchasing things? What's the cycle? Those are the key things if you want to cash in. Then the biggest thing is to do it now. You want to start building the database so six years from now you have a strategic weapon your competitor doesn't have. You'll have the advantage of knowing who your customers are, what they're buying. You'll be able to build a bigger audience and build "intellifriend" programs and other cross-marketing programs.

Jesse

To follow up, the key here is relationship. One attribute that really sends me to a store is to have a personal relationship, to know who I'm dealing with. However, you can replicate that on line if you're proactive with your customers so once they buy something, you stay in contact. You help them upgrade—all the value-adds. You continue that relationship. I'm not seeing a lot of that now.

Dan

Anonymity is another issue. What if I want to be anonymous? What if I want to buy, God forbid, girdles or something like that, and I don't want anyone to know? I can remain anonymous.

Bryan

Jesse's point is extremely well taken; it's the key issue. It's the nature of what is happening to that relationship that you really need to look at. Taking a proactive stance is the only way you can effectively deal with that.

John

But be polite about it too. Give them choice.

Jesse

It must be a requested relationship.

Bryan

Right.

Tish

It's interesting how we all agree on the big picture, but the implementation is totally different. We're still totally experimenting on how to fulfill that.

Jesse

The one thing that really disappointed me about what happened with push technology was it wasn't the technology that was bad; it was the way it was handled. A BackWeb, for instance, which has a polite distribution technology and personalized delivery capability, enables a company to be proactive with its support. But nobody's going to touch any push technology now because they're getting spammed by it and marketers don't know how to use it.

Bryan

It becomes an issue of making sure when you're setting up systems like this that you can track and maintain a relationship with the customer. It's not just fulfillment. It's about learning more about who that individual is and being able to service him or her at a higher level than you could in a normal retail situation. It shouldn't be looked at as a low-cost measure to get product out to someone more cheaply. It's a way to enhance the buying experience.

Key Recommendations

- Proactively evaluate the pros and cons of using e-commerce yourself so you will know how to make doing business on your site a pleasurable experience.
- Put as much information as possible on your site to enhance its use as a research tool.
- Begin creating relationships and building a client database now.

Topic 4:   Technology

Technology will continue to mutate at a furious pace. *How will you manage change?*

Dan

Here's the issue: a lot of companies look at their Internet efforts as a technology effort. It is not a technology effort; it's a communication effort. It's about talking to people, vendors, whoever, processing information, communication. Whether it be purchasing, whether it be research, whatever it is you're trying to do with the Internet, the goal is to lay down the foundation of how to communicate. The technology will adapt to that. Clients will come in, and we know when they've been on an airplane because they've read the latest *PC Computing*. They pull out an article and want us to put the latest technology into their Internet site. It makes no sense. It doesn't really fit. The idea is to communicate.

Bryan

The fundamental shift is from *how* questions to *why* questions. Why are you doing it as opposed to how are we doing it.

Dan

To cope with the furious change of technology, the key is to have a plan and lay the foundation of what you want to do. Then, as new technology comes, map that to your plan.

Bryan

Right.

Dan

Does this fit in with my plan? Does this enhance the goals and the objectives I've laid out?

Jesse

Have a message and find the technology to implement it rather than find the technology and then create a message based on the capabilities of the technology.

Dan

We've literally had people walk in and say, "I'd like you to build a Web site, and I want you to build it on this platform, using these tools." "But what do you want it to say?" "Well, I haven't thought about that yet."

Bryan

You want to get out of the fire-ready-aim mode and make sure you're doing it the right way around.

Dan

Usually the last thing we talk about with a client is technology. Don't even talk about it. Don't bring it up. We'll deal with that later after we figure out what we want to do.

John

We don't start with the technology at all. We say, "What are the business objectives you're trying to achieve, and what are some of the strategies we use in achieving that?" Then you bring it back to technology. The caveat is, you take a larger context of how the technology serves a business goal, not just in terms of communication but in terms of infrastructure and operational capabilities. From order fulfillment to merchandising. If you look at how that type of thing may affect the company, a lot of times *how* will affect *why*. A lot of times you will have a fundamental change that has such an impact that you may have to look at your business process at that point and say we're going to have to go back and look at this whole thing and change what we've done because of the technology and how it's impacting not just us, but our competitor.

Bryan
Can you give us a specific example?

John
One is electronic software distribution (ESD), as well as how companies are starting to tie into suppliers and vendors within an existing network in terms of getting your supplies, how to communicate the just-in-time inventory concepts. For example, before, if you ran out of a certain internal supply, you had to check inventory, call the vendor, order, have it delivered. Whereas now, you may have a direct line that ties in when supplies go low. It will communicate directly to your vendor to say, "Restock this." You could even put business logic in that may say, depending on the season and how our sales forecast is going, "Give us extra, give us less, give us new colors…."

Jesse
The issue is, how do you deal with forward compatibility, which is always going to be an issue. What's too far ahead and what's just far enough ahead? Do you wait for the right thing?

Bryan
There's no way you can anticipate everything that potentially is going to happen. It's just unrealistic to think the world works that way. It's an issue of being nimble and making sure you've built enough flexibility into your planning to be able to take account of as many changes as possible. That's the best anyone can do.

Tish
We're not suggesting just the automation of a current business process, but to step back. It's very easy for us to just think about the business. But eventually you have to jump in. Then you really need to look at technology and understand design. Traditionally, the management information system (MIS) departments of organizations have been overworked and understaffed

because they're normally not part of the core competency of whatever a particular company is trying to execute. If a company is selling shoes, it has put all its money into selling shoes, and the MIS that supports that is traditionally very low on the food chain. With that in mind, it's very important that executives start to move a little more into the areas of design of technology so they can help to direct their MIS groups and appreciate how important the MIS group is. The technology is important. That way you can also design scalability, and that helps to have the technology people and the business people much closer together in their communication.

Dan

When I started the fine.com International four years ago, I went out and taught myself HTML and started picking up the other technologies. I already knew how to program databases. Now a lot of the technology has surpassed my knowledge. When I go back into our pit, I see these kids just cranking away on the Dynamic HTML and Java and VBScript. It's impossible to keep up with it as an executive. I feel bad for the CEO of a major corporation that has to do that or even wants to do it. The key is is to find a partner. This may sound self-serving, but find someone who can come in and understand what your business is and figure out how to apply technology to your business instead of technology for technology's sake.

Tish

We're sort of throwing technology into this bucket, and there are many different steps in looking at technology. HTML vs. fundamental database design. It's very different. If you look at a four-step process, there is strategy, analysis, design, and implementation. What I'm suggesting is that executives don't need to go and learn HTML. But if they can move into that process at the strategy stage and potentially the analysis stage and a little bit of design, then they can start thinking about where their business is going and let the implementers implement.

Dan

If you're a CEO, it's almost impossible to keep up with all the little technologies out there that could help you. You do need to be at the strategic level and the design level and then know how to go out and find the people to implement it. Rely on people who can come in and help you understand your business, not just technology, and people who can understand what your strategic goals are.

Conquering the Digital Frontier: Seven Issues to Face En Route to Web Success

Adam

We need to remain agnostic about new technology: it has to be proven before we will believe. We utilize change when it has a user benefit to it, and only if it seems to have a reasonable shelf life. We keep our clients informed of the various changes but recommend only those products that are relevant to their objectives and are quality investments.

Bryan

It's really important to potentially be able to help a corporation reengineer how to approach its inside technology because that's going to be left behind. Once your job is done as vendor and you walk away, there'd better be a support system in place to make sure it doesn't fall apart. It becomes an issue for decision makers. It's actually an advantage to realize technology changes in shifts, and you don't have to be rigid about how you apply it. Traditionally, that is where things go wrong inside organizations. Technology is looked at as something that essentially is stratified and you do it only one way. You can't grow. People have to change their attitudes toward what that means inside the organization so that MIS does not become an enclave to prevent change but rather enables it and learns to be more flexible and responsive. If that doesn't happen, then anything that's done inside the organization won't really improve.

John

There's such a potential for technology to aid in increasing profit. Number one, experiment, because things are changing. In a changing environment you have to experiment and try new things because if you don't, you're not going to find out. The second is you have to prepare for failures. Inevitably, not all your trials are going to succeed. That's part of the process, and all of us who are sitting at this table probably understand we all have our failures. It's possible some of these things may not work because we're trying them for the first time. We're the pioneers; there's no one ahead of us. It's important to realize that, and that's a cultural change in a lot of companies.

Tish

Although I personally agree with John's comment, there could be a lot of pushback from the masses. They kind of want someone else to do that, to make those mistakes for them. It will be a hard sell.

Dan
I'll be radical. I've got two final comments on this. One is that we should move toward simplicity. Yesterday in the car, we were driving along, and someone was talking about a site that had four different operating systems on it. It was crazy. Simplicity for me is how can we keep a site simple so people can maintain it and we can scale it. I also push for standardization. Let's just get over the politics and the religious fights here and say, if we can standardize on certain platforms, then we can make it easier for all of us to develop and to integrate our systems and actually build more powerful communication tools.

Jesse
Let's not lose sight that more important than the technology is the messaging, and this needs to integrate well with the traditional message. This is the Internet, and you can take advantage of technology to expand upon that message and create an interactive environment, or a personalized environment for it. But it starts with the message, with a marketing campaign.

Tish
It's not all about marketing. It seems in this industry that a lot of folks come in from the ad agency world, but there are other people coming into it from all sorts of different angles, from consulting, from back-end systems integration. When I talk with colleagues, the majority of the folks in this industry are coming from the ad agency world, but there are more and more players coming from the different ends.

Jesse
At the same time, in everything you do there is a message. In every interaction there is a form of communication. The most minute interaction still reflects on that corporate culture, and you want to have at every point some consistency in your message. Whether it's a marketing campaign or whether it's a human resources outreach, you want that synergy there.

Tish
Are you suggesting it's content-related?

Jesse
To a certain degree, it is content.

Conquering the Digital Frontier: Seven Issues to Face En Route to Web Success

Tish

What I'm suggesting is it can be a usability issue. It doesn't matter how pretty and how well branded it is.

Jesse

You're just saying it has to be integrated.

Tish

Yeah.

Jesse

They're both very, very crucial aspects.

John

Don't worry so much about those HTML 3.2 specs, 4.0 specs, or whatever. What is the objective you're trying to achieve, and do these things fulfill that?

Bryan

It's also about communicating and making sure the corporation engineers itself for change. Change is inevitable.

Dan

How will you manage change? You have to wait to make sure your audience is ready to change before you do. If you try to go out and push the limit and say, we're going to standardize on Internet Explorer 4.0, and damn be the rest of you; you have to adapt to me, and only 25 percent of your audience can get IE 4.0, you've screwed yourself. You've got to be ready for your consumers to change.

Tish

But it's not all consumers.

Dan

It could be your employees. If your employees aren't ready for it, if your legacy systems aren't ready for it, you can't push ahead. You can push ahead, but you can only push ahead when people are ready to step up to the plate.

Jesse

If you have compelling enough content, they will come. If nobody pushes the boundaries, then we're stagnant.

Dan

Some people have to be out there pushing the boundaries. That's fine. Those people can go ahead, and they have the money to burn. That's their opportunity to do that. But for us, what we try to do is to be conservative. You've got to reach as much of the audience as you can. If you have to go without frames, if you have to go without Java… You have to wait until the majority of the audience catches up. That's the way we approach it. Other people approach it differently.

John

For your clients, that is their objective. That's the target market you're trying to reach.

Bryan

There are solutions we need in order to reach different audiences. There are technology solutions to make that possible. Active Server Pages, for example. It's a classic. You serve the appropriate content to the individual at the end if it serves the purpose of communicating your message more effectively.

John

Anytime you need to make a change, there's going to be inevitable resistance. But there are times when you're going to have to do it. You saw that to a certain extent with the layoffs and the restructuring that went on in the 1980s and the early 1990s. Those things will happen again. Sometimes it makes sense. It's going to be tough, but you've got to do what you've got to do.

Key Recommendations

- Plan the foundation of what you want to communicate, and map the technology to that.
- Remain flexible, and design for scalability.
- Understand Internet technology, and work with Internet development partners who understand your business.
- Integrate your internal technologies with your Internet efforts.

Topic 5:   Legal Issues

The global network may require a completely new level of legislation. *Will your business suffer or prosper?*

Dan

Frankly, I'm really worried about the legislation and the government stepping into the Internet. If they do, how that will screw up all these issues we've put in place for our customers. What we're trying to do is be proactive in keeping governments, not just the U.S. government, but *governments* out of this. It's something that's been successful so far. We've gotten pretty much the federal government and Al Gore to head up an issue that says, hands off, but we still have the state governments poking their noses in, putting taxes in, telling us what we can say, what we can't say. Other governments are poking their noses in, saying you can't distribute this kind of information in our country. It's a tough thing because it's going to call for an effective "U.N. of the Internet." And hopefully, if there is one, it won't mess us all up.

Bryan

Well, actually, for specific businesses, could we be more positive about this? Is there, in fact, an initiative a corporation could take to ensure its plans are not going to be compromised in the future by pushing for legislation?

Jesse

The problem is, states have their own initiatives. Unless there is across-the-board continuity, it's like having your corporations based out of Delaware for protection.

Bryan

Those are states' rights issues, though. They're never going to give up that ability to have their own legislation. It's a real problem because it needs to be a single point of law. Are you going to have a problem if you're actually advertising a product that's illegal in a state?

Jesse

Well, we've seen that with pornography, where the gentleman in one state puts pornography on line and because somebody views it in another state, he is now liable, and he's been arrested and tried for that.

John

If we're having a problem getting 50 states to agree on one thing, imagine trying to get all the other countries. This could be really fragmented around the world. How do you deal with the fact that someone in another place—another country, another state—can see and interact with your content and that laws in that locality affect the content you have and how you interact with your customers?

Dan

Any legislation would cause your company to suffer. Look at the track records of the government and the way it's stuck its nose in the legislation. Some of the stuff doesn't make any sense at all. Then there's the issue of being able to comply with that. When we set up our first big commerce site, the level of detail we had to go into to program for taxes on the city, state, and county levels was a nightmare. Then to have to deal with Canadian and Mexican and international…. That's easy right now. It's going to get worse.

Jesse

Let's look at the airline industry, for instance, and how much more secure it is for an individual to fly on a major airline out of a country such as the United States or Britain as opposed to, say, a third world country where the inspection standards and the regulations are different. Now, can legislation create a safer environment as some may argue for us and a safer environment to shop so consumers know they're going to get what they pay for?

Dan

It could provide that. However, you'd have to trade something off. Do you want to trade those things off or not? There are areas where legislation might help. For example, in e-commerce, if there were a common set of security protocols. The U.S. Post Office has talked about becoming our electronic post office and guaranteeing security, guaranteeing when I get a letter from you, I know it's from you, and helping eliminate spam or reclassifying it. There may be some ways where you could prosper, but generally if the entire world gets together and decides to legislate the Internet, businesses are in trouble.

John

There is going to be some of type of legislation. It's pretty inevitable that will happen. What hopefully this level of legislation will do is to create some standards that will cut across the line. The existing laws are inadequate to deal with the issues we're facing. That's one of the reasons for the pornography case that gets tried in a completely different place, or in certain countries using certain words or depicting a certain figure may be very defamatory, for example. At that point the legal issues start to come in. Hopefully this will help companies prosper. But at the same time, they're also going to have to suffer because that may require changes in what they do. This is going to change.

Bryan

We shouldn't always be negative when we look at this. If there were legislation to allow something like the Internet Free Market Act to make sure you could sell anywhere you wanted to, that could be a huge benefit. If you don't have that in place and this becomes a serious way of doing business and you're locked out of markets because that legislation wasn't enacted or put in place, then you suffer—suffer dramatically.

Dan

What we have to do is almost predict what's going to happen. Take a look at the U.N. How well has it put together legislation and enforced a common set of standards in the world? It's done a really bad job. How are we going to get people like Saddam Hussein to sit at the table and figure out what can be said on the Internet and what can't be said on the Internet and agree with the U.S. and Canada, Mexico, and Japan, and Europe? It's going to be a bad thing except for when it can protect people against, for example, fraud and certain other issues. But there are already laws there to protect people.

Bryan

Well, that's actually my point. This becomes a strategic question as opposed to our being able to answer it right here. What legislation exists now that, if it were enforced with the Internet, would actually cause you to suffer or prosper? Then take the next step. Should that become a part of a general legislation to make sure either that it is not applied to the Internet or that it is?

Dan

Imagine 1000 lawyers from around the world sitting in a room and figuring out what we can and can't do on the Internet. Is that a good or a bad thing?

Tish

This orange juice carton has nutritional facts on it. That is sort of along the same lines of what you were saying. If there were a protocol or a standardization, a better-business type of legislation, no matter what your bells and whistles were, the bottom line would be the product costs X, consumers pay taxes here, or whatever. Then there is some potential for some upside as well, which is to standardize on business practices.

Bryan

Do we need to focus on business legislation? What about standards?

Tish

The other thing I was thinking about was standards with things like education. Suppose universities had to offer all their courses on line. There's some potential upside to that because there could be access to universities around the world for people who normally wouldn't have access. Then again, nobody can afford a computer who can't go to university, so it probably wouldn't work.

John

But perhaps it could be public access.

Tish

Yeah, public access is sort of where I'm getting at with that. But who pays for that is the kicker.

Dan

Well, in order to put this label on this orange juice box, they had to raise taxes to create an agency to maintain that thing.

Tish

That's not necessarily a bad thing. It can be short-term pain and long-term gain.

John

We should look at it positively. There's already a trend toward a globalization of products in the world. People are standardizing. Tish brought up a great example of the labels. Corporations are already aware of a lot of these issues, and they're at first being made to standardize. Perhaps this is just an outgrowth of globalization. Perhaps it may be a lot easier than we foresee.

Dan
Yeah. That could be a really good thing. I just don't see how it's going to happen on a global basis. The U.S. can step up and say, "We're going to legislate the world." The world's going to say, "No way." We're in for a little bit of suffering before we start prospering from global legislation.

Jesse
The current protocols that are in place for your business are going to apply to the Internet. If not now, soon.

Adam
If history is any indication, once global issues are impacted by legislation, we all may suffer. It is still too early to tell what limits may or may not be imposed on the global network, and probably unwise to guess as to whether that hypothetical legislation will create prosperity or suffering.

Dan
I'm really interested to see what's going to happen when Clinton gets out next term if the Republicans get in. They've been pushing to start legislating the Internet and start taxing it. It'll be interesting to see if they get that through and what starts happening with this.

Bryan
What about the possibility of taxation of Internet Service Providers (ISP)? Access would become much more expensive. Are there potentially haves and have-nots as a consequence of that? Does that affect the customers you can reach because they can no longer afford access? Those are huge issues.

John
Are there technological solutions that may help deal with some of these issues? Right now it's really difficult to stop people from foreign countries from accessing Web pages if they want to get in. But if you want to make changes at that level, that has to be changed at the router protocol level. Those things are possible. There's a larger issue. The Internet has been decentralized, and no one really controls it. We're starting to see if there is going to be some type of overall structure, some kind of centralized decision making. I know I'm wary of that.

Dan

My company built the extranet for the Washington State Liquor Board. You should have seen the 60 years' worth of laws, judgments, and rules that had to be built into the database to comment sale of liquor in the state. It was this huge three-ring binder. Just to sell liquor in the state. Now, imagine having to take that and apply that on the Internet and then how many different products we'd have to do that for, cigarettes and all the others….

Bryan

What we're saying is that it is probably inevitable that will happen. It hasn't been enforced to date. What happens with virtual vineyards, for example, if they try to deliver alcohol in Connecticut? It's against the law there. It's a felony to sell alcohol in that way. It can't be done by mail or delivered to your home. It has to be bought and purchased in a state-controlled store. Those are the kinds of things you need to look at when you're planning; that way you can make sure you're not in potential violation of existing legislation.

Key Recommendations

- Tread carefully.
- Stay informed.

Topic 6:   Distribution

The Internet will open new channels of distribution. *What are the challenges and opportunities your business will face?*

Jesse

The primary issue is going to be cannibalization of existing distribution channels.

Dan

You've got a company like Nordstrom, and one of its prime motivations for not going on line is that it's worried it will draw the people out of the stores and get them to start purchasing on line. Then Nordstrom would have all this expensive brick and mortar set up around the country, staffed to the hilt and ready to roll, but the people aren't coming through the doors. The opportunity is to use the Internet to create a new audience, both geographically and demographically. Bring those people into the Internet, and then also use the Internet to enhance your stores so you can push people in through the revolving doors as well as getting them to buy on line. It becomes a complementary business vs. one that cannibalizes your current status.

Jesse

Complementary is the key word. There was a study that showed one in five people who walked onto a car show floor bought a car. If you think about that for a second, the Internet is an incredible medium to drive traffic to the showroom floor. But I don't think one in five that go to your Web site are going to buy. Your odds are going to be better if you get them on the showroom floor.

Adam

We will have to work closely with our clients to manage the conflicts of interest these new channels create. As they wrestle to maximize online profits without alienating their traditional distribution channels, there is an opportunity for us to help them use the Web to effectively build their businesses. We can also help clients to use new channels to integrate into their traditional channels so all parts of an enterprise benefit.

Tish

There's a great article *The Economist* put out I think on May 10 last year looking at how the middleman is, in fact, not gone but is evolving. Amazon.com is a great example of that. It can be an incredibly lucrative evolution. My advice to a senior executive would be to discuss the issue with an existing line of distribution and suggest ways that new lines of revenue could be realized. Not have it as a negative experience but a positive experience, and to work with middlemen to figure out what that's going to be.

Jesse

Several things could happen. One, it then becomes incumbent on current channels of distribution to provide more of a value-add. Or else, you can use the Internet as the distribution channel for that value-add, and then, therefore, you are again working in a complementary fashion.

Dan

Look at some of the challenges and opportunities of cutting out the middleman. One of the challenges is the middleman has always provided a value. If it wants to stay in place, it has to add value. If a company decides to eliminate the middleman, then it has to be willing to step up to the plate. It's going to have to reapply some of the money it's going to save by cutting the middleman out to support a new customer. The opportunity for companies is if you can go direct to the customer, then you get to know the customer, and then you can serve that customer better, hopefully. You can start building a relationship. You get face to face with the customer. The challenge is, a lot of companies are not prepared to step up to the plate and service the customer.

Jesse

We need to also keep in mind, though, that the middleman for the retail outlet is probably better equipped to handle issues such as new customer generation than the Internet, which currently is much more reactive. Your Web site is there to accommodate the customer that comes to you. You can't just let go of existing distribution channels. You're still going to need to support them, which again brings it back to the need to complement.

John

A good recommendation might be to look at doing a pilot program. We realize with some of the sites we built that the client hasn't thought about something, and they find out once we build it. The site may change in terms of what a company's initial expectations were once they actually have a program set up and running.

Jesse

It's crucial to educate and allow your middleman to participate in that pilot program because quite often what I've seen is the instant reaction of, "Oh, no, you're competing with me." There's a lack of knowledge of how they can work together. Perhaps by taking on traffic on the Internet, you are also branding the middleman. It's an additional opportunity to brand your company and your product. People are going to go there for research, but they're still going to feel uncomfortable, and they're still going to walk into the stores, and they're going to avail themselves of that middleman. You can work well together.

Conquering the Digital Frontier: Seven Issues to Face En Route to Web Success

Tish

In following that thought, the notion of the channel is very important. There is the opportunity currently to use that as the "field" in the feedback loop for product evolution. It shouldn't be a knee-jerk reaction, but rather an evolution. "You scratch my back, I'll scratch yours. I need field information as a supplier of software."

John

A lot of companies are getting that actual feedback information from the consumers. For example, let's take a product that's sold by a third party merchandiser, a retailer. What would be very important is for you to get that information in terms of how well does your product sell, what kind of feedback do you get from your customers. There are companies that are great at that. They get instant information at the point of sale, and analyze that data, even on a daily basis, to look at the demands they have and how well a certain product is doing. That shortens the overall cycle in terms of how well you're able to make decisions. Everything is there—R&D of a certain product, how well does it meet the market expectation, how well does this advertising effort work. That's one of the opportunities that would come from looking at the channels of distribution.

Dan

The opportunity here is for manufacturers to get to know who their customers are and to help them get better customer service. There's a theory that says 20 percent of your customers account for 80 percent of your business. We did a study for a company, a manufacturer of car antennas. We found that one percent of their customer base accounted for 90 percent of their sales. One percent! Still, they couldn't tell who those customers were because they had a distribution system that didn't allow them to find out what the names of those customers were. They weren't effectively helping their customers because they didn't know who were the customers they had to keep and what were their issues. By cutting the middleman out or by evolving to a more direct system, they were able to get closer to those customers and really hold onto them and then help other customers move up into that category by trying to mirror them and show them the benefits of selling more of their product vs. their competitors. The Internet provides a great opportunity for that. But the challenge is, can it actually replace the value the middleman gave? The other huge opportunity is geographic distribution. For most small businesses, 95 percent of their business comes from within a 10-mile radius. If you really have a valuable product and you're able to pick up new geographic regions, the world is in your palm. You can grab that with the Internet and move to it quickly, where you could never have done that before through any other type of advertising.

Tish

Here's an issue, a real-life situation. Let's take the financing of cars or trucks. Normally it takes forever for all the paperwork to go through on financing. We built a system to help automate that. Who pays for that? What I'm getting at is the evolution of your relationship with your middleman. Who's responsible for financing that? Is it the parent company, is it a 50-50 split?

Jesse

That's a decision that's going to happen internally company by company. But if you think about it, if you are speeding up the bureaucracy, you're freeing people to participate more in new business generation and sales. Everybody stands to gain.

Tish

Who pays for it?

Jesse

My guess is the parent company. Maybe it's amortized across the board.

Tish

So far it's been the parent company, but I bet you if there were some way of amortizing it or whatever, you'd see a lot more of that happening.

Jesse

Let's keep in mind that a distribution channel is not necessarily related to just sales. It's customer retention issues, it's customer support. It's being proactive in areas that the middle person cannot be. Perhaps then it's taking the relationship that's initiated by the middleman and continuing it in a more viable and cost-effective medium, which is the Internet, wherever possible.

Tish

Here's another situation. The shoe industry is very paper-based right now, and the retailers and the manufacturers and everybody use faxes and phone. There's an opportunity for the wholesaler to talk directly to the retail store.

Then there are these holding companies in between. There are so many mom-and-pops in that industry still. Who should pay for the opportunity for these mom-and-pop shops to get on line and order? Should it be the manufacturer? Should it be a person in the distribution chain? Or should it be the mom-and-pops?

Dan
Who's going to benefit the most?

John
There are some models for this. Intel for example. It does comarketing. If you're making a computer with an Intel chip, it will pay for a portion of your advertising.

Jesse
It's co-op marketing, just like it's co-op distribution.

John
Yeah, exactly. You may start to see some of these types of co-op marketing efforts on line.

Dan
When we talk about distribution, we're also talking about communication. How are we getting our information that's being distributed to us differently or enhanced or complementary to other areas? There was an article in *USA Today* about content and the challenges these folks were facing in terms of attracting subscribers and the issues that face those content delivery folks. They're perhaps a little too forward. They're not there yet.

Bryan
I wanted to actually narrow it to just talk about what television networks are using this for, and just very briefly to touch on the experiments NBC is doing with content, where it's extending its show brands into Internet versions and using that as a means to essentially pilot concepts. NBC actually had for the first time a crossover from one of those Web shows to broadcast. The character worked out successfully on the Web, and now that character is appearing on air. It opens up very interesting channels for NBC to think about doing television in a different way, which now includes direct viewer response as opposed to the abstracts it's had to deal with through metering systems. The company can now hear directly from the audience and cater programming to those individuals.

John

As companies get more information directly from consumers, they may not be used to dealing with that kind of information.

Bryan

You have to be set up to respond to it.

John

A lot of times companies may get too much information. That's one of the challenges.

Jesse

I hate to use the cliché that content is king, but with distribution you're going to have to really fine-tune your message and give a very, very compelling message because that distribution medium is now open to every single individual. We're getting swamped. Let's bring spam into play here. I get probably 30 e-mails a day on some of my e-mail addresses, and rarely is one of them pertinent, but I have to go through them to make sure I don't miss it.

Dan

The thing that excites me about the new channels of distribution is electronic software distribution. If I make certain types of software or tools for people, and I want my clients to have the most recent update of those tools, there is the ability to be able to distribute that through the Internet on an ongoing basis. People can subscribe to it, and it would automatically update their computers. It's a terrific opportunity. The challenge is convincing your customers to trust you and allow you to take care of that for them.

Jesse

There are also some technological issues that come along with that when you're distributing software. There's the issue of that end user distributing it. That needs to come into play. Then there's also, Did that end user actually receive it? Was there any problem in the distribution itself via the Internet? Is there any way of monitoring and confirming that the customer actually received it and it works?

Dan

I just read an article about how they're starting to deliver music on line. They've set up the technology so you can download it and they can monitor what you're distributing and what you're not distributing. They're serializing the code. It's a great way because now I can go buy a song, bring it right down to my computer, and press it onto a digital video disc (DVD). I don't have to go to the store to buy it.

Bryan
There are opportunities that are just starting now. There's a company that will do compilation disks for you. You can select the tracks you want. The company cuts it and sends it to you. In the future, of course, you'd be able to get that directly.

Dan
In Japan they're putting digital video discs-recordable (DVD-Rs) in the computers already. It's just that the copyright laws here don't allow us to have the DVD-R, just the DVD. But if we could record that or put it onto a CD, then I can take that and just stick it in my car and play it. I know the technology is now coming up to snuff so they can monitor the distribution and charge for it. In fact, there are companies now that are starting to do that. That's a new way of distribution.

Bryan
From the content perspective, there's an opportunity for artists to be able to communicate directly with their audiences without a label or a corporation being in the way. That's an exciting opportunity as well. Not only is it a business opportunity, it's also a way of being able to get closer to the end user, to the client, to the customer, to the fan in a way that you never could before. It doesn't necessarily mean the label has no role. It means the artist has an opportunity to do something that's different.

Jesse
The other issue then becomes recording. We're getting really, really focused on one industry here with music.

Bryan
Think about it as information.

John
Traditional outlets will continue to be there. What I mean by "traditional" is that even if you're making direct sales, you're still going to—your record still may be on sale, possibly through a retail outlet that has a branded name. This is the place people come to buy records. You're going to see maybe more permutations of this. But these traditional music distribution channels will still exist, perhaps in new forms.

Bryan

Instead of just focusing on what we've said about music, we could think of it as any form of information you want to sell. It changes the nature of the relationship as a consequence.

Key Recommendations

- Work with middlemen to find ways to make your Internet efforts complement your other means of distribution.
- Create a pilot program to test the functionality you plan to implement and smooth the transition.

Topic 7: Liabilities and Accountabilities

The Internet can leave companies exposed to an entirely new realm of liabilities and accountabilities. *How will you protect yourself?*

Jesse

As Dan mentioned earlier, you have to have a crisis communications plan in place before you even get involved with distribution of anything on line because the power of the individual has never been greater than on the Internet. I've seen it time and time again: an individual can dramatically affect a company's sales or reputation on line by going into a company's chat room, service and support areas, or news groups, and it's impossible to stop an individual. You need to have a plan in place on how to respond in a situation like that.

Bryan

There's a couple that actually put up the Ford Truck Web site because they were complaining about a truck being defective. Ford refused to acknowledge there was a problem. They set up the Web site and got a recall. That's pretty powerful stuff.

Dan

My company is dealing with this with Amway right now. One of the reasons Amway wanted to have a much-improved corporate site was that its 1 to 1.2 million distributors were sick of the anti-Amway sites out there, which were actually better than the Amway sites, and were really poking a lot of holes into their strategy. What we had to do was examine the anti-Amway sites and figure out what are they saying and communicating, and how can we address that in a positive light on the Amway corporate site. It was really the anti-Amway sites that drove us to build a new site for Amway. But one of the things companies have to realize is they're exposed anyway in the real world. The Internet is no different. They can't be afraid to go on line. They can't be afraid to have a chat room. We were involved in one of the early implementations of the Microsoft Exchange site, the community site. There was this worry that if we set up a chat room in the Exchange site, people would start complaining and bitching and moaning about Exchange. In fact, the opposite was true. What happened was when people got in there and started bitching and moaning, the pro-Exchange people would jump all over them and push them out and make them feel uncomfortable. But it was a much better experience with the company because people really got to get in there and exchange their views and be open. Companies can really learn from that. Ford's problem wasn't that this couple put up an anti-Ford site. It was that it didn't listen to what its customers were saying.

Jesse
I've had the very same experience you've had where the proponents get in there and information typically does get corrected. A lot of companies do go to the Internet as an opportunity to have an interactive environment and get feedback. If that's true of your agenda here, and oftentimes it is, take it to the next step and really go out and solicit opinions. Don't just provide a Webmaster contact. If you're really interested in what the community is doing, go and take a look, check out not just your Web site, but go and look in the newsgroups and find out what people are saying about you, and respond to them.

Dan
Volvo put up its site in its early days a couple years ago. What it found was people were using it as an opportunity to complain. There are the lemon laws in a lot of states that if you complain, the manufacturer has to take care of it. Volvo was not physically prepared to handle the number of issues that arose through the Internet site, and so it had a negative experience with that. The thing we always tell our clients is get ready to transact and get ready to transact in a lot of ways. With Safeway we have a person who just answers e-mail all day long. That's all that employee does.

We've created prepared copy blocks that can be included in e-mail and have been approved by legal. We personalize the message, but we always make sure we include these canned messages so we cover ourselves.

Jesse

That's great that companies are taking that kind of a stance because how many others here have had the experience of clients not being equipped to take e-mail, so they don't want to put any contact information on their direct link. I, as a developer, end up getting that e-mail saying, "We want to contact these people." The audience will go to any lengths. The fact of the matter is, people need to be heard, and it's part and parcel of developing a Web site and going on the Internet: you need to give them an opportunity to contact you.

Bryan

Even without having a Web site set up, this exposure exists anyway.

Tish

I agree with Jesse. Acknowledge this is an issue and assign head count or plan around it, whether it's using resources within the company or external resources. The issues will change. The exposures will change as we change the architecture of the sites and use different methods. It's just important that it's identified.

Jesse

There's another issue I come up against all the time, which is how do you weight the input you receive? I've heard some people say for every e-mail you get, there are probably 100 people who are not contacting you but are having a similar experience. Do you react to every single e-mail you get? You can't. We're not in the position of handling customer service and support either. It's a fine line. Are you going to respond to everybody? When do you hit the panic button?

Dan

How are you going to protect yourself from all these liabilities? First of all, you need to find yourself a really good communications lawyer. Not only just the Internet but communications. Some of that's reasonable. One of the nice things about our lawyers is they say, "You *can* say that. It's okay, do it." You have to balance that risk. The other thing that is scary is not so much on the legal side but the liability of putting your business on line. The other day Amazon.com had an eight-hour blackout. Think of the money it lost during that time period.

Conquering the Digital Frontier: Seven Issues to Face En Route to Web Success

Jesse

E-trade. That was huge. When the recent market sell-off was happening, Web sites were overwhelmed and couldn't handle a large percentage of their traffic. There were a lot of disgruntled customers out there saying, "I lost a lot of money."

John

The important word in this topic is "accountabilities." Companies are being held accountable for the quality of the service or product they deliver. We've all talked about how the Internet really gives individuals power. It's so easy to communicate with a large number of people and to reach those audiences. Being on the Internet also shortens the time frame in which a company has to react. Things happen much, much faster. The interaction becomes instantaneous. Internally the company has to be set out to equip it. A lot of companies are not. You get a letter, there's a process you go through. But people expect to be responded to in a very short time frame on the Internet, and that's something that has to be taken into account.

Dan

If I'm a CEO or a CIO or a COO of a major corporation or any business, one of the big issues is commerce. Everyone is going out and trying to do e-commerce, and there's a whole level of security that needs to be put in place. If you are not prepared to deal with that, you should not go out and do e-commerce because you're putting yourself at risk and you're putting your customers at risk. You need to know your facts and have your ducks in a row before you go out and try to do any level of e-commerce.

John

Dan's point will extend to other types of transactions—for example, anytime you're exposing your customer's information. The Social Security site is a great example. At first it opened up its records so people could log on to its Web site, type in their Social Security number, and see what kinds of earnings they have. Currently, if you want to do it, you have to get a form and mail it. It takes weeks for something to be sent back. But again, the issue is, how secure is this?

Dan

Jesse, can you talk a little bit more about the crisis communications plan? Have you actually put one of those together? I'm just curious to find out, for example, how you prepare for things like that.

Tish

It's a PR thing.

Jesse

It's very much a PR thing. It's an Internet-savvy PR thing, and it varies by who your customer base is. But it does entail response. Knowing where your newsgroups are, knowing where your audience is on line, and being willing to instantly access that audience when you see a need and respond and be proactive and let people know they're being heard.

Dan

For Intel, when it found a flaw in the Pentium chip, to ignore it was the worst thing in the world. The next time there was a flaw, Intel acknowledged it right away and took care of the problem and the goodwill went much further. In your crisis plan you have to have ways of being able to acknowledge, being able to react.

Jesse

I've been on both sides. I've represented companies who had both responses. What ends up happening is you get this swell of public abuse. This is probably the wrong word. But, it carries on and on, and then it goes to the press because these people will then go to traditional media and it gets written up. Then you're really under fire for something that started as an individual who was unhappy on the Internet and may have found a bug. But, what's really happening here is when people are coming at you and saying there's a problem, if you're ignoring it, not only are you opening yourself up and you're not being accountable, but you're missing a golden opportunity. More often than not, your customers are in essence doing your R&D for you. This could and should be a positive experience. To say we don't have enough people to staff that right now is absolutely ridiculous. On the other hand, I've represented companies who've taken that crisis situation where their customers do go on the Internet and the newsgroup and start complaining about a product not working as it's been promoted to work, and I've had the client go on and instantly say, yes, you are right. We were unaware of it. Thank you very much. This is what we're going to do. It's a very, very scary thing to do because not only do you go specifically to where that accusation was made, but the idea is to go to where your customers are across the board because then you are proactively letting them know you are aware there is a problem, which you intend to address, and you are doing this before other customers start to surface publicly with the same issue. Chances are, if you are proactive, you also gain consumer loyalty. You also take the wind out of the sails of the individual publisher who's intent on taking the issue from the Internet to a more traditional medium such as the print press, where the damage is significantly greater.

Dan

I had kind of a personal experience with that when ACT, a contact management product now owned by Symantec, first went to Windows about five or six years ago. I was a member of CompuServe, and there was an ACT forum. When they went out, it was the worst product I've ever seen launched. It was so bad even the manual was not in line with what was in the actual program. It was terrible, and they ignored all of us, and it was an outpouring. It took about two weeks. You couldn't get through to ask any questions on the help line and no one knew any answers and everyone was guessing and everyone was badmouthing the company. It took two weeks until the president came on line on CompuServe to say they were fixing some of the problems. But he didn't apologize for it. Do you know how much inconvenience that company caused to so many thousands and thousands of people? They could have come out right away. The Internet exposed them because it allowed all these people to gather interactively and really share their emotions and bond together with this negative feeling toward the company.

John

That brings up something we touched on before. Community. One thing to be aware of is how it's so much easier to form a community on the Internet, and that is natural because of the cost—the traditional means of creating a community can be very expensive, and it's very geographically based. That is not true with the Internet.

Dan

I have a question for the group. One of the liabilities of being on line is that it makes it much easier for competitors to copy you. We've had some of our clients say, "We don't want to go on the Internet. We don't want to tell a lot of stuff on the Internet about our products because then our competition will find out and they'll imitate us."

Tish

I've heard that too.

Dan

How have you dealt with that, Tish?

Tish

It takes a while to get a company on line, and so you can sort of deal with it in an iterative way. We'll work through where their sensitivities are and that sort of thing because you don't get them on line overnight. We look at their competition, and we start to put a strategy together that's acceptable for them based on what they want to reveal and what they don't want to reveal. It also goes beyond that because whatever you show can also show your weaknesses as well as your strengths. It's part of a comprehensive strategic plan. Their sensitivities are just part of that plan.

Jesse

I had that happen as well. Companies may be reticent to let their clientele know on line in a public forum that there is a bug because they're afraid their competitors will take that information and manipulate it and promote it themselves. But, you've got to believe their competitors already have that information if the customers do. They're out buying your products. They're out talking to people. If the information is available from a 1-800 number, from a brochure, or from anywhere else, they're going to get it there just as well.

Tish

Here's another issue. We did a freight forwarding site for a small startup that did not want to put the competitive prices on line because it was too easy for its customers to compare in real time. It was very interesting because the business model sounded really great, but when it came time to actually roll it out, the company had to pull back on the real-time price comparison, the functionality.

Dan

Because of a fear of competitive threat it, in essence, yanked out the depth of the program.

Tish

Exactly.

Dan

Leaving it gutless for the customer to use.

Jesse

If you're not competitive, then maybe you need to look at the fact that you're not competitive instead of trying to stifle that information.

Tish

One of the things we do now, particularly with commerce types of comparisons, is to really show your strengths and allow the customer, the user, to differentiate. Really try to focus on the areas that differentiate your product. You should know where you stand with your competitors anyway and make sure you focus on that message. But that's a part of a total plan.

Jesse

It's safe to assume if your customers are on line doing research, either they are educated consumers or their intent is to become educated. It's time to stop underestimating consumers. Hiding or failing to disclose information is not going to be very viable anyway. They're going to find it and resent you all the more. Again, it is how you present yourself. If you are not competitive in price, then sell the attributes you are competitive on. But don't think you can hide information from them because then they're going to find out, and the damage is going to be even greater.

Tish

That fear you were mentioning is something that's pretty prevalent.

Dan

When I'm looking to acquire a company, I go to the Internet first, and I'll go through the list of Web sites. If they don't have a decent Web site, I will immediately click off and dismiss the company. Companies are exposing themselves if they don't have a good presence that reflects the company. Otherwise, people will just pass over them and immediately dismiss them. I'm acting like what I do is what everyone else does, but I can only assume other people act the same way.

John

I agree. Especially a company that has a well-known brand. It's so important to represent who you are appropriately because there are certain expectations the customer has.

Dan

Your Web site is kind of like your clothes. It's how people perceive you.

Tish

In early 1995, we were involved in building some of the first sites for microsoft.com, which Microsoft wanted to have live, and they were reviewed by Steve Ballmer, Microsoft's executive vice president of sales. I'll never forget watching him lose it about how he really wanted this to be the face and not show the weaknesses but the strengths. Most of the marketing people didn't get it internally, and he didn't let a lot of stuff go live as a result of that, but it was really nice that we kind of got it early on. It was very scary.

Jesse

It doesn't have to be a scary experience if you work with a developer you trust.

Adam

Extreme vigilance is the best form of protection. Being aware of potential liabilities is the first step in safeguarding against them.

Key Recommendations

- Have a crisis communication plan in place.
- Stay informed about evolving legal issues.
- Find a good communications lawyer.

There You Have It

When the Microsoft Site Builder Network first talked about rounding up authors to write a book, we were a little concerned that individual issues might get in the way of a successful group effort. After all, the participants are successful entrepreneurs working in a hugely competitive industry, some of them within the same geographical market.

Fortunately, personalities and business rivalries never undermined the group's ability to focus on putting this book together. Our roundtable discussions proved to be focused and productive. The participants were intent on asking tough questions and were determined to give their best efforts to address the issues they had raised. The success of these discussions hinged on the tremendous enthusiasm these people have for the emerging field within which they have worked for the past several years—years during which they have each helped shape the vast changes taking place in the ways the world does business. Having watched them work together over the course of this project, I can tell you that like Site Builder Network—the group that brought them all together—they are wholeheartedly determined to help you make your business a success.

About the Author

Tony Leininger has been with the Microsoft Site Builder Network since shortly after its inception. In addition to writing about Web design and development for the SBN Web site, he spends a good deal of his time looking through Windows.

APPENDIX

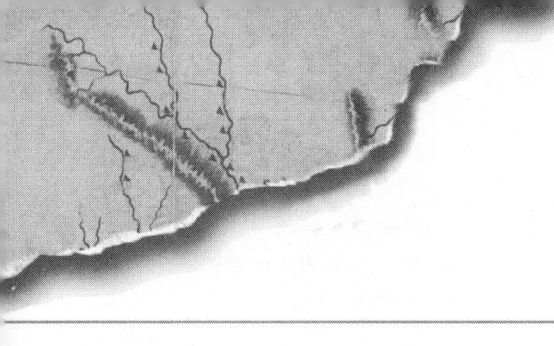

Author Roundup

We've corralled the best and brightest entrepreneurs from among Microsoft's Site Builder Network level 3 members to write *How the Web Was Won: Conquering the Digital Frontier*. They've been around since the Internet was started, riding roughshod over technical, design, and business challenges and blazing a trail for those who've followed.

Ron Bloom

Ron Bloom is the president and chief operating officer of THINK New Ideas. Prior to joining THINK New Ideas, Mr. Bloom served as chief operating officer of On Ramp, one of the world's most prestigious Internet solutions providers. Ron has helped lead the company in its Internet and intranet pioneering efforts, creating the world's first cybercast, integrating next-generation marketing and communications into online communications, and helping On Ramp become chosen as one of *FORTUNE* magazine's "Top 25 Emerging Technology Companies of 1995."

Ron has steered many entrepreneurial organizations, serving as president of MediaTime Advertising and Communication, in Chicago, Illinois; president of Prototype Computer Aided Design; vice president and creative director of Jeffrey Nemetz and Associates Advertising in Chicago, Illinois; president of TMF Communications, Los Angeles, California; and president and founder of Ron Bloom Productions, a production and consulting firm. His visionary outlook has helped to shape marketing and communications on the Internet.

Ron majored in philosophy with a minor in business administration and has become a respected contributor, speaker, and author in the interactive community.

John Kim

John Kim's first experience with computers was in the early 1980s on a Magnavox Odyssey game console playing with an assembly language cartridge. He quickly graduated to 6502 Assembly language on an Apple II+ and continued to program in many languages on various platforms (Microsoft Windows, UNIX, Macintosh). He has been on line since the early heydays of bulletin boards, The Source, and ARPANET.

John is highly skilled in Java, HTML, Director, C++, and all things interactive. As director of engineering, he lends to Red Sky Interactive (RSI) his extensive knowledge of just about any program or platform you could name. RSI is an interactive strategy, design, and production company, which develops award-winning Web sites, CD-ROMs, and kiosks for companies such as Land's End, Nike, and Absolut Vodka.

Cerise Vablais

Cerise Vablais is the manager of the special campaigns team of the Microsoft Site Builder Network and also manages the Site Builder Network Level 3 partners.

Cerise has worked at Microsoft in varying capacities since 1993, including stints as a freelance technical writer, online producer, and software test engineer. She also owned her own multimedia company, Soggy in Seattle Productions, Inc., and created and developed an award-winning CD-ROM game, "Treasure Quest."

Jesse Albert

Jesse Albert is the general manager of Media Revolution. A seasoned public relations agency veteran and multimedia consultant, Jesse helped start, manage, and grow the boutique digital communications agency, successfully developing high-profile clientele in the entertainment, consumer, business to business, and technology marketplaces. Jesse is responsible for the strategic growth of the agency, while also pursuing new business opportunities and strategic corporate alliances.

Prior to Media Revolution (*www.mediarevolution.com*), Jesse founded Advanced Media Marketing, Inc., a Santa Monica–based Internet marketing consultancy. Jesse's emphasis while at Advanced Media Marketing was on creating innovative new media solutions to enhance traditional marketing communications. His clients included Epson America, *GameFan* Magazine, Candle Corporation, and Xatrix Entertainment.

Previously Jesse pursued a career in public relations and worked for several Los Angeles–based agencies. At Hajjar/Kaufman Advertising, his primary client was Canon Computer Systems, Inc. For Canon, he managed strategic and tactical aspects of the computer manufacturer's public relations program, including editorial and analyst-consultant relations, product launches, review programs, and trade show support.

With Manning Selvage & Lee, Albert designed and implemented public relations programs for various accounts, including Epson America, Inc.

Jesse was named by *Daily Variety* as one of "20 Multimedia Executives to Watch in 1997." He earned his bachelor's degree from the University of Southern California.

In a former life, Jesse was involved in artist tour production, traversing North America with popular bands, including Aerosmith.

Based in Santa Monica, California, Media Revolution is a leading digital communications agency developing customized interactive solutions for industry leaders, including Twentieth Century Fox, Universal, DreamWorks, Aramark, Countrywide, Sega GameWorks, and many others. The company develops compelling new media marketing and productivity solutions, including Web sites, ad banners, intranets, extranets, online games, original content, and enhanced CDs.

Tish Hill

Luticia (Tish) Hill is one of the twenty-something cofounders of Sitewerks—A Bowne Company, a Seattle-based Internet development company. Tish has taken the company from a two-person start-up to its recent acquisition by Bowne Internet Solutions, an international Internet services firm.

With an educational background is in computer systems analysis and information science, Tish moved into mulitmedia production in the early 1990s, working for US West and Microsoft, before cofounding Sitewerks in 1995. At Sitewerks, Tish works in setting and implementing corporate strategy, as well as maintaining strong client relationships and new business development. Sitewerks is a leader both in the high-tech industry and in the business world. The company concentrates not only on the work they do but also on the people doing the work.

Dan Fine

Dan Fine founded fine.com International in 1994 and since its inception has served as its chief executive officer and chairman of the board. fine.com is an international company with offices in Seattle; Los Angeles; Washington, D.C.; Tokyo; and London. Dan took the company public on NASDAQ in late 1997. Prior to founding the company, he served as vice president of marketing and principal of Kobasic Fine Hadley, an advertising agency. Kobasic Fine Hadley was formed in 1990 after the merger of Kobasic Hadley and Fine Advertising, an agency founded by Dan in 1987. Before founding Fine Advertising, Dan worked in New York City for Levine, Huntley, Schmidt & Beaver Advertising, a division of Grey Advertising.

Dan holds a bachelor's degree from Washington State University. He speaks frequently at seminars around the United States and teaches integrated marketing communications at the University of Washington Extension College.

Bryan McCormick

Bryan McCormick began his career in multimedia 10 years ago at Optical Data Corporation, where he was responsible for scripting and later architecting HyperCard-based software packaged together with the company's laserdisc titles for the education market. Those titles included Windows on Science and the Space Disc series.

In 1990, he joined the fledgling ABC News InterActive unit and later assumed responsibility for running software development there. While at ABC, he worked on the award-winning AIDS disc Earthquake and The Powers of the Supreme Court, among others.

In 1992, Bryan formed BAM! Software, which produced the Writer's Solution for Prentice Hall. The cross-platform software—written from scratch—ranks as one of the most ambitious efforts in courseware development to date, consisting of 14 CD-ROMs with over ten thousand assets each and 7 laserdiscs spanning five grade levels.

In 1995, BAM! Software merged with Broadway Video to create the Broadway Interactive Group. There Bryan and his team produced such award-winning projects as the Tommy CD-ROM (Interplay and Kardana Productions, 1995), the tenth anniversary Enhanced-CD reissue of Paul Simon's *Graceland,* and the groundbreaking live comedy Web site for MSN, This Is Not a Test.

In addition to his accomplishments in the title business, Bryan has also lectured on various topics in multimedia throughout the United States, Canada, and Japan. He has also written for *Microsoft Interactive Developer,* for which he wrote the first piece to appear on Cascading Style Sheets (MIND, October 1996).

Adam Heneghan

Adam Heneghan, COO of Giant Step, is responsible for the development of Giant Step's innovative digital business-to-business and business-to-consumer solutions.

Adam founded Giant Step with his brother Eric in 1991. Based in Chicago, Giant Step currently employs more than 60 people. Adam plays an integral role in all aspects of the business, including the management of engineering, programming, architecture, and design within Giant Step.

Under Adam's codirection, Giant Step has served as interactive architects for Microsoft, McDonald's, Oldsmobile, United Airlines, Kellogg's, and Jenn-Air, among others. Based on his impressive body of work, Adam is a highly sought speaker at industry events and product reviews. He is often called on to describe how and why a new product is significant to the interactive community. Giant Step is also recognized as the first agency to offer a complete digital solution that integrates consulting, development, design, hosting, and support.

Adam and his brother became interested in computers at an early age, in part because of their father, a renowned architect who praised computers as valuable creative tools, not just as calculating devices. Adam continued to pursue his love of computers and technology while studying business at Indiana University, graduating in 1991 with a degree in management. That same year, Adam attended the Macworld conference and confronted new trends in video editing and CD-ROMs. These insights, together with his natural affinity for integrated technology and architecture, eventually led the Heneghan brothers to create Giant Step.

Tony Leininger

Tony Leininger is a member of the special campaigns team of Microsoft's Site Builder Network. He coordinates and writes the Site Builder Network case studies and is the voice behind SBN's Designer of the Month interviews, part of the Site Builder Network Design Workshop.

Before coming to Microsoft, Tony worked in children's social services and in professional theater—acting, directing, and handling literary management. A graduate of Hanover College, he plays the piano, sketches, and gardens in his spare time.

He would like to publicly thank and acknowledge the fine teachers and mentors he has had the good fortune to work with over the years, including J. David Wagner, Thomas G. Evans, Catherine B. Rutledge, Jon Cranney, Wendy Lehr, Dale Redpath, and Cyd Wicker.

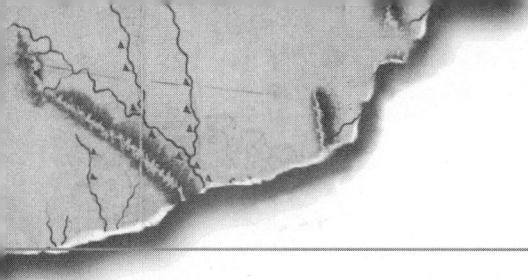

Index

Note: Italicized page numbers refer to figures or illustrations.

Numbers

24-x-7 communication with customers, 120

A

ABC News Interactive, 137, 139, 141, 148, 154
accountabilities and liabilities, 240–48
Active Server Pages (ASP), 59, 188
ACT program, 245
adult chat rooms, 41
Adult Verification Services (AVSs), 42
AdultWatch, 42
adult Web sites, 39–47
   anonymity and, 40
   appeal of, 40
   income sources of, 41–43
   membership fees, 42
   number of, 44
   number of visitors to, 45
   as pioneers of Web technology, 45
   regulation of, 46–47
   time spent on, 45
   variety and, 41
Advanced Media Marketing, 52
advertising agencies, 102–4, 191, 192
advertising of CD-ROMs, 153–54
Advocates, in customer life cycle, 113, *113*
airline industry, 228
Alien-Resurrection.com, 53–54
Allen, Brian, 107
Amazon.com, 28, 233, 242

America Online (AOL), 16
Amistad Web site, 53–54, *54*, 66–70, *68*, 74
Amway, 240–41
Andreesen, Marc, 8, 9, 12
animations, 69–73
anonymity
   adult sites and, 40
   e-commerce and, 109, 218
anticipating
   additional services, 31
   number of visitors, 30
AOL (America Online), 16
Apple, 144
   HyperCard, 136–37, 141
application development, 88, 89
Architecture Context Diagram (ACD),
   building a Web site and, 126
ARPANET, 5
Atari, 146
audience. *See also* customers
   building a Web site and, 124
   knowing your, 57, 58

B

backbone, 5
BackWeb, 218
Ballmer, Steve, 248
bandwidth, 194
   improvements in, 76–77
banking industry, 91, 211–12
Barksdale, James, 9

Barton, Kathy, 57, 58, 63
BB Edit, 75
Berners-Lee, Tim, 8
Bezos, Jeff, 131
Broadway Video Entertainment, 165
brochure requests, 179
brochureware, 53, 70
Broderbund, 146
browsers, 8, 17. *See also* Internet Explorer; Netscape Communicator
   building a Web site and versions of, 127
   compatibility with, 34–36
   reliability of Web sites and, 27
   security of, 32
budget, building a Web site and, 128
Budweiser, 11–12
building Web sites, 119–30
   computing environment, 126–27
   creativity, 125
   fulfillment and customer interaction, 128–29
   measurement and research, 124–25
   objectives and strategies, 123–24
   plan (blueprint) for, 123–30
   project resources, budget, and timeline, 128
   promotion and site maintenance, 129
   proposal, 120–21
   team for, 122
Burnett, Leo, 170
business objectives, building a Web site and, 123

C

Cameron, James, 100
Carnegie Mellon University study of pornography, 46
Casio, 15
CBS television, 14
CD-I, 139

CD-ROMs, 139, 169
   cost of producing and selling price of, 155
   cross-platform, 149
   early history of, 139–44
   marketing and advertising, 153–54
   poor quality of, 151–52
   popular perception of, 150
   quality assurance and, 152
   repurposing and, 144–50
CDs, Enhanced, 157–58
censoring software, 46
centralization vs. decentralization, 200
chat rooms, adult, 41
Clark, Jim, 9
click-thrus, on adult sites, 43
co-marketing, 118
comic books, interactive and personalized, 61
commerce. *See* e-commerce; marketing
commerce sites, reasons consumers purchase goods from, 109
communication
   with customers, in Web site proposal, 120
   technology and, 224–25
Communications Decency Act (CDA), 42, 46
community
   creating a, 245
   sense of, 118
compatibility, 26
   with different browsers, 34–36
competitors, building a Web site and review of, 124
computing environment, building a Web site and, 126–27
connection to the Internet, 5
   high-speed, 76–77
constructing a Web site. *See* building Web sites
content
   controlling, 174
      Hallmark site, 186–87
   distribution channels and, 237–39
   multimedia, 133–35, 138, 139, 141–43, 154

content analysis, building a Web site and, 125
Continental Savings Bank, 121
convergence, 205–13
convergence of computers and other appliances, 198
co-op marketing, 237
credit cards, browser security and, 32
Criterion Collection, 144
Curry, Adam, 12
customer acquisition cost, 111
customer life cycle, 113
customers. *See also* audience; marketing
  building lasting relationships with, 114–19
    co-marketing opportunities, 118
    community, sense of, 118
    feedback, 114
    frequent buyer (or viewer) programs, 114
    merchandising your store, 118–19
    multiple entry paths, 116
    Paretta's Law, 117
    predicting behavior, 115
    reminder messages, 114
    rewarding your best customers, 116
    saving your customers time and trouble, 115–16
  feedback from, 235
  survey of, 102
customer satisfaction, 121
customer service, building a Web site and, 128
cybercasts (NetCasts), 13–15
cybererotica.com, 45

D

database marketing, 110
data security, 33
decryption of credit card information, 32
designing Web sites, 23, 88, 89
developers of the future, 92. *See also* solution providers; Web development
development tools, 188–91
  building a Web site and, 127
digital cameras, 15
digital solution providers. *See* solution providers
digital technologies. *See* technology (new technologies)
Digital Versatile/Video Disk (DVD), 158, 239
digital video discs-recordable (DVD-Rs), 239
Disney, 152
distribution channels, 232–40
  middleman and, 233–36
documentation, scalability of Web sites and, 31–32
Domain Name System (DNS), 11–12
DreamWeaver, Macromedia, 75
DreamWorks, 66, 67
Dynamic HTML, 75

E

e-commerce, 87, 213–19, 243
  distribution channels and, 232–40
Economist, The, 233
electronic software distribution (ESD), 221, 238
e-mail, 241, 242
  "in-character," 60
  spam, 238
  tracking, Oldsmobile site and, 183–84
encryption
  browser security and, 32
  of credit card transactions, 32
Enhanced CDs, 157–58
episodic Web sites, 58–59, 64, 159
Epson America, 52–53, 203
ET game, 146
E-trade, 243
Explora (Gabriel), 141
extranets, 35, 85, 86
Exxon, James, 46

F

feedback from customers, 114, 235, 241
   Oldsmobile site and, 182
   successful Web sites and, 173
film industry, 50
fine.com International, 105, 110, 111, 114, 118, 127, 131
firewalls, 34
First Amendment rights, 46
Flash, Macromedia, 56, 65–73, 75
Ford Truck Web site, 240
frequent buyer (or viewer) programs, 114

G

Gabriel, Peter, 141
games, Shockwave, 64
gateway pages, 59
General Motors, 180, 214
general store, 108–9
   fantasy about, 101–2
Giant Step, 170, 191–93, 195, 214
   development tools used by, 188–91
   Web sites created by, 175–88
globalization, 198, 199–205
goal setting, successful, 171–72
Graceland (enhanced CD), 158
Grammys online event, 13–15
graphic design, building a Web site and, 126
graphics department, Web site–building team and, 122
Greene, Mike, 13
growth of the Internet, 27

H

hackers, 33
Hallmark, 184–88, *185, 187,* 195
A Hard Day's Night (CD-ROM), 144
Highway 61 (CD-ROM), 151–52

hosting environment, building a Web site and, 127
hosting services, 191, 192, 204
HTML, 222
HyperCard, 136–37, 141
hyperlinking, 8

I

IKEA, 70
immediacy of commerce sites, 109
immersive CD-ROMs, 152
immersive Web sites, 54, 58, 60, 64
Independence Day (movie) Web site, 57–62, *61, 63,* 114, 202
information services department, Web site–building team and, 122
infotainment, 13
integrated marketing communications, 110
Interactive Response Marketing (IRM), 110–19
   applying, 112
   building lasting relationships with customers and, 114–19
   customer life cycle and, 113
   databases and, 112
   objectives accomplished with, 130–31
interactive technologies, 110–11
interactive Web sites, 61. *See also* immersive Web sites
international Web traffic, 201
Internet, 87
   early history of, 5–7
Internet Service Providers (ISPs), 28
intranets, 35, 85, 86–87
I Photograph to Remember (Meyer), 142, 144

J

JMR Creations, 44
Johnny Mnemonic, 146
Jurassic Park (CD-ROM), 150

K

KMPS (radio station), 105, *106*

L

laserdiscs, 137–38
legal issues (legislation), 227–32
liabilities and accountabilities, 240–48
Lieberman, Jonathan, 44, 45
LifeSavers Web site, 56
lifetime value (LTV), 111
limitations of technology, 55–56
Lion King (CD-ROM), 152
Living Books series, 146
localization, 199, 200, 202
loyalty programs, 179
    Hallmark, 185, 186
    United Airlines, 175, 178

M

Macromedia, 65–73
Macromedia Director, 71–73
Macromedia DreamWeaver, 75
Macromedia Flash, 56, 65–73, 75
maintenance, site, 129
management information system (MIS) departments, 221–22
Manning, Selvage, and Lee (MS&L), 52
marketing, 69–70. *See also* commerce sites; customers; e-commerce; Interactive Response Marketing (IRM)
    building a Web site and, 123
    of CD-ROMs, 153–54
    database, 110
    distribution channels and, 232–40

marketing strategist, Web site–building team and, 122
mass customization, 112
Mays, Ken, 121
McKenna, Regis, 119
Media America, 14
Media Revolution, 49–55, 61, 65, 76
Media Ventures Entertainment Group, 52
membership fees for adult Web sites, 42
message boards, 182, 186
Meyer, Pedro, 142, 143
Microsoft, 17
Microsoft Certified Solution Providers (MCSP), 82
Microsoft Developer Store, 118
Microsoft Exchange, 241
Microsoft Internet Explorer, 17. *See also* browsers
Microsoft NetShow, 73, 74
Microsoft Network (MSN), 16, 164–66
Microsoft Site Builder Network, 248
Microsoft Site Server, 74
    Personalization Server component of, 116, 176, 177
    suite, 116
    Usage Analyst component of, 178
Microsoft SQL Server, 59, 65, 107, 177, 183, 188
Microsoft Usage Analyst, 178
Microsoft Visual InterDev, 188, 189
Microsoft Visual Studio, 188
Microsoft Web site, 248
    event database, 81–82
Microsoft Windows NT, 107, 188, 190
    security and, 33
middleman, 214, 216, 217, 233–36
Mileage Plus program (United Airlines), 175, 178

Mosaic, 8, 12, 105, 156
movie trailers, online, 56, 62
MTV, 12
multimedia, 54–56, 62, 69–71, 133–37. *See also* CD-ROMs
   benefits and cost effectiveness of, 63–65
   ten years ago, 136–38
multiple entry paths for customers, 116
music, online distribution of, 238–39
Myst, 152

N

naming conventions on the Web, 12
NARAS, 14, 15
NASDAQ, 117, *117,* 129, 202
National Academy of Recording Arts and Sciences (NARAS), 13
Naughty Linx, 44
NBC, 237
NetNanny, 46
Netscape, 15
   founding of, 9
Netscape Communicator, 34. *See also* browsers
networks, 161–63
new technologies. *See* technology (new technologies)
Nike, 25
Nordstrom, 232–33

O

Oldsmobile, 179–84, *181,* 194–95
On Ramp, 12, 13, 15, 18
organizations, lists of vendors provided by, 93–94

P

Paretta's Law, 117
partners, business, 84
   choosing, 83, 96–97
passwords, 34
personalization, 27, 59, 61, 87, 120, 172, 194
   Hallmark site and, 185–86
   Oldsmobile site and, 180
   United Airlines site and, 176–78
Personalization Server, Microsoft, 116, 176, 177
Philips Electronics, 139
PhotoWorks, 106
pioneers, 6–7
planning. *See also* anticipating
   new technologies and, 220
   scalability of Web sites and, 31
plug-ins
   detection of, 35, 59
   downloading, 60
political issues, globalization and, 203
pornography, 227. *See also* adult Web sites
   regulation of, 46–47
postcards, electronic, 31
predicting customers' behavior, 115
privacy, 6
promotion of Web sites, 129
proposal for building a Web site, 120–21
Prospects, in customer life cycle, 113, *113*
prototyping, rapid, 28
publishers
   early, 9–11
   multimedia, 144, 145, 148–50
push technology, 24, 76, 218

Q

QuickTime, 73, 140, 141, 144

R

rapid prototyping, reliability of Web sites and, 28
RealAudio, 15, 73
RealFlash, 73
RealNetworks, 73
RealSystem 5.0, 73
Recreational Software Advisory Council on the Internet (RSACi ratings), 46–47
Red Sky Interactive, 22, 23, 35
  team approach used by, 25
redundancy, reliability of Web sites and, 27
references for solution providers, 94–95
regulation of pornography, 46–47
reliability of Web sites, 26–29
reminder messages, 114
Repeat customers
  in customer life cycle, 113, *113*
reports, building a Web site and, 124
repurposing, CD-ROMs and, 144–50
return on investment, building a Web site and, 128
rewarding your best customers, 116
RFM (recency, frequency, and monetary) formula, 116
Rifkin, Jay, 52
risk assessment, building a Web site and, 124
Rolling Stones, 13
rollovers, 36
Rundgren, Todd, 141, 142

S

SafeSurf, 47
Safeway Corporation, 129, 241
sales, expanding, as rationale for building a Web site, 120. *See also* e-commerce; marketing
scalability of Web sites, 26, 29–32, 222
scheduling, reliability of Web sites and, 29
Schumacher, Fred, 105
Schwartz, Evan, 118
search engines, 44
Seattle FilmWorks, 106, *107*
Secure Electronic Transaction (SET), 33
security, 26, 32–34
  browser, 32–33
segmentation, of Oldsmobile site, 181–82
Senn, Rob, 13
server platform, building a Web site and, 127
servers
  reliability of Web sites and, 27
  security and, 33
settlers, 7
sex sites. *See* adult Web sites
Shockwave, Macromedia, 60, 64, 71–73
shopping. *See* e-commerce
shopping carts, 45
shopping club, 102
Simon, Paul, 158
Site Analyst, 188
Sitewerks, 84, 88, 91, 92
Skyworks Technologies, 56
Social Security site, 243
solution orientation of successful Web sites, 172–73
  Hallmark site, 186
  United Airlines site, 178
solution providers, 83
  areas of expertise of, 88–90
  choosing, 92–96
  of the future, 92
spam, 238
specialization, strategic, 90–92
speed, maximum acceptable delay, 30
Spielberg, Steven, 66

Spot, The, 159–62
staff, of solution providers, 96
standards, Internet, 26–27
strategy, Internet (strategic objectives), 88, 90–92, 205
   building a Web site and, 123
streaming technologies, 73
streaming video and audio, 74
successful Web sites, 170–88
   elements involved in creating, 170–74
   Oldsmobile, 179–84
   United Airlines, 175–79
Suspects, in customer life cycle, 113, *113*
SYNFLOOD, 33
systems integration, 88, 89

T

tables, 35
taxes, 228, 230, 231
team approach
   to building a Web site, 122
   Red Sky Interactive's use of, 25
technology (new technologies), 219–26. *See also specific technologies*
   business-related uses for, 83–86
   CEOs and, 222
   limitations of, 23–24
   simplicity and, 224
Telecommunications Act of 1996, 42
television, 77, 140–41, 237
   interactive, 78
   the Web compared to, 163–64
testing
   for bugs in Web sites, 125
   scalability of Web sites and, 31
THINK New Ideas, 9, 18
This is Not a Test, 165

timeline, building a Web site and, 128
time spent on adult sites, 45
Tommy, 148–49
Toshiba computers, 24
tracking, 174
   Oldsmobile site and, 183–84
   United Airlines site and, 178–79
trade journals, finding solution providers at, 93
trade shows, finding solution providers at, 93
trailers, movie, 56, 62
Twentieth Century Fox Home Entertainment, 51–52, 57, 58, 114, *115*

U

United Airlines, 175–79, *177,* 194
Universal Media Initiative, 73
UNIX, 6, 190
   security and, 33
uptime guarantee, 28
user interface, 124

V

value added, 214, 215–16, 218, 233, 234
vector-based programs, 67
vendors, collaboration with, 28
video, online, 45
visits (visitors). *See also* customers
   anticipated number of, 30
   repeat, 59
Vollman, Michael, 67
Volvo, 241
Voyager, 142, 144

W

Wang, Perry, 75
Wang, Sharon, 69
Washington State Liquor Board, 232
Web development, 191–93
Web servers, security and, 33
Web sites
    building (*see* building Web sites)
    designing, technological legacy of the
        Internet and, 23
WebTV, 77, 194, 208, 210–12
Welsh, Michelle, 72
Windermere Real Estate, 107, *108*

Y

Yang, Sharon, 51
Yim, Jason, 51–52, 55
Yuen, Yush, 50

Z

Zimmer, Hans, 52

The manuscript for this book was prepared and submitted to Microsoft Press in electronic form. Text files were prepared using Microsoft Word 97. Pages were composed by Microsoft Press using Adobe PageMaker 6.52 for Windows, with text in Garamond and display type in Frutiger. Composed pages were delivered to the printer as electronic prepress files.

Cover Graphic Designer
Tom Draper Design

Interior Graphic Designer
Kim Eggleston

Interior Graphic Artist
Michael Victor

Principal Compositor
Abby Hall

Principal Proofreader/Copy Editor
Shawn Peck

Indexer
Maro Riofrancos

The *professional's companion* to Microsoft Internet Explorer 4.

This exclusive Microsoft® collection provides complete technical information on Microsoft Internet Explorer version 4.0 for the network administrator, the support professional, and the internet service provider. The MICROSOFT INTERNET EXPLORER RESOURCE KIT gives you a technical resource guide packed with authoritative information and an indispensable CD-ROM containing Microsoft Internet Explorer 4, the Microsoft Internet Explorer Administration Kit, valuable utilities, accessory programs, and source code that help you save time and accomplish more—all of which makes it easier for you to deploy and support customized versions of Internet Explorer in your organization.

U.S.A.	$49.99
U.K.	£46.99 [V.A.T. included]
Canada	$71.99
ISBN 1-57231-842-2	

Microsoft Press® products are available worldwide wherever quality computer books are sold. For more information, contact your book or computer retailer, software reseller, or local Microsoft Sales Office, or visit our Web site at mspress.microsoft.com. To locate your nearest source for Microsoft Press products, or to order directly, call 1-800-MSPRESS in the U.S. (in Canada, call 1-800-268-2222).

Prices and availability dates are subject to change.

Microsoft®*Press*

Microsoft Press has titles to help everyone— from new users to seasoned developers—

Step by Step Series
Self-paced tutorials for classroom instruction or individualized study

Starts Here™ Series
Interactive instruction on CD-ROM that helps students learn by doing

Field Guide Series
Concise, task-oriented A–Z references for quick, easy answers—anywhere

Official Series
Timely books on a wide variety of Internet topics geared for advanced users

All User Training

All User Reference

Quick Course® Series
Fast, to-the-point instruction for new users

At a Glance Series
Quick visual guides for task-oriented instruction

Running Series
A comprehensive curriculum alternative to standard documentation books

Microsoft Press® products are available worldwide wherever quality computer books are sold. For more information, contact your book or computer retailer, software reseller, or local Microsoft Sales Office, or visit our Web site at mspress.microsoft.com. To locate your nearest source for Microsoft Press products, or to order directly, call 1-800-MSPRESS in the U.S. (in Canada, call 1-800-268-2222).

Prices and availability dates are subject to change.

start faster and go farther!

The wide selection of books and CD-ROMs published by Microsoft Press contain something for every level of user and every area of interest, from just-in-time online training tools to development tools for professional programmers. Look for them at your bookstore or computer store today!

Professional Select Editions Series
Advanced titles geared for the system administrator or technical support career path

Microsoft® Certified Professional Training
The Microsoft Official Curriculum for certification exams

Best Practices Series
Candid accounts of the new movement in software development

Microsoft Programming Series
The foundations of software development

Professional — Developers

Microsoft Press® Interactive
Integrated multimedia courseware for all levels

Strategic Technology Series
Easy-to-read overviews for decision makers

Microsoft Professional Editions
Technical information straight from the source

Solution Developer Series
Comprehensive titles for intermediate to advanced developers

Microsoft Press
mspress.microsoft.com

mspress.microsoft.com

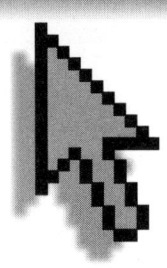

Microsoft Press Online is your road map to the best available print and multimedia materials—resources that will help you maximize the effectiveness of Microsoft® software products. Our goal is making it easy and convenient for you to find exactly the Microsoft Press® book or interactive product you need, as well as bringing you the latest in training and certification materials from Microsoft Press.

Microsoft Press online

Where do you want to go today?®

Microsoft® Press

Register Today!

Return this
How the Web Was Won
registration card for
a Microsoft Press® catalog

U.S. and Canada addresses only. Fill in information below and mail postage-free. Please mail only the bottom half of this page.

1-57231-917-8   **HOW THE WEB WAS WON**   *Owner Registration Card*

_____
NAME

_____
INSTITUTION OR COMPANY NAME

_____
ADDRESS

_____
CITY   STATE   ZIP

Microsoft Press
Quality Computer Books

For a free catalog of
Microsoft Press® products, call
1-800-MSPRESS

BUSINESS REPLY MAIL
FIRST-CLASS MAIL   PERMIT NO. 53   BOTHELL, WA

POSTAGE WILL BE PAID BY ADDRESSEE

NO POSTAGE
NECESSARY
IF MAILED
IN THE
UNITED STATES

MICROSOFT PRESS REGISTRATION
HOW THE WEB WAS WON
PO BOX 3019
BOTHELL WA   98041-9946